CASIAN ANTON (born July 30, 1988) private analyst in International Relations with concerns in the study of interdisciplinary methodology, world state and structures of explanation. QTS in Humanities (2016 in England, 2011 in Romania, Petru Maior's University of Târgu Mureş), MA in *Security and International Relations* ('Lucian Blaga' University of Sibiu, Romania, 2013), BA in *International Relations and European Studies* (Petru Maior's University of Târgu Mureş, Romania, 2011), Erasmus Student to *University of Social Science and Humanities* (Warsaw, Poland, 2012-2013).

Casian Anton

On The Famous Feud

BLACK AND WHITE EDITION

Probably the most advanced analysis ...

TO MRS HAMILTON ROWY:
THE G.O.A.T. OF
ENGLISH:

ENJOY THE LECTURE!
CASIAN ANTON, ~~DEC 202~~ 😊
FEB 2023

Author: Casian Anton

Cover: was created inside the app Adobe Express (standard license)

Printed by Amazon

© 2022 CASIAN ANTON via Revi Project 88

"On The Famous Feud" (Black and White Edition)

ISBN: 9798844567995

Revi Project 88 (London, UK): *is dedicated to create knowledge and advance the understanding of various topics in the field of Social Science & Humanities (International Relations as a specific area of study). All the activities within this project is to guide, exchange, sustain and share unique and original ideas that can help people to understand the world.*

Online orders: www.amazon.com
Contact: www.reviproject88.com
Social Media: Revi Project 88 (Twitter, Facebook, Instagram, Tumblr)

FIRST EDITION

**To Kanye West, Kim Kardashian West,
Taylor Swift, Katy Perry and
Western Mass-Media:**

"This goes out to all you people going bed with
a ten and waking up with a two."
(Katy Perry, *This Is How We Do*, 'Prism,' 2013)

"We think we know someone, but the truth
is that we only know the version of them
that they've chosen to show us."
(Taylor Swift, *reputation*, volume 1, 2017)

"A wise man should be humble enough to admit
when he's wrong and change his
mind based on new information."
(Kanye West, *Twitter*, February 2016)

"Cause all of my enemies started out friends."
(Taylor Swift, 'The Archer', *Lover*, 2019)

"You play stupid games, you win stupid prizes"
(Taylor Swift, 'Miss Americana & The Heartbreak Prince', *Lover*, 2019)

"Lifelike, this is what your life like, try to live
your life right, People really know you,
push your buttons like typewrite"
(Kanye West, 'Follow God', *Jesus is King*, 2010)

"Use this gospel for protection, It's a hard road to Heaven"
(Kanye West, 'Use this Gospel', *Jesus is King*, 2019)

"I just wanted you to know"
(Kanye West, 'Famous', *The Life of Pablo*, 2016)

"[…] Just thought you should know"
(Taylor Swift, 'Miss Americana & The Heartbreak Prince', *Lover*, 2019)

"If you wanna see the true character of person watch
the way they treat someone who can't do anything for them.
Question everything, Follow the innate feelings inside you,
Free to take ideas and update them at your will,
Truth is my goal"
(Kanye West, *Tweets from Twitter*, 2018)

Revi Project 88

Table of Contents

Introduction: on the **FAMOUS** feud

21 months after the release of her multi-platinum and blockbuster album, namely *1989*, Taylor Swift became one of the most famous pop artist in the world, being named the 21st century Pop Princess, America's Sweetheart, an innocent and clean model for the young female generation of the Western world, but also for other parts of the world. However, a video posted in July 2016 on the Snapchat account of the famous Kim Kardashian[1], changed the narrative line of Taylor Swift and her positive image around the world. The video contained heavily edited parts of the telephone conversation from January 2016 between Kanye West and Taylor Swift and the background narrative of the creation of the controversial song *Famous*. In February 2016 Taylor Swift rejected the story of the events revealed by Kanye West on his Twitter account. However, hours later, Kanye West tweeted that Taylor Swift gave her blessing about the song. In July 2016, in the video posted by Kim Kardashian, Taylor Swift's voice confirmed Kanye West's side of the story by saying over the telephone conversation: "Umm, yeah I mean go with whatever line you think is better. It's obviously very tongue in cheek either way. And I really appreciate you telling me about it, that's really nice." […] "And you know, if people ask me about it I think it would be great for me to be like,' Look, he called me and told me the line before it came out. Jokes on you guys, We're fine.'" […] "You guys want to call this a feud; you want to call this throwing shade but right after the song comes out I'm going to be on a GRAMMYs red carpet and they're going to ask me about it and I'll be like, 'He called me.'" The telephone conversation from January 2016, the release of the song *Famous* in February 2016 and the different views of the actual telephone conversation published by Taylor Swift and Kanye West, was the catalyst and the start of the second part of the feud (the first part was in September 2009). The Western mass-media, fans of both sides and ordinary people reacted with negative and positive comments and memes forming two social forces: the social force of Kim Kardashian and Kanye West and the social force of Taylor Swift.[2]

---

[1] The ex-wife of the famous rap artist Kanye West; in June 2016, a month before the videos published by Kim Kardashian, there was already a trailer of an interview with GQ magazine in which she announced the existence of a video evidence showing a different face of Taylor Swift.

[2] Various parts from this report were also used in *Black and White Music: A Journey Behind the Musical Notes,* Second Edition, August 2022, Amazon (printed edition). The reason behind this use is simple: it was a single report in two parts: 1. *On the Famous Feud* and the 2. *Music of the Famous Feud* (a comparison research of the music released by Kanye West and Taylor Swift, then later extended

Kim Kardashian and Kanye West's social force have declared the release of a small edited part of the telephone conversation as a final blow to Taylor Swift, because Kim Kardashian, through one short video posted on Snapchat, successfully demonstrated a white female character with two faces and the role of the false white victim she played throughout her entire musical career.[3]

In July 2016, hours after Kim's video from Snapchat, Taylor Swift published her response with a screenshot (on Instagram) suggesting that it was written before Kim Kardashian's revelation. Taylor Swift's post on Instagram did not help her side of the story and reinforced the idea that she knew there was evidence of her involvement in the song *Famous*, which she declined to confirm it as expected by Kanye West, Kim Kardashian and a minor number of Western mass-media journalists and bloggers.[4]

Taylor Swift's social force did not let the guard down and continued to support Taylor Swift's point of view: she heard the song for the first time at the same time as the general public and did not approve the lyrics used by Kanye West in the song *Famous*: 'I feel like me and Taylor might still have sex / Why? I made that bitch famous (God damn) / I made that bitch famous.' Taylor Swift replied: 'Where is the video of Kanye telling me he was going to call me 'that bitch' in his song? It doesn't exist because it never happened. You don't get to control someone's emotional response to being called 'that bitch' in front of the entire world. Of course I wanted to like the song. I wanted to believe Kanye when he told me that I would love the song. I wanted us to have a friendly relationship. He promised to play the song for me, but he never did. While I wanted to be supportive of Kanye on the phone call, you can't 'approve' a song you haven't heard. Being falsely painted as a liar when I was never given the full story or played any part of the song is character assassination. I would very much like to be excluded from this narrative, one that I have never asked to be a part of, since 2009.'

The conflict between the three celebrities is important because it covers a major topic in the USA: the allegations made by black people about the persistent racism of the white people against them and other minorities. In the *Famous* case, between Taylor Swift (the 'privileged white woman': a philosophical concept addressed to white women in the USA and used by

---

to other artists). In this chapter the reasons are used from *Black and White Music: A Journey Behind the Musical Notes,* but modified to accommodate specific explanations and needs for this report.

[3] Ellie Woodward, 'How Taylor Swift Played The Victim For A Decade And Made Her Entire Career', *Buzzfeed,* January 31, 2017, available at: https://www.buzzfeed.com/elliewoodward/how-taylor-swift-played-the-victim-and-made-her-entire-caree?utm_term=.eqJNKE2B6#.kiP4wE0YB, last accessed: June 26, 2022.

[4] From now on, I will use *Western mass media* with the following definition: it is about the journalists and bloggers and their articles used *only* in this report; for the negative views about Taylor Swift: it is about the journalists and bloggers with the negative articles exposed in chapter *V. The Famous Feud: Strategies of Interpretation and Communication*.

black activists, such as Black Lives Matter, as a possible evidence to justify the poor life of black women in comparison with white women which have a higher chance of success because the system is created in a way to give white women a better outcome) and Kanye West (the black man persecuted by white people, including by Taylor Swift by refusing to confirm his narrative about the background details of the song).

In some Western mass-media agencies and the social force of Kim Kardashian and Kanye West, Taylor Swift's response was unconvincing leading to several articles about the causes and reasons for the feud between them. In July 2016, the popular opinion agreed with Kanye West and Kim Kardashian's side of the story. The mechanisms for interpreting the parties involved in the *Famous* feud are multiple and there is still a great interest in debating the perpetrators and the victims of the feud.

In this report I investigated the *Famous* feud between Kim Kardashian, Kanye West and Taylor Swift from the following items of research:

1. to expose, to extract, to understand the role of the Western mass-media about: **a.** the key moments of the *Famous* feud; **b.** detailed and specific information about the *Famous* feud; **c.** to find what is missing from the *Famous* feud timeline;
2. to analyse the narrative line of the feud in order to identify patterns of behaviour: Kanye West's behaviour toward Taylor Swift, and Taylor Swift's behaviour toward Kanye West;
3. to assess three points of view of Kanye West, Kim Kardashian and Taylor Swift:

   3.1 *Kanye West wrote on Twitter*: '3rd thing I called Taylor and had a hour long convo with her about the line and she thought it was funny and gave her blessings';

   3.2 *Kim Kardashian in the interview with GQ magazine* from 16 June 2016 and during her show *Keeping Up with The Kardashians* (season 12, episode 11): 'She totally approved that. […] 'She totally knew that that was coming out;'

   3.3 *the affirmation made by Taylor Swift in July 2016*: 'Being falsely painted as a liar when I was never given the full story *or played any part of the song* (underline by author) is character assassination';

4. to analyse the *Famous* song to see how much Taylor Swift knew about the song before its release;

5. to analyse the impact of the *Famous* feud on the albums sales and songs for Kanye West, Taylor Swift and Katy Perry;
6. to discover the mechanisms and strategies of interpretation and communication used by Kim Kardashian, Kanye West, Taylor Swift and the Western mass-media;
7. to explore possible reasons for creating, supporting and promoting the *Famous* feud by Kim Kardashian, Kanye West, Taylor Swift and the Western mass-media;
8. to confront and challenge the core argument of the 'false white victimhood' attributed to Taylor Swift;
9. to confront and challenge the core argument of Ellie Woodward about the existence of a false worldview attributed to Kanye West which is that of a: 'black man terrorising the "innocent" white woman' because of Taylor Swift;
10. to find out who is the victim and who is the perpetrator of the *Famous* feud.

This report was born out of the urgent need to provide clearer, more transparent information and better-founded examples to explain the *Famous* feud for the general public in a different way than what Kim Kardashian, Kanye West and Taylor Swift offered through music, interviews and other media content.

Black and white people are in need of answers and this report is a meditative resource about the *Famous* feud. In this report interested people about Taylor Swift, Kanye West and Kim Kardashian will find the space to read about it and confront their knowledge with the investigation's findings. The report can be used to calm the realities of racism and can provide a point of reference in future discussions and evolutions of this feud.

This report explored the background strategies of Kanye West, Kim Kardashian and Taylor Swift to maintain popularity and fame in an ever-changing world: sacrifices, intelligence, methods of communications, side effects and a minimal view of the efficiency of their strategies in the long term.

By no means this report is made with the intentional purpose to present the players of the feud in a negative light. I followed and interpreted raw numbers, analysed interviews by Kanye West, Kim Kardashian, Taylor Swift and articles written by journalists and bloggers. This report aligns with the investigations released by various Western mass-media news agencies, such as the Rolling Stone, The Daily Beast and more.[5]

'On the **Famous** feud' report it is a unique and original investigation, there is no other research which explores this conflict on various levels; most probably, at the time of publishing, this report might be one of the most advanced analyses of the *Famous* feud.

---

[5] For the full list of articles connected to this report, see chapter *V.1 The Famous Feud in Western Mass Media*.

The road of the Famous Feud report:

- the first idea of the report I had it in September 2016 after reading few negative articles about Taylor Swift (including the interview of Kanye West and Kim Kardashian West for Harper's Bazaar) at a time when I heard one song from her catalogue, *Red*; by the end of November 2016 I outlined the whole plan of the research; in December 2016 I bought the first album in my life, *1989,* with the purpose to create a music comparison between Kanye West and Taylor Swift; in the end I listened to their albums and I was impressed by their music and I made my own playlists with favourite songs;
- the first version of this report was completed in early June 2017 and I planned to release it the same day with the album *Witness* by Katy Perry for the world to 'witness' this report, but Taylor Swift decided to release her music on all digital platforms and ruined my plan, so I decided that it is better if I publish the report later same year, after the atmosphere is better for my conclusions;
- the next date was August 30, 2017: on the one-year anniversary of Kanye West's speech at the MTV Music Awards where he deceived the audience about the conclusions of the telephone conversation with Taylor Swift and her implicit agreement *that she knew everything he had planned*; I considered this day a symbol and a suitable reaction to create a balance of the feud; however, on August 21, 2017 Taylor Swift decided to return with a new album, *reputation*; I decided it was better to wait for Taylor Swift to make her own move given that she was the main target of the West family (Kanye West and Kim Kardashian West were married at the time); I postponed the launch until July 2018: I thought it was long enough for Taylor Swift to present her own strategy for rebuilding her reputation and create her own response to Kanye West and Kim Kardashian;
- in August 2018 I started a new job and, unfortunately, I did not have time to revisit the report and publish it; from this moment I let the report to rest in the folder;
- in April 2019 I returned to the report and decided that it is better if I include more information about the feud and for this reason the data used in this report include many sources from different years, 2016-2022; the new information in the report can be observed after the 'date of publication' and the date of the 'last accessed' of the online resources used;
- in the middle of March 2020, the Covid 19 pandemic forced me to work from home and I had time to revise the report's findings; I added new information and planned to publish it on July 16: the symbol day of the *Famous* feud; however, news were pouring on Twitter that Kanye West had decided to announce a new album and I wanted to listen to it hoping to find information that could change the report's

conclusions, but the album was postponed for July 2020 and, since the pandemic forced me to work from home, I decided that if I waited 3 years, I could wait until July; however, on July 23, Taylor Swift announced the *folklore* album and, again, I postponed the report for another date;

- over the summer of 2020, I added *folklore* to the report and set a release date for late August 2020, but Kanye West decided to announce the *Donda* album, and I waited again to give Kanye West the same option as I did with Taylor Swift's *folklore*; at the same time the volume of work increased and I had to postpone the launch date again;
- in December 2020 Taylor Swift decided to release her second surprise album, *Evermore*, and I decided to add it to the report; at this point I decided not to plan any more launches, to give up the report and to deal with other much more important research ideas;
- in July 2021, while on vacation, after listening to the new version of the song *The Lakes (Original Version)*, I remembered the report and came up with the plan to divide it: the first part to be *On the Famous Feud*: an analysis of the feud and events between Kanye West and Taylor Swift (around 200 pages); the second part about black and white artists and the source of their music (around 200 pages);
- in August 2021 I published the second part of the report under the name *Black and White Music: A Journey Behind the Musical Notes* and I added new research reasons;
- in April 2022 I decided that *Black and White Music* had enough time and space to breathe into the public mind and be browsed by readers, but this time I will not plan any release date; I will let everything to flow without caring if someone will read it or if it will have a positive impact on participants, the fans, the general public and the Western mass-media.

In the first chapter, **THE PLAYERS AND THE METHODOLOGY OF THE FAMOUS FEUD**, I described the main research methods and the limits of the research.

In the second chapter, **THE FAMOUS FEUD TIMELINE**, I investigated the timeline of the *Famous* feud in the Western mass-media from three points of view:

a) the key moments of the *Famous* feud,
b) detailed and specific information about the *Famous* feud,
c) what is missing from the *Famous* feud timeline.

To achieve this purpose, I created a *1. General timeline of the Famous feud in the Western mass-media*: United Kingdom (UK), United States of America (USA); Australia is not part of

Western mass-media, but I decided to include it as an optional view of the *Famous* feud presented in a country outside what is considered 'Western world (countries on the West of Europe, but still English as a main language)'; *2. I analysed the events of the timeline* for each research target (USA, UK, Australia)*, 3. then I compared the results between the research targets* to create a general view of Western mass-media from the three points of view written above. The final results were added in a table and in the form of a figure and were used as an extra source of information to analyse and compare the events of the feud in the Western mass-media.

In another section of this chapter, I wrote the details of events from the *Famous* feud. This timeline includes only the conversations and interviews of Kanye West, Kim Kardashian and Taylor Swift. Further to chapter one, I investigated the narrative line of the relationship between Kanye West and Taylor Swift from September 2009 (MTV Music Awards) to November 2017 (the release of Taylor Swift's *reputation* album) and between Kim Kardashian and Taylor Swift from June 2016 to November 2017, with the purpose to find patterns of behaviour that either might show unknown information, or what we know already can be presented in a new way that might be use for a better and easier understanding of the feud.

In chapter three, ***HOW MUCH TAYLOR SWIFT KNEW ABOUT THE FAMOUS SONG***, I evaluated four points of view:

1. Kanye West wrote on Twitter: '3rd thing I called Taylor and had a hour long convo with her about the line and she thought it was funny and gave her blessings';
2. Kim Kardashian in the interview with GQ magazine from 16 June 2016 and during her show *Keeping Up With The Kardashians* (season 12, episode 11): 'She totally approved that. […] 'She totally knew that was coming out;'
3. the affirmation made by Taylor Swift in July 2016: 'Being falsely painted as a liar when I was never given the full story *or played any part of the song* (underline by author) is character assassination';
4. general knowledge of the *Famous* song in percentage: the content of this section was created with the purpose to check in percentage how much Taylor Swift knew about the *Famous* song.

The information presented in chapter three is also for lovers of details, numbers and charts.

In chapter four, ***THE IMPACT OF THE FAMOUS FEUD***, I investigated:

1. the impact of the *Famous* feud on music album sales: the first week in the USA between Taylor Swift and Kanye West;
2. global sales of the songs that are the cause of the feud: *Famous* for Kanye West, *Look What You Made Me Do* for Taylor Swift and *Swish, Swish* for Katy Perry;
3. the impact of the *Bad Blood – Swish, Swish* feud on global album sales between Taylor Swift and Katy Perry;
4. the number of producers and songwriters of the songs involved in the *Famous* feud: *Famous* for Kanye West, *Look What You Made Me Do* for Taylor Swift;
5. the sources of inspiration and originality of the albums released after the MTV VMA event in 2009: Taylor Swift's album: *Speak Now*, and Kanye West's album: *My Beautiful Dark Twisted Fantasy*;
6. the rating available on Metacritic;
7. the connection between the *Famous* feud and the *Bad Blood – Swish, Swish* feud, Taylor Swift versus Katy Perry.

Although being presented as a feud of Taylor Swift with Katy Perry, actually this feud is linked with the *Famous* feud which is explored in extenso.

Chapter five, **FAMOUS** *FEUD: STRATEGIES OF INTERPRETATION AND COMMUNICATION* is about revealing the mechanisms and strategies of interpretation and communication of the *Famous* feud used by Kanye West, Kim Kardashian, Taylor Swift and the Western mass-media. There is strong evidence in favour of Taylor Swift, however, too many journalists came to conclusions about Taylor Swift that shocked me, for example Amy Zimmerman in her article published by *The Daily Beast* wrote about Taylor Swift: 'has been tapping into virginal white victim tropes her entire career.'[6] After reading this article, I decided to explore more news sources to see how Taylor Swift is presented by various journalists. I found over one thousand articles written about the feud and I arranged them in two categories: USA and UK with the name of the news agency and a link to the website source. I gathered links about the *Famous* feud from the following news agencies: Slate Magazine, People, Vanity Fair, Cosmopolitan, Glamour Magazine, Elle, Vulture, Marie Claire, Forbes, Ok! UK, Radar Online, GQ, The Sun, Metro, Evening Standard, Telegraph, Daily Star, The Guardian, The Independent, Express, AOL.co.uk, Mirror, Huffington Post, Daily Mail, Pagesix, Billboard, CBS News, Business Insider, Harpers Bazaar, New York Daily, Gossip Cop (the best source for accuracy, I gathered 33 links about the feud; the articles are not available at the time of publication of this report, all of them were deleted from the website), Rolling Stone, People,

---

[6] Amy Zimmerman, 'Taylor Swift's History of Suing Friends, Fans, and Foes—and Now Kimye?', *The Daily Beast*, July 23, 2016, available at: https://www.thedailybeast.com/taylor-swifts-history-of-suing-friends-fans-and-foesand-now-kimye, last accessed: June 26, 2022.

E Online, Lifestyle, The Atlantic, TMZ, W Magazine, Latinpost, Daily Beast, Buzzfeed, Los Angeles Time, US Magazine and TIME.

From over one thousand articles, I managed to read over 500 articles. Simply put: I got sick of the drama and I could not read anymore. The statements released by Taylor Swift and her management team regarding her involvement in the *Famous* song released by Kanye West are also analysed. This text analysis is done with the purpose to expose the inability of journalists and bloggers to follow and understand the logical flow of Taylor Swift's statements and reach logical conclusions regarding this feud. After the text analysis, I created a table with a list of the negative content written by various journalists (names included) and published in popular and highly acclaimed news agencies in the USA and in the UK (name of the news agencies, title and date of publication is included). In the end, I offered snap-shots with negative representation of Taylor Swift by various journalists through their articles about the *Famous* feud despite the lack of hard and clear evidence of her true involvement in the creation of the *Famous* song.

In chapter six, **FAMOUS** *REASONS FOR A* **FAMOUS** *FEUD*, I wrote reasons to justify the strategies used to fuel voluntarily and involuntarily the feud by Kanye West, Kim Kardashian, Taylor Swift and the Western mass-media. All the reasons are speculative and some negative. Maybe there is a possibility that these speculative reasons to have some truth and could help in making a better understanding of the events between Kanye West, Kim Kardashian and Taylor Swift. There are more negative reasons for Kanye West because he started the feud and Taylor Swift was in defence mode. Also, in this chapter, I found an interesting pattern that is happening in 2008, 2009 and 2016 and involves Taylor Swift, Kanye West and Beyoncé.

Finally, *WHO IS THE* **FAMOUS** *VICTIM AND WHO IS THE* **FAMOUS** *PERPETRATOR*, I reformulated the purpose of this report and the conclusions I reached for each item of research.

.

I. The players and the methodology of the **FAMOUS** feud

I.1 The players of the **FAMOUS** feud

I.1.1 Ye (Kanye West in this report)[7]

Kanye West is Grammy Award-winning (24) rapper, record producer, entrepreneur, fashion designer and one of the greatest and most influential hip hop musicians of all time. Kanye West's views about the music industry, politics, race and personal life received significant media coverage being a frequent source of controversy.[8] In October 2013, Kanye West was officially engaged to Kim Kardashian, a few months later they married in Florence, Italy. On February 19, 2021, Kim Kardashian filed for divorce and was declared legally single on March 2, 2022.[9]

I.1.2 Kim Kardashian[10]

Kim Kardashian is the star of the reality show 'Keeping Up with the Kardashians', model, media personality and businesswoman (creating brands such as KKW Beauty, KKW Fragrance and SKIMS). Kim Kardashian was under the loop of the Western mass-media and news coverage before she met Kanye West (engaged in October 2013), for example her friendship with Paris Hilton. However, the mass media attention grew higher than before in

---

[7] Born Kanye Omari West; June 8, 1977. I decided to keep the former name because the information in this report happened when his name was Kanye West and not the current name, Ye. For more information, read Guardian Staff and Agencies, 'Kanye West officially changes name to Ye', *The Guardian*, October 19, 2021, available at:
https://www.theguardian.com/music/2021/oct/19/kanye-west-changes-name-ye, last accessed: June 26, 2022.
[8] Kanye West, *Wikipedia*, available at: https://en.wikipedia.org/wiki/Kanye_West, last accessed: June 26, 2022.
[9] Nancy Dillon, 'Kim Kardashian Declared Legally Single From Kanye West: 'Thank You So Much'', *Rolling Stone*, March 2, 2022, available at: https://www.rollingstone.com/music/music-news/kim-kardashian-kanye-west-divorce-final-1315042/, last accessed: June 26, 2022.
[10] Born Kimberly Noel Kardashian (formerly West; born October 21, 1980). I decided to keep the former name because the information in this report happened when her name was Kim Kardashian West and not the current name.

2007 due to a video leaked online showing her sexual intercourse with former boyfriend, rapper Ray J.[11] However, the high leap into the Hollywood world was not because of this video, but more to her ability to adapt to fashion trends, the marriage to Kanye West and, mostly, her vision to identify opportunities for women in the USA; currently she is involved in a four-year law apprenticeship that is supervised by the legal nonprofit #cut50 to become a lawyer with the purpose to improve the prison system in the USA.[12]

I.1.3 Taylor Swift[13]

Taylor Swift is one of the best-selling musicians of all time (more than 200 million records sold worldwide), her concert tours are some of the highest-grossing in history; received 11 Grammy Awards (including three *Album of the Year*, first women in the history to win this award for a third time), an Emmy Award, 34 American Music Awards (the most for an artist), 29 Billboard Music Awards (the most for a woman), Woman of the Decade and Artist of the Decade. Like Kanye West, Taylor Swift has received critical praise and widespread media coverage; however, for Taylor, the media coverage was also due to being involved in various relationships that did not end well all the time and many songs from her catalogue are her side of the story.[14]

I.1.4 '**FAMOUS** Feud': a definition

'Famous feud': is the long-term dispute, conflict, bitter disagreement due to different views about awards for music recognition, events behind recorded phone calls, forced interference in the narrative line of Kanye West (from September 2009 until present), Taylor Swift (from September 2009) and Kim Kardashian (from spring 2016 until present).

The 'Famous feud' concept was coined by Western mass-media starting with February 2016 and the release of the song *Famous* by Kanye West in which he used the following lyrics in reference to Taylor Swift for which he takes credit for her career: 'I feel like me and Taylor might still have sex / Why? I made that bitch famous (God damn) / I made that bitch famous.'

---

[11] Kim Kardashian, *Wikipedia*, available at: https://en.wikipedia.org/wiki/Kim_Kardashian, last accessed: June 26, 2022.
[12] Sara Bliss, 'Kim Kardashian Is Becoming A Lawyer: What Her Move Can Teach You About Making A Career Leap', *Forbes,* April 18, 2019, available at: https://www.forbes.com/sites/sarabliss/2019/04/18/kim-kardashian-is-becoming-a-lawyer-what-her-move-can-teach-you-about-making-a-career-leap/, last accessed: June 26, 2022.
[13] Taylor Alison Swift (born December 13, 1989).
[14] Taylor Swift, *Wikipedia*, available at: https://en.wikipedia.org/wiki/Taylor_Swift, last accessed: June 26, 2022.

In this report, I used 'Famous feud' to describe all the events between Kanye West, Taylor Swift and Kim Kardashian.

I.1.5 Western Mass-Media: a definition

I define 'Western Mass-Media': news agencies / blogs / magazines (online and printed) from English-speaking countries: United States of America (USA), United Kingdom (UK) and Australia; also: journalists and bloggers from these countries.

In terms of specific 'Western Mass-Media', I included the following news agencies / blogs / magazines (online and printed): Slate Magazine, People, Vanity Fair, Cosmopolitan, Glamour Magazine, Elle, Vulture, Marie Claire, Forbes, Ok! UK, Radar Online, GQ, The Sun, Metro, Evening Standard, Telegraph, Daily Star, The Guardian, The Independent, Express, AOL.co.uk, Mirror, Huffington Post, Daily Mail, Pagesix, Billboard, CBS News, Business Insider, Harpers Bazaar, New York Daily, Gossip Cop (the best source for accuracy, I gathered 33 links about the feud; the articles are not available, all of them were deleted from the website), Rolling Stone, People, E Online, Lifestyle, The Atlantic, TMZ, W Magazine, Latinpost, Daily Beast, Buzzfeed, Los Angeles Time, US Magazine, TIME.

I.2 The methodology of the **FAMOUS** feud

In this subchapter I described the research methodology used in this report.

To find the existence of patterns:

- I used key dates of the *Famous* feud (based on the precise date (day, month, year) when the events happened) available in the table with the *Famous* feud timeline; the dates were used to create a figure with a 3D narrative line which shows the dynamic between the players of the *Famous* feud; the creation of one large figure (Figure 9) allowed me to see the whole narrative line of the main players of the feud; the starting point of the patterns is in September 2009 with Kanye West and Taylor Swift and continues as today even if the figure does not contain information about the feud after November 2017;
- I linked and compared the events from Kanye West's life with the events from Taylor Swift's life; in other words, what events existed in Taylor Swift's narrative line when Kanye West interfered in her narrative line;

- surprisingly, Taylor Swift is not the only artist which has to deal with Kanye West's interference in the narrative line, he does it with other people[15] as well.

The information collected from the credit page will be used for the rest of this report without recitation.

The main research methods are:

- counting
- division
- subtraction
- adding
- conversion into percentage;
- the average method.

The Album Release Dates:

- I used the information to find patterns that could show how artists are releasing their albums: similarities, differences and patterns (predictable, fixed, changing and surprise);
- I used the findings to see if there is a positive and negative interference in the narrative line of the album release between Kanye West, Taylor Swift and Beyoncé.

Famous Reasons for a Famous Feud:

- during the investigation, I wrote various reasons why the *Famous* feud was created and supported for more than 10 years; the reasons are based on the data used in this report; all the reasons are speculative and some negative, maybe there is a possibility that these speculative reasons to have some truth and could help in making a better understanding of the events between Kanye West, Kim Kardashian and Taylor Swift.

The Race of the Samples:

- this is used only for the comparative study between Taylor Swift and Kanye West: I investigated only their albums released in 2010 where I wanted to expose how many black and white people inspired the artists in creating their music.

---

[15] I used 'people' instead of artists, because I'm not sure if all the information collected and the people involved in it can be added in the 'artist' category.

The Limits of the Research:

- all the information in this report should not be used as a source of final truth: only a few research ideas under certain conditions were used to show information (perhaps unknown until now) about the background narrative and strategies of interpretation and communication (connections, similarities, differences) used by the players of the feud;
- Metacritic website does not include all the reviews written about the albums, there are reviews with higher and lower grades which are not included, and therefore the real and final grade could be higher or lower than what it is available on Metacritic and in this report;
- the information and conclusions of this report is limited and should be used only in terms of the data used here;
- readers should use 'maybe' and 'suggest' as strategy of interpretation regarding the content of this report even if the specific keywords ('maybe' and 'suggest') are not found in the text all the time;
- in this report some information was updated with news from 2022, other with news from 2021 and some left as first date used in 2017; for a better clarification, read the footnotes to find out the date when the information was collected and verified for the last time;
- the conclusions of this reports are based on the evidence available at the time of publishing and based on what I was capable to collect and interpret, however, it is possible that in reality, in the full conversation between Kanye West and Taylor Swift, there may be more than 25 minutes as we have today on Youtube, and to be more information that will either will reject, approve or reject and accept different parts of the findings;
- there may be a wrong interpretation of the information used and I could not see or think about it as a wrong way to use it;
- this report explored mostly interpretation / comparison / mathematical / maybe / suggestion / correlations and cannot provide / assure / guarantee all the time a clear causal evidence and link to support the findings.

II. The **FAMOUS** feud timeline

In this chapter I investigated the timeline of the *Famous* feud in the Western mass-media from three points of view:

a) the key moments of the *Famous* feud,
b) detailed and specific information about the *Famous* feud,
c) what is missing from the *Famous* feud timeline.

To achieve this purpose:

1. I created *A general timeline of the Famous feud in the Western mass-media*: United Kingdom (UK), United States of America (USA); Australia is not part of Western mass-media, but I decided to include it as an optional view of the *Famous* feud presented in a country outside what is considered 'Western world (countries on the West of Europe, but still English as a main language)';

2. *I analysed the events of the timeline* for each research target (USA, UK, Australia);

3. *I compared the results between the research targets* to create a general view of Western mass-media from the three points of view written above.

The general methodology of this chapter is described below:

- I searched on Google.com the keywords: 'taylor swift Kanye west timeline';
- I accessed articles written only in newspapers in the United Kingdom, the United States and Australia;
- I collected the key dates of the *Famous* feud written in the Western mass-media from February 11, 2016 (the beginning of the feud) until November 10, 2017 (on the day Taylor Swift released the album *reputation* considered by the Western mass-media and fans as a response to Kanye West and Kim Kardashian for revealing to the general public an edited part of the phone conversation between her and Kanye

West, but also to Katy Perry (wrote a song called *Swish, Swish* (2017) as a response to Taylor Swift's 2014 song *Bad Blood*;
- the final results were added in a table and in the form of a figure and were used as an extra source of information to analyse and compare the events of the feud in the Western mass-media.

II.1 The '**Famous** Feud' Timeline in the Western Mass-Media

II.1.1 United Kingdom

TABLE 1. THE **FAMOUS** FEUD TIMELINE IN THE UNITED KINGDOM NEWS

NEWS	AUTHOR	TITLE WITH LINK	DATE OF PUBLICATION	LAST ACCESSED
THE INDEPENDENT	Olivia Blair	Taylor Swift and Kanye West Feud: A Brief History of the Pair's Relationship	16/07/2016	24/09/2017
MIRROR	Rebecca Pocklington	Kanye West and Taylor Swift's Feud From The Start: A Timeline Of Their Biggest Rows Over The Years	18/07/2016	24/09/2017
HUFFINGTON POST	Julia Brucculieri	A Comprehensive Outline Of Everything That Just Went Down In The Kimye-Taylor Swift Feud	18/07/2016	24/09/2017
FEMALE FIRST UK	Daniel Falconer	The Taylor Swift and Kanye West Feud (featuring Kim Kardashian) – A Timeline	18/07/2016	24/09/2017
VOGUE UK	Lucy Hutchings	Taylor Swift Vs. Kim and Kanye: A Timeline	18/07/2016	24/09/2017
OK! MAGAZINE UK	Hayley Kadrou	Taylor Swift and Kanye West: A Timeline of Their On-Off Feud	18/07/2016	24/09/2017
Elle UK	Unsah Malik	Taylor Swift Vs. Kimye: A Timeline Of Everything	02/08/2016	24/09/2017
METRO	Emma Kelly	A Brief History Of Taylor Swift And The 'Snakes' – Who Will Be Targeted On Reputation?	24/08/2017	24/09/2017
COSMOPOLITAN	Emma Dibdin	A Timeline of Taylor Swift and Kanye West's Feud	28/08/2017	24/09/2017
POPSUGAR UK	Ryan Roschke	A Timeline Of The Drama Between Kanye West And Taylor Swift	30/08/2017 – updated 3/09/2017	24/09/2017

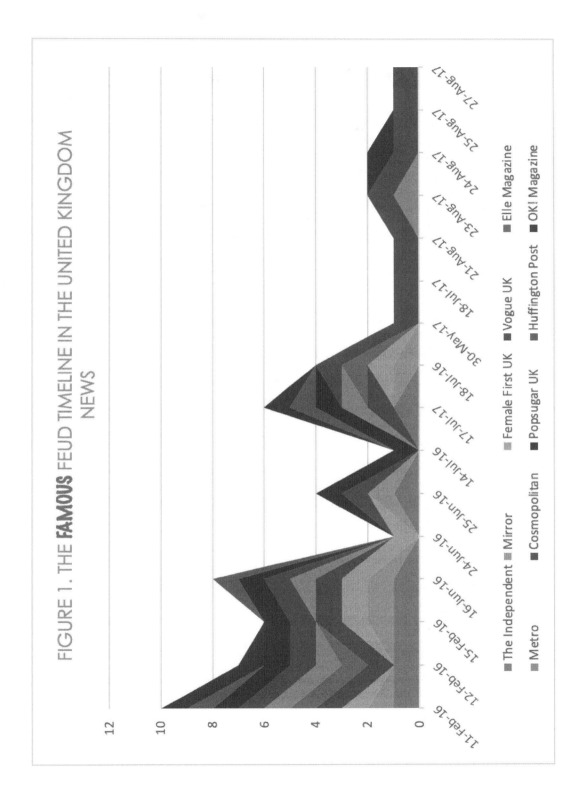

FIGURE 1. THE **FAMOUS** FEUD TIMELINE IN THE UNITED KINGDOM NEWS

II.1.2 United States of America

TABLE 2. THE **FAMOUS** FEUD TIMELINE IN THE UNITED STATES OF AMERICA NEWS

NEWS	AUTHOR	TITLE WITH LINK	DATE OF PUBLICATION	LAST ACCESSED
BILLBOARD	Erin Strecker Adelle Platon	Kanye West & Taylor Swift: A Complete Timeline of Their Relationship	9/08/2015 – updated until July 17, 2016	24/09/2017
CBS NEWS	-	Kanye West vs. Taylor Swift: A Timeline	16/02/2016	24/09/2017
ROLLING STONE	Keith Harris	Taylor Swift vs. Kanye West: A Beef History	16/02/2016 – updated August 2017	24/09/2017
BUZZFEED	Jemima Skelley	The Whole Kanye And Taylor Mess Just Got Even Worse	18/07/2016	24/09/2017
BUZZFEED	Sam Stryker	We Have All The Receipts In The Feud Between Taylor Swift, Kim Kardashian, And Kanye West	18/07/2016	24/09/2017
BUZZFEED	Ellie Bate	The Kim-Kanye-Taylor Feud, Explained For People Who Don't Know What The Hell Is Going On	18/07/2016	24/09/2017
TELL TALES ONLINE	-	Kanye West And Taylor Swift: A Timeline Of Their Feud	24/02/2016 – updated August 2017	24/09/2017
TEEN VOGUE	De Elizabeth	Taylor Swift and Kanye West Feud: A Breakdown of Every Event	18/07/2016	24/09/2017
US MAGAZINE	Nicholas Hautman	Kanye West and Taylor Swift's Tumultuous Relationship: A Timeline of Their Ups and Downs	18/07/2016	24/09/2017
HOLLYWOOD LIFE	Chris Rogers	Taylor Swift Vs. Kimye: Everything You Need To Know About Explosive Feud — Timeline	18/07/2016	24/09/2017
THE ODISSEY	Jolie Delia	A Timeline Of Every Taylor Swift Feud Ever	18/07/2016	24/09/2017
WIRED	Brian Raftery	Buckle Up: The Kanye West/Taylor Swift Feud Will Continue Until the End of Time	18/07/2016	24/09/2017
ESQUIRE	Matt Miller	A Very Brief Recap of the New Twist in the Kanye West / Taylor Swift Feud	18/07/2016	24/09/2017
NME	Helen Thomas	Taylor Swift and Kanye West: The Good, The Bad, And The Ugly In Their Long-Standing Feud	18/07/2016	24/09/2017
THE WRAP	Rasha Ali	Taylor Swift and Kanye West: A Timeline of the Epic Feud (Photos)	18/07/2016	24/09/2017

II. THE **FAMOUS** FEUD TIMELINE

THRILIST	Dan Jackson	Why Kim Kardashian Annihilated Taylor Swift On Snapchat	18/07/2016	24/09/2017
COMPLEX	Complex	A Timeline of Kanye West and Taylor Swift's Feud Over the „Famous' Lyric	18/07/2016	24/09/2017
THE FADER	David Renshaw	A Brief History Of The Kanye West And Taylor Swift 'Famous' Rift	18/07/2016	24/09/2017
MOVIEPILOT	Varia Fedko-Blake	Kimye Vs. Taylor Swift: A Full Rundown Of The Rockiest Relationship In The Business	18/07/2016	24/09/2017
TIME	Cady Lang	A Comprehensive Guide to the Kanye West-Taylor Swift-Kim Kardashian West Feud	19/07/2016 – updated 29/07/2016	24/09/2017
LA TIMES	Christie D'Zurilla	Kanye West vs. Taylor Swift: A Timeline Of The Drama, Which Now Includes Kim Kardashian West	19/07/2016	24/09/2017
HARPER BAZAAR	Emma Dibdin	The Complete Timeline of Kanye West and Taylor Swift's Feud	19/07/2016	24/09/2017
CAPITAL FM	-	Watch: A Complete Timeline Of The Taylor Vs Kanye & Kim Beef (Just As It's Getting So Complicated)	19/07/2016	24/09/2017
HFG	copa0077	A Timeline Of Taylor Swift And Kanye West's Feud	31/05/2017	24/09/2017
PEOPLE	Grace Gavilanes	Taylor Swift and Kanye West's Rocky History: A Timeline	Updated 24/08/2017	24/09/2017
PEOPLE	Laura Cohen	A Timeline of the Complicated Relationship Between Taylor Swift and Kim Kardashian West	Posted 25/08/2017	24/09/2017
GLAMOUR MAGAZINE	Carolina Nicolao	Taylor Swift vs Kanye West: A Timeline Of Their Ongoing Feud	25/08/2017	24/09/2017
BUSTLE	Sabienna Bowman	A Timeline of Kanye West & Taylor Swift's Feud To Help You Process 'Look What You Made Me Do'	It does not have a publication date, however at the moment of data collection the publication date was „a month ago'	24/09/2017
FOX NEWS	-	Taylor Swift's Celebrity Feud History: From Kanye West to Katy Perry, And Beyond	25/08/2017	24/09/2017
POPSUGAR	Ryan Roschke	A Timeline Of The Drama Between Kanye West And Taylor Swift	30/08/2017 – updated 3/09/2017	24/09/2017
NEW YORK DAILY NEWS	-	A Timeline Of The Drama Between Kanye West And Taylor Swift		24/09/2017

WIX	Brenda Santana	Kanye West v. Taylor Swift: A Historical Timeline	No date of publication	24/09/2017
HELLO! MAGAZINE	-	A Timeline Of Taylor Swift, Kanye West and Kim Kardashian's Rocky Relationship	No date of publication	24/09/2017

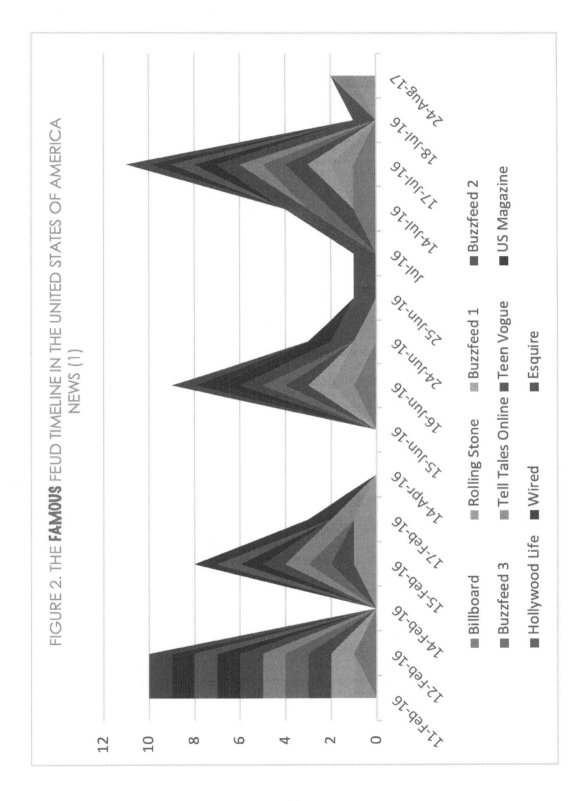

FIGURE 2. THE **FAMOUS** FEUD TIMELINE IN THE UNITED STATES OF AMERICA NEWS (1)

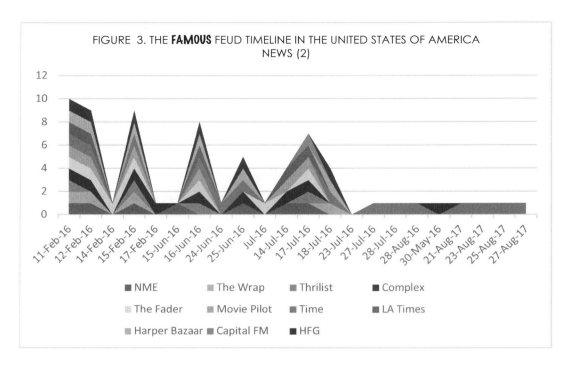

FIGURE 3. THE **FAMOUS** FEUD TIMELINE IN THE UNITED STATES OF AMERICA NEWS (2)

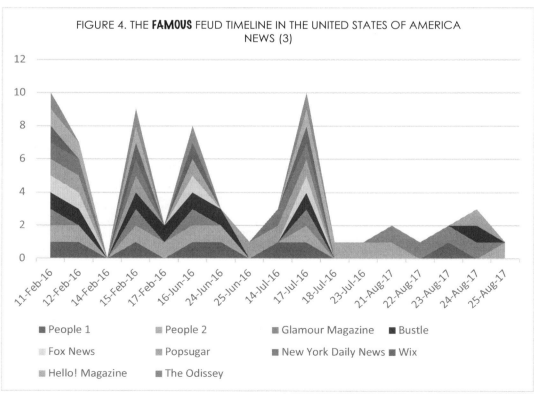

FIGURE 4. THE **FAMOUS** FEUD TIMELINE IN THE UNITED STATES OF AMERICA NEWS (3)

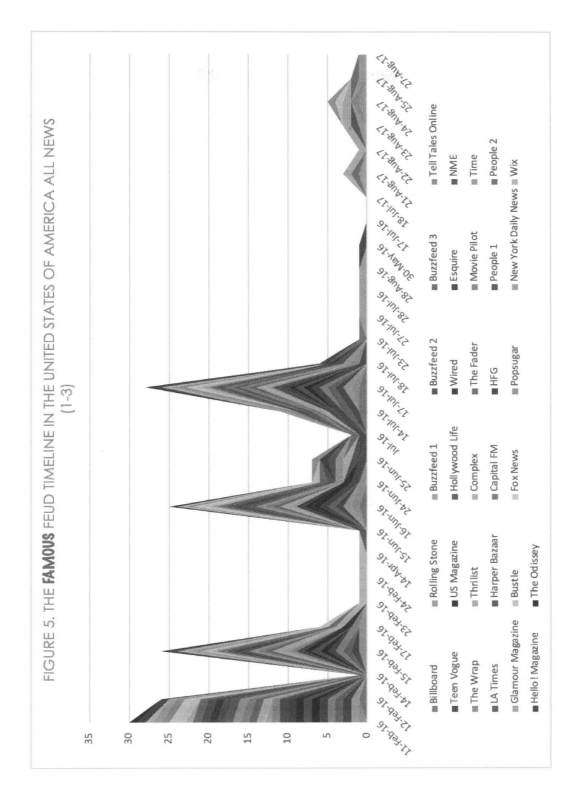

FIGURE 5. THE **FAMOUS** FEUD TIMELINE IN THE UNITED STATES OF AMERICA ALL NEWS (1-3)

II.1.3 Australia

TABLE 3. THE **FAMOUS** FEUD TIMELINE IN AUSTRALIA NEWS

NEWS SOURCE	AUTHOR	TITLE WITH THE LINK	DATE OF PUBLICATION	LAST ACCESSED
POPSUGAR AUSTRALIA	Ryan Roschke	How Did We Get Here? A Timeline of the Taylor Swift and Kanye West Drama	19/07/2016	24/09/2017
YAHOO AUSTRALIA	Sarah Norton	A Timeline Of The Tumultuous Kanye West vs Taylor Swift Feud	19/07/2016	24/09/2017
VOGUE AUSTRALIA	Vogue Staff	Frenemies: A Complete Timeline Of Kanye West And Taylor Swift's Friendship	28/08/2017	24/09/2017

FIGURE 6. THE **FAMOUS** FEUD TIMELINE IN AUSTRALIA NEWS

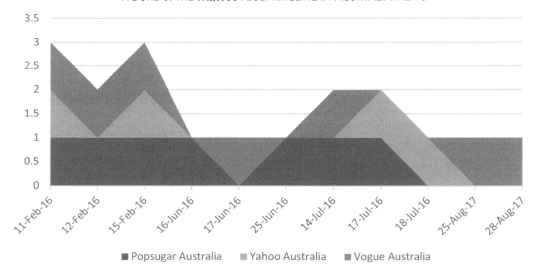

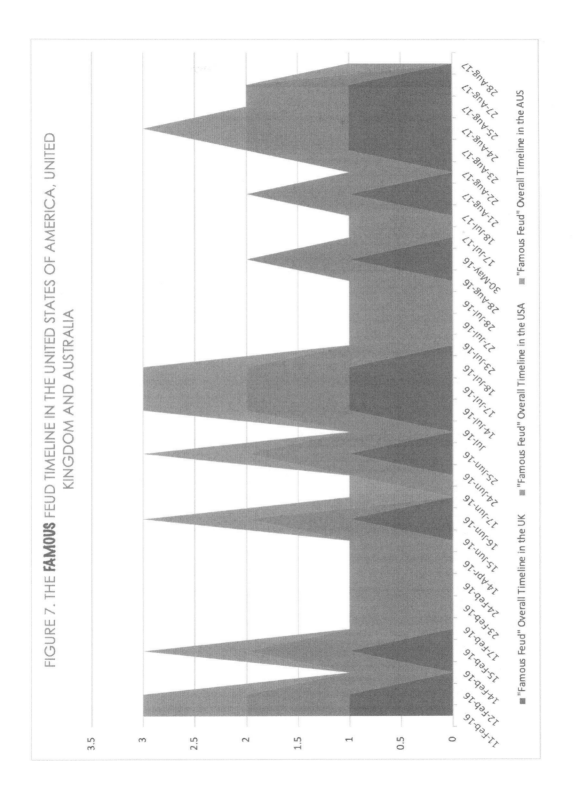

FIGURE 7. THE **FAMOUS** FEUD TIMELINE IN THE UNITED STATES OF AMERICA, UNITED KINGDOM AND AUSTRALIA

II.1.4 Western Mass-Media Timeline: Conclusion

The conclusions of the timeline presented by the Western mass-media (general, not specific to each news source) is rendered for each purpose detailed in the methodology written at the beginning of the chapter.

a. key moments of the *Famous* feud:

- the Western mass-media focused on the important elements of the feud, respectively the beginning and the confession of Kanye West about the involvement of Taylor Swift in making the song and her negation (February 2016);
- presented the edited video as evidence of the telephone conversation (July 2016) and wrote that Taylor Swift knew Kanye West had a song that she knew and accepted it, except the word 'bitch' and the line 'I made that bitch famous';

b. detailed and specific information on the *Famous* feud:

- each newspaper exposed the two key moments (accusation and proof), but the difference between the news sources is the following: some news sources exposed the timeline in the smallest details (for example *Complex* is the only news source which includes Taylor Swift's response from April 2016 to the *Famous* feud in 2016) or focused on only three key important events such as Thrilist (February, June, and July 2016);
- among the news sources with a detailed and updated timeline for 2017 I found for example Rolling Stone, Popsugar, Time, Bustle, Glamour Magazine and People;
- some news sources collected and added in the timeline the dates of a feud event, depending on when new information was provided by Kanye West, Kim Kardashian or Taylor Swift (for example *Rolling Stone* wrote in the timeline the launch of the video of the *Famous* song on June 24, 2016 when it was published on Tidal; *Time* wrote June 25, 2016 (probably on this date the journalist saw the video), *The Fader* has July 1, 2016 (the release date of the music video of the *Famous* song on Youtube));
- the timeline presented by the mass-media in a different format (either all events, the important events or the association of an event from the feud with the day when the journalists collected the information about the events from the feud) can be confusing for readers, especially for readers who access multiple news sources to verify the information, however, this presentation of information about the players in the feud does not change the finding: high neutrality about the feud;

c. what is missing from the *Famous* timeline:

- Taylor Swift's response from April 2016 (she refused to add more information) to the *Famous* feud in 2016 in the timeline of all the news agency (except Complex);
- the wrong position of the telephone conversation between the artists from January 2016 to July 2016: all the timelines wrote the phone conversation from January 2016 in July 2016 because in this month the phone conversation was made public; for a better view of the dynamic between the artists involved, the conversation should be changed to its original place, January 2016; this aspect is important as it accurately reproduces the order of events and help to identify the communication strategy of the two artists and who misled first.

II.2 The '**Famous** Feud' Timeline

In this chapter I wrote the events of the *Famous* feud. Because both artists have deleted the public content on their social media pages (Twitter, Instagram, Facebook), readers will be sent to news sources where evidence is still to be found. This timeline includes only the conversations between Kanye West, Kim Kardashian and Taylor Swift. The conclusions of this section are written after the table and the figure with the *Famous* timeline.

TABLE 4. **FAMOUS** FEUD TIMELINE 2009 - 2017	
SEPTEMBER 13, 2009	
TAYLOR SWIFT	KANYE WEST
-	While Taylor Swift was giving her acceptance speech for Best Female Video *You Belong with Me* at MTV Video Music Awards, Kanye West got onto the stage and interrupted her; he took her microphone, saying: "Yo, Taylor, I'm really happy for you and I'mma let you finish, but Beyoncé had one of the best videos of all time! One of the best videos of all time!" (Kanye West was referring to the music video for 'Single Ladies (Put a Ring on It)'. He then handed the microphone back to

Taylor Swift. Kanye West posted an apology on his blog.[16]

SEPTEMBER 14, 2009	
TAYLOR SWIFT	KANYE WEST
The interview with E Online News after the MTV show: "I was standing on stage and I was really excited because I had just won the award and then I was really excited because Kanye West was on the stage," […] "And then I wasn't so excited anymore after that." The reporter asked Taylor Swift if she has hard feelings about Kanye West. Taylor responded: "I don't know him and I've never met him." The reporter continued asking Taylor if she was a fan before the event from the stage. Taylor responded: "Yeah, It's Kanye West." The reporter continued asking Taylor if she is still a fan and 'I take a no?' Taylor responded: "You know I just… I don't know him and I don't want to start anything because I just, you know, I had a great night tonight."[17]	Kanye West posted a second apology on his blog; he appeared on The Jay Leno Show later that night, where he delivered another apology to Taylor Swift: "Dealing with the fact that I hurt someone or took anything away, you know, from a talented artist – or from anyone – because I only wanted to help people.' '…My entire life, I've only wanted to do and give something that I felt was right and I immediately knew in this situation that it was wrong."[18]
SEPTEMBER 15, 2009	
TAYLOR SWIFT	KANYE WEST
On September 15, 2009, two days after the outburst, Swift talked about the matter on	

---

[16] Jayson Rodriguez, 'Kanye West Crashes VMA Stage During Taylor Swift's Award Speech', *MTV*, September 13, 2009, http://www.mtv.com/news/1621389/kanye-west-crashes-vma-stage-during-taylor-swifts-award-speech/, last accessed: October 24, 2017; Daniel Kreps, 'Kanye West Storms the VMAs Stage During Taylor Swift's Speech', *Rolling Stone*, September 13, 2009, https://www.rollingstone.com/music/news/kanye-west-storMs.-the-vmas-stage-during-taylor-swifts-speech-20090913?rand=84857, last accessed: October 24, 2017.

[17] Breanne L. Heldman, 'Kanye West Steals Taylor Swift's Thunder…but Not for Long', *E Online*, September 14, 2009, available at: https://www.eonline.com/news/143965/kanye-west-steals-taylor-swift-s-thunder-but-not-for-long, last accessed: October 23, 2017.

[18] Jayson Rodriguez, 'Kanye West Tells Jay Leno He's 'Ashamed' of VMA Outburst', *MTV*, September 14, 2009, http://www.mtv.com/news/1621529/kanye-west-tells-jay-leno-hes-ashamed-of-vma-outburst/, last accessed: October 24, 2017.

The View. Asked what she was thinking the moment it happened, she stated:

'Well, I think my overall thought process was something like, 'Wow, I can't believe I won, this is awesome, don't trip and fall, I'm gonna get to thank the fans, this is so cool. Oh, Kanye West is here. Cool haircut. What are you doing there?' And then, 'Ouch.' And then, 'I guess I'm not gonna get to thank the fans''[19]

Taylor Swift (after The View) told ABC News Radio: "Kanye did call me and he was very sincere in his apology, and I accepted that apology."[20]

Following Taylor Swift's appearance on *The View* show, Kanye West contacted her to apologize personally. Taylor Swift accepted his apology.

SEPTEMBER 4, 2010	
TAYLOR SWIFT	KANYE WEST
-	Kanye West wrote a series of tweets addressed to Taylor Swift and VMA incident: "It starts with this... I'm sorry Taylor." "I wrote a song for Taylor Swift that's so beautiful and I want her to have it. If she won't take it then I'll perform it for her." "She had nothing to do with my issues with award shows. She had no idea what hit her. She's just a lil girl with dreaMs. like the rest of us." "She deserves the apology more than anyone... Who am I to run on stage? I would never ever again in a million years do that. Sorry to let you down. It is distasteful to cut people off as a general rule. What's the point of dressing tastefully if I'm going to act the complete opposite? Yes I was that guy. A 32 year old child.

---

[19] Jocelyn Vena, 'Taylor Swift Tells 'The View' Kanye West Hasn't Contacted Her', *MTV*, September 15, 2009, http://www.mtv.com/news/1621550/taylor-swift-tells-the-view-kanye-west-hasnt-contacted-her/, last accessed: October 23, 2017.
[20] Sheila Marikar, 'Taylor Swift: Kanye West Called, 'Was Very Sincere in His Apology'', *ABC News*, September 15, 2009, http://abcnews.go.com/Entertainment/FallConcert/taylor-swift-talks-kanye-west-vmas-view/story?id=8580064, last accessed: October 23, 2017.

When I woke up from the crazy nightmare I looked in the mirror and said GROW UP KANYE ... I take the responsibility for my actions. Beyoncé didn't need that. MTV didn't need that and Taylor and her family friends and fans definitely didn't want or need that."[21]

SEPTEMBER 12, 2010	
TAYLOR SWIFT	KANYE WEST
During MTV VMAs, Taylor Swift sang 'Innocent', a song widely believed (mass media and fans of Taylor Swift and Kanye West) to be about Kanye West and her forgiveness for what Kanye West did to her a year ago: "It's alright, just wait and see Your string of lights is still bright to me You're still an innocent Lives change like the weather It's okay, life is a tough crowd 32 and still growin' up now I hope you remember Today is never too late to Be brand new."[22]	-

OCTOBER 19, 2010	
TAYLOR SWIFT	KANYE WEST
-	Appearing on *The Ellen Show*, Kanye West said that following the oversized reaction to 'the Taylor Swift incident,' he had to leave the country, living overseas for a while. *Ellen DeGeneres:* "Why?" *Kanye West:* "I feel in some ways I'm a soldier of culture. And I realize no one wants that to be my job. I'll never go onstage again, I'll never sit at an award show again, but will I feel feuded about

[21] Monica Herrera, 'Kanye West Bares All on Twitter: 'I Wrote a Song for Taylor Swift',' *Billboard*, September 4, 2010, https://www.billboard.com/articles/news/956495/kanye-west-bares-all-on-twitter-i-wrote-a-song-for-taylor-swift, last accessed: October 24, 2017; Daniel Kreps, 'Kanye Unveils New Track, Offers Song to Taylor Swift', *Rolling Stone*, September 7, 2010, http://www.rollingstone.com/music/news/kanye-unveils-new-track-offers-song-to-taylor-swift-20100907, last accessed: October 24, 2017.
[22] Taylor Swift, 'Innocent', Genius, https://genius.com/Taylor-swift-innocent-lyrics, last accessed: October 24, 2017.

things that meant something to culture that constantly get denied for years and years and years? I'm sorry, I will. I cannot lie about it in order to sell records."[23]

OCTOBER 20, 2010	
TAYLOR SWIFT	**KANYE WEST**
-	Kanye West had an interview with *Access Hollywood*: *Kanye West:* 'Why are the last four Albums of the Year: Taylor Swift, Dixie Chicks, Ray Charles and Herbie Hancock? Like, you know, with all due respect… that's inaccurate.'[24]

NOVEMBER 5, 2010	
TAYLOR SWIFT	**KANYE WEST**
-	Kanye West had an interview with the radio station KDWB: *Kanye West:* "My moment with Taylor, 12 years old, eighteen year old girl me um cutting her off it show like a lack of compassion with everything she went to to deserve this one moment that shouldn't you know that [inaudible] have 100 magazine covers and sell a million first week, but um um that shouldn't even categorize with the greatest living artists that we have to date even be put in the same category you know it's it's just it's just disrespectful was retarded and I for me you can see the amount of work that we put into this." *Kanye West:* "It's like, what's so arrogant about that moment? If anything, it's selfless. I'm walking around now with half an arm, trying to sell albums and having to walk in rooms and be afraid of my food getting spat in, like people going 'I lost all total respect for you,' and nobody wants to just sit and look at the reality."

[23] The Ellen Show, 'Kanye West Talks About the Taylor Swift Incident', *Youtube*, October 19, 2010, https://www.youtube.com/watch?v=rej2Ts_TpwQ, last accessed: October 24, 2017.
[24] Simon Vozick-Levinson, 'Kanye West says Taylor Swift, Dixie Chicks, Ray Charles didn't deserve Grammys', *Entertainment Weekly*, October 21, 2017, http://www.ew.com/article/2010/10/21/kanye-west-grammys-taylor-swift/, last accessed: October 24, 2017; see here the official interview: *Access Hollywood*, 'Kanye West Talks Grammys, Hopes For Wider Artist Recognition', October 24, 2010, http://www.accesshollywood.com/articles/kanye-west-talks-grammys-hopes-for-wider-artist-recognition-91822/, last accessed: 24 October 2017.

Kanye West: "The audacity of it losing anything … I guarantee if it was the other way around, and Taylor Swift was 15, 12, 15 years into the game, and on her 40th video or 50th video, and she made the video of her career, do you think she would have lost to a brand new artist? Hell no!"[25]

NOVEMBER 24, 2010	
TAYLOR SWIFT	KANYE WEST
-	During a secret show slash release party at the Bowery Ballroom in New York City last night, 1.00 am, Kanye West continued his rant by expressing his continued issues with singer Taylor Swift and said: "Taylor never came to my defense at any interview. … And rode the waves and rode it and rode it."[26]

JUNE 11, 2013	
TAYLOR SWIFT	KANYE WEST
-	In a *New York Times* interview Kanye West stated about Taylor Swift VMA's moment that he doesn't have any regret about his interruption and that it was a situation where he gave into peer pressure to apologize. When asked if he'd take back the original action or the apology, if given the choice, he answered, "You know what? I can answer that, but I'm – I'm just -- not afraid, but I know that would be such a distraction. It's such a strong thing, and people have such a strong feeling about it. *My Beautiful Dark Twisted Fantasy* was my long, backhanded apology. You know how people give a backhanded compliment? It was a backhanded apology. It was like, all these raps, all these sonic acrobatics. I was like: 'Let me show

---

[25] Sneakerhut37, 'New Interview - Kanye West speaks his mind November 5, 2010 (Part 1)', *Youtube*, November 8, 2010, https://www.youtube.com/watch?v=Uq3W-E782kc, last accessed: May 28, 2010.

[26] Jason, 'Kanye Blasts Taylor Swift & Matt Lauer (Video)', *Rap Basement*, November 24, 2010, http://www.rapbasement.com/kanye-west/112410-kanye-west-blasts-taylor-swift-and-matt-lauer-during-secret-show-in-new-york-city-watch-here.html, last accessed: May 28, 2010; *Post Staff Report*, 'Rapper Kanye West disses Taylor Swift … again: Report', November 24, 2010, https://nypost.com/2010/11/24/rapper-kanye-west-disses-taylor-swift-again-report/, last accessed: May 28, 2010; *US Weekly Staff*, 'Kanye West SlaTaylor Swift Again', November 24, 2010, https://www.usmagazine.com/entertainment/news/kanye-west-slaMs.-taylor-swift-again-20102411/, last accessed: May 28, 2010.

you guys what I can do, and please accept me back. You want to have me on your shelves."[27]

FEBRUARY 8, 2015	
TAYLOR SWIFT	KANYE WEST
Taylor was at the Grammy Awards and Kanye West was present as well.	Kany West was present at the Grammy Awards. Kanye West said in a telephone interview with Ryan Seacrest about Taylor Swift: "She wants to get in the studio and we're definitely going to go in', […] 'I don't have an elitism about music, I don't discriminate."[28]

APRIL 29, 2015	
TAYLOR SWIFT	KANYE WEST
In an interview with *Entertainment Tonight*, Cameron Mathison asked Taylor Swift about the rumored collaboration between her and Kanye West. Taylor Swift answered: "He has said that… We're never been in the studio together, but he's got a lot of amazing ideas, he's one of those people who's just like idea, idea, idea, like what you think of this, what you think of that, he's very creative and like I've think we've talked about it but we've also about so many other things, I think I completely respect his vision as a producer, so that's all I know now, I have no idea how the next album is gonna be though."[29]	- -

AUGUST 11, 2015	
TAYLOR SWIFT	KANYE WEST
During a cover interview with *Vanity Fair*, Taylor Swift said about Kanye West: "I feel like I wasn't ready to be friends with him until I felt like he had some sort of respect for me, and he wasn't ready to be friends with me until he had some sort of respect for me – so it was the same issue, and	-

[27] Jon Caramanica, 'Behind Kanye's Mask', *New York Times*, June 11, 2013, https://www.nytimes.com/2013/06/16/arts/music/kanye-west-talks-about-his-career-and-album-yeezus.html?_r=0, last accessed: May 28, 2018.

[28] On Air with Ryan Seacrest, 'Kanye West Explains Grammys Stunt, Plans to Work With Taylor Swift', *Youtube*, February 11, 2015, https://www.youtube.com/watch?v=Qg1hZ329eCU, last accessed: October 23, 2017.

[29] Entertainment Tonight, 'Taylor Swift on Rumored Kanye West Collaboration: 'He's Got a Lot of Amazing Ideas'', *Youtube*, April 29, 2015, https://www.youtube.com/watch?v=WsqOI5ZGFZs, last accessed: October 23, 2017. Bruna Nessif, 'Is This Taylor Swift and Kanye West Collaboration Happening or What?! Watch Now', *EOnline*, April 30, 2015, https://www.eonline.com/news/652354/is-this-taylor-swift-and-kanye-west-collaboration-happening-or-what-watch-now, last accessed: October 23, 2017.

we both reached the same place at the same time' […] And then Kanye and I both reached a place where he would say really nice things about my music and what I've accomplished, and I could ask him how his kid doing. … We haven't planned [a collaboration, added by the author] … But hey, I like him as a person. And that's a really good, nice first step, a nice place for us to be."[30]

BEFORE THE MTV VMA AWARDS AUGUST 2015	
TAYLOR SWIFT	KANYE WEST
In an interview for Rolling Stone, September 2019, Taylor Swift said: "But the 2015 VMAs come around. He's getting the Vanguard Award. He called me up beforehand – I didn't illegally record it, so I can't play it for you. But he called me up, maybe a week or so before the event, and we had maybe over an hourlong conversation, and he's like, "I really, really would like for you to present this Vanguard Award to me, this would mean so much to me," and went into all the reasons why it means so much, because he can be so sweet. He can be the sweetest. And I was so stoked that he asked me that."[31]	-

AUGUST 30, 2015	
TAYLOR SWIFT	KANYE WEST
Taylor Swift presented the Video Vanguard Award for Kanye West and invoked the original incident in her speech: 'I first met Kanye West six years ago – at this show, actually! [..] *The College Dropout* was the very first album my brother and I bought on iTunes when I was 12 years old…I've been a fan of his for as long as I can remember	During the acceptance speech, Kanye West said: 'First of all, thank you Taylor for being so gracious and giving me this award this evening. I often think back to the first day I met you, also. I think about when I'm in the grocery store with my daughter and I have a really great conversation about fresh juice and at the end,

---

[30] Josh Duboff, 'Taylor Swift: Apple Crusader, #GirlSquad Captain, and the Most Influential 25-Year-Old in America', *Vanity Fair,* August 11, 2015, https://www.vanityfair.com/style/2015/08/taylor-swift-cover-mario-testino-apple-music, last accessed: October 23, 2017.

[31] Brian Hiatt, 'The Rolling Stone Interview Taylor Swift', *Rolling Stone*, September 18, 2019, available at: https://www.rollingstone.com/music/music-features/taylor-swift-rolling-stone-interview-880794/, last accessed: October 21, 2019.

because Kanye defines what it means to be a creative force in music, fashion and, well, life. So, I guess I have to say to all the other winners tonight: I'm really happy for you, and imma let you finish, but Kanye West has had one of the greatest careers of all time.'[32]

they say, 'Oh, you're not that bad after all. […] You know how many times MTV ran that footage again? Because it got them more ratings. You know how many times they announced Taylor was going to give me the award. Because it got them more ratings.'[33]

After the show, Kanye West sent to Taylor Swift a huge flower arrangement.

JANUARY 2016	
TAYLOR SWIFT	KANYE WEST

Kanye West calls Taylor Swift.

Kanye West: "[To someone outside room] Lock that door and then stand on the other side of it until I knock for you … No, lock the doors up."

Kanye West: "[Resuming a conversation in progress with Swift, her end initially unintelligible.] …old school s—, yeah. I'm doing great. I feel so awesome about the music. The album's coming out February 11, I'm doing the fashion show February 11 at Madison Square Garden, we're dropping the album February 12th that morning. It's like…"

Taylor Swift: "[Inaudible.]"

Kanye West: "Oh, thank you so, so much. Yeah. It feels good. It feels like real Ye, Apple, Steve Jobs-type music. So my next single, I wanted you to tweet it. It's a good Friday to drop it. It's a good Friday song. So that's why I'm calling you, that I wanted you to put the song out."

Taylor Swift: "Oh, wow. Like, um, what would people… I guess it would just be, people would be like, "Whyyyy is this happening?" They would think I had something to do with it, probably."

Kanye West: "Well, the reason why it will be happening is because it has a very controversial line at the beginning of the song about you."

Taylor Swift: "[Apprehensively.] What does it say?"

Kanye West: "So it says… and the song is so, so dope. And I've literally sat with my wife, with my whole management team, with everything and tried to rework this line. I've thought about this

---

[32] Cady Lang, 'A Comprehensive Guide to the Kanye West-Taylor Swift-Kim Kardashian West Feud', *Time*, July 19, 2016, updated: July 29, 2016, https://time.com/4411055/kanye-west-taylor-swift-kim-kardashian-feud/, last accessed: October 23, 2017.

[33] Rolling Stone, 'Read Kanye West's Blunt, Poignant VMA Video Vanguard Award Speech', August 31, 2015, https://www.rollingstone.com/music/music-news/read-kanye-wests-blunt-poignant-vma-video-vanguard-award-speech-42495/, last accessed: October 23, 2017.

line for eight months. I've had this line and I've tried to rework it every which way. And the original way that I thought about it is the best way, but it's the most controversial way. So it's gonna go Eminem a little bit, so can you brace yourself for a second?"

Taylor Swift: "[Sounding resigned.] Yeah."

Kanye West: "Okay. All right. Wait a second, you sound sad."

Taylor Swift: "Well, is it gonna be mean?"

Kanye West: "No, I don't think it's mean."

Taylor Swift: "Okay, then, let me hear it."

Kanye West: "Okay. It says, um,… and the funny thing is, when I first played it and my wife heard it, she was like, "Huh? What? That's too crazy," blah, blah, blah. And then like when Ninja from Die Atwoord heard it, he was like, "Oh my God, this is the craziest s—. This is why I love Kanye," blah, blah, blah, that kind of thing. And now it's like my wife's favourite f—ing line. I just wanted to give you some premise of that. Right?"

Taylor Swift: "Okay."

Kanye West: "So it says "To all my Southside [N-word] that know me best, I feel like Taylor Swift might owe me sex."

Taylor Swift: "[Laughs, relieved.] That's not mean."

Kanye West: "Okay. Well, this is the thing where I'm calling you, because you're got an army. You own a country of mother—ing 2 billion people, basically, that if you felt that it's funny and cool and like hip-hop, and felt like just "The College Dropout" and the artist like Ye that you love, then I think that people would be like way into it. And that's why I think it's super-genius to have you be the one that says, "Oh, I like this song a lot. Like, yeah, whatever, this is cool, whatever." It's like, I got like s— on my album where I'm like, "I bet me and Ray J would be friends, if we ain't love the same bitch"."

Taylor Swift: "Oh my God! I mean, I need to think about it, because you know, when you hear something for the first time, you just need to think about it. Because it is absolutely crazy. I'm glad it's not mean, though. It doesn't feel mean. But oh my God, the buildup you gave it, I thought it was going to be like, "That stupid, dumb bitch." But it's not. So I don't know. I mean, the launch thing, I think it would be kind of confusing to people. But I definitely like… I definitely think that when I'm asked about it, of course I'll be like, "Yeah, I love that. I think it's hilarious." But, um, I need to think about it."

Kanye West: "You don't have to do the launching and tweet. That was just an extra idea I had. But if you think that that's cool, then it's cool. If not… I mean, we are launching the s— like on just good Fridays on SoundCloud, on the site, s— like that."

Taylor Swift: "You know, the thing about me is, anything that I do becomes like a feminist think-piece. And if I launch it, they're going to be like, wow, like, they'll just turn into something that… I think if I launch it, honestly, I think it'll be less cool. Because I think if I launch it, it adds this level of criticism. Because having that many followers and having that many eyeballs on me right now, people are just looking for me to do something dumb or stupid or lame. And I don't know. I kind of feel like people would try to make it negative if it came from me, do you know what I mean? I think I'm very self-aware about where I am, and I feel like right now I'm like this close to overexposure."

Kanye West: "Oh. Well, this one, I think this is a really cool thing to have."

Taylor Swift: "I know, I mean, it's like a compliment, kind of. [Chuckles.]"

Kanye West: "I have this line where I said… And my wife really didn't like this one, because we tried to make it nicer. So I say "For all my Southside [N-word] that know me best, I feel like me and Taylor might still have sex." And my wife was really not with that one. She was way more into the "She owes you sex." But then the "owe" part was like the feminist group-type shit that I was like, ahhhhh."

Taylor Swift: "That's the part that I was kind of… I mean, they 're both really edgy, but that's the only thing about that line is that it's like, then the feminists are going to come out. But I mean, you don't give a f—. So…"

Kanye West: "Yeah, basically. Well, what I give a f— about is just you as a person, as a friend…."

Taylor Swift: "That's sweet."

Kanye West: "I want things that make you feel good. I don't want to do rap that makes people feel bad. Like of course, like I'm mad at Nike, so people think, "Oh, he's a bully. He ran on stage with Taylor. He's bullying Nike now," this $50 billion company."

Taylor Swift: "Why are people saying you're bullying Nike?"

Kanye West: "Because on "Facts," like, I say, "Yeezy, Yeezy, Yeezy, they line up for days / Nike out here bad, they can't give s— away.""

Taylor Swift: "Yeah, yeah, yeah. I mean, that's just what you do, though. I mean, I wouldn't say that it's possible to bully a company like Nike. But I mean… um, yeah, I mean, go with whatever line you think is better. It's obviously very tongue-in-cheek either way. And I really appreciate you telling me about it. That's really nice."

Kanye West: "Oh, yeah. I just had a responsibility to you as a friend. I mean, thanks for being like so cool about it."

Taylor Swift: "Thanks. Yeah, I really appreciate it. The heads-up is so nice. You'd be surprised how many people just do things without even asking or seeing if I'd be okay with it, and I just really appreciate it. I never would have expected you to tell me about a line in one of your songs. That's really nice that you did."

Kanye West: "You mean like unexpected s— like you taking the time to give someone a really, really valuable award and then they completely run for president right afterwards? Like unexpected in that kind of way? [Laughs.] [A few months earlier, at the 2015 MTV Awards, Swift presented West with his lifetime achievement award, followed by a rambling speech in which he acknowledged he had smoked pot beforehand and was going to run for president.]"

Taylor Swift: "[Laughs.] We have not talked about what happened."

Kanye West: "I just thought that was wavy. It was vibey. The funny thing is, I thought about the weed and the president, both of those things I thought about in the shower the day before and just started laughing like crazy. I was like, I gotta say that I had just smoked some weed and then say I'm gonna run for president… So those are my bases of… I knew I wanted to say the thing about going to like the Dodgers game with my daughter and like getting booed and that being scary, and I knew I wanted to say like me changing and thinking about people more since I had a daughter. And then I wanted to say the weed thing. And then I wanted to say the president thing. And everything else was just like off the cuff."

Taylor Swift: "Oh my God. It was definitely like it stole the show… And then the flowers that you sent me. I Instagrammed a picture of them and it's the most Instagram likes I've ever gotten. It was like 2.7 million likes on that picture of the flowers you sent me. Crazy."

Kanye West: "It's some connection or something that I think is really important about that moment when we met on stage. There's something that I think is really important about that, and where humanity is going, or now where me and Kim are, and having a family and just everything, the way things are landing. So it's always… Relationships are more important than punchlines, you know."

Taylor Swift: "Yeah, I mean, I don't think anybody would listen to that and be like, "Oh, that's a real diss" — like, "She must be crying about that line." And I think because of how crazy and strange and fateful the way we met was, I think we have to pick our moments to do stuff together and make sure it's only really cool stuff."

Kanye West: "Yeah, exactly. We can't have it like be somebody else's idea that gets in front and they're like… Because if you're like a really true, creative, visceral, vibey type person, it's probably hard for you to work at a corporation. So how can you give a creative ideas and you're working in a house of non-creativity? It's like this weird… So whenever we talk directly… Okay, now what if later in the song I was also to have said, uh… "I made her famous"? Is that a…"

Taylor Swift: "[Apprehensively.] Did you say that?"

Kanye West: "Yes, it might've happened. [Laughs.]"

Taylor Swift: "Well, what am I going to do about it?"

Kanye West: "Uh, like, do the hair flip?"

Taylor Swift: "Yeah. I mean… Um… It's just kind of like, whatever, at this point. But I mean, you've got to tell the story the way that it happened to you and the way that you've experienced it. Like, you honestly didn't know who I was before that. Like, it doesn't matter if I sold 7 million of that album ["Fearless"] before you did that, which is what happened. You didn't know who I was before that. It's fine. But, um, yeah. I can't wait to hear it."

Kanye West: "I mean, it's fun. It's definitely… You're ready to trend. That's all I can say."

Taylor Swift: "Uh, what's the song called?"

Kanye West: "Uh, it might be called 'Hood Famous.'"

Taylor Swift: "Oh, cool. Is it going to be like a single-single, or is it going to be a SoundCloud release? What are you doing?"

Kanye West: "Oh, this one right here is like f—ing Song of the Year-type territory."

Taylor Swift: "Oh my God. Amazing. That's crazy. Oh my God. Speaking of Song of the Year, are you going to the Grammys?"

Kanye West: "Uh, you know what? I was thinking to not do it. But I think that this song… You know what? I'm going to send you the song and send you the exact wording and everything about it, right? And then we could sit and talk through it. But if the song goes and f—ing just…"

"[The video goes out momentarily, as the filmer's phone battery apparently dies. When it resumes, they are still discussing whether West might attend the Grammys.]"

Taylor Swift: "… they just look at us and go… [Unintelligible] …Even if we've made an incredible achievement, it's harder for people to write down our names for some reason. That's just human nature. It's envy. It's asking people in our industry to vote for the people who are already killing it."

Kanye West: "Yeah. It's like so many people wanted Meek Mills (sic) to win because Drake was just killing it for so long, and they were just like, "We just need, like, Meek Mills (sic) to, like…" But I think, you know, okay… So that has my mind going through a lot of places to problem-solve. I was talking to Ben Horowitz – do you know this guy? He's a VC. Ben Horowitz out of San Fran. But he's down with that."

Taylor Swift: "I know that name. I don't know him."

Kanye West: "It's just like the San Fran clique, you know, that type of thing, like he stays down the street from Mark Zuckerberg and s– like that. So I was talking to him and I was like, "Bro"… Like me, I'm in personal debt. I'm in debt by a good like 20, 30 million, ever since the fashion, and still have not made it out of it. So that's part of the reason why I had to go to Roc Nation and the touring deals evolved, and it allowed the whole town to try to feel like they could control Kanye or even talk to me like I'm regular or have agents do it, but they saw they couldn't. It's like even in debt, he moves around like he's like a billionaire. I'm like, yeah, I'm a cultural trillionaire! I might have financial debts. So I told Ben Horowitz, I was like, "You guys, you, Mark Zuckerberg or whoever, Tim Cook, you guys have to clean that up." So I'm sending Ben Horowitz my current balance. That means that I'm not up 50, not up 100 million, not up 200 million, not up 300 million. No –negative 20 million, currently. I, Kanye West, the guy who created the genre of music that is the Weeknd, that is Drake – the guy who created… Every single person that makes music right now, favourite album is "The College Dropout." Every single person that makes music. But I'm rich enough… Like, I went into debt to my wife by 6 million working on a f–ing house, less than like a few months ago, and I was able to pay her back before Christmas and s– like that. So, you know, when I talk about Nike, the idea that they wouldn't give me a percentage, that I could make something that was so tangible, when Drake was just rapping me into the motherf–ing trashcan, that I could have something that was tangible that showed my creativity and expressed myself, that also could be a business that I could have a five-times multiple on and actually be able to sell it for like a hundred million, 200 million or a billion dollars, that was very serious. Every conversation, every time I'd scream at Charlemagne (Tha God) or scream at (radio host) Sway, that was really, really, really serious. And it also was with my family. I felt like, look, if I'm just the angry black guy with some cool red shoes from Nike five years ago, I was going to be visiting my daughter, as opposed to be living with her. It would've been like, enough is enough. It wouldn't have been cool anymore, because it would have been a group of people, including my wife, that all had at least like 500, 400 million in their account. And then you get the angry black man at the party talking about "I'm the one that put Kim in the dress! I'm the one that did this!" But it never realized itself. So that's one of the things I just talked to Ben… And I talk about it on the album. Talk about personal debt and s–. Just the idea like, "Oh s–, this dude with this f–ing Maybach that makes f–ing $50 million a tour still hasn't lined it up or came out of the point when AEG and Live Nation wouldn't give him a deal." The debt started after "Watch the Throne" [West's joint album with Jay-Z], because I got no deal. But I still was doing my creative projects on my own, shooting a film, doing a fashion show, just trying to be very Disney, be very visceral, be creative. And…"

Taylor Swift: "I mean, I'm sure you've thought about this up and down, but I mean, is there a way to monetize these in a way that you thought would still feel authentic but make them into a multibillion dollar company?"

Kanye West: "Well, that's what we're going to do. That's what we're in the plans of. I'm 100% going to be like a multi, multi, multi-billionaire. I think it's fun that I can like be like Charlie Sheen and be like, "Hey, like, I got AIDS." You know, like…. To me, I told Drake that the other night. I was like, "Yo, Drake, I'm in personal debt." And for me to tell Drake, the f—ing number one bachelor in the world that can f—ing rap anybody into a trashcan, that lives four blocks down the street from my wife and like basically f—s all of her friends, that I'm in personal debt, it's such a like putting down the sword or putting down the hand or opening, showing the hand. That I don't have my poker face on with any of you guys. I'm just me. I'm just a creative. You know, everything I did, even when it was mistimed, whatever it might've been from a… It's always like from a good place, and I know that I'll overcome it and I know that the world will overcome it. Because, like, I'm going to change the world. I'm going to make it… I'm gonna make people's lives better on some post-Steve Jobs, Howard Hughes-type shit. Like, I'm going to do things with education. I'm going to do things that help to calm down murders in Chicago or across the globe. Things that help to calm down police brutality, to equalize the wealth amidst the class system. Because there's a bunch of classes of wealthy people that hate Obama because he's more social and he wants the people who don't have anything to have everything. And in my little way, by learning how to design, design is something that's only given to the rich currently. The exact color palette that Hermes uses versus the color palette that Forever 21 uses — a color palette is extremely important. Color is important. You know, the knowledge of proportions… you know, the size of our house versus the size of someone else's houses, and just the dynamics of that proportion. Like, I don't want this conversation to go too, too long, but I wanted to give you a bit of where I'm at and the perspective that I'm at and the way… the fact that I am the microprocessor of our culture. Meaning like, I can figure out how to give Rihanna a Mary J. Blige-type album. I can figure out how to get the fashion world to accept my wife, and thus the whole family. I can figure out a lot of impossible… I can figure out how to make something that you're wearing to the airport, five years after the entire globe was like, "Hang that [N-word] alive and f— him, and let's watch him die, slowly, publicly." So, it's a lot. I figured that out for myself, so it's a lot of s— that we collectively, with the power that you have and your fans, the power my wife has, the power that I have, that we can do to really make it where it's not just the rich getting richer, but… You know, make it not just a f—ing charity, not singing for Africa, but change things in a way that people can experience s— themselves, a piece of the good life. You know?"

Taylor Swift: "Yeah. I mean, they're amazing ideas and amazing concepts, and I definitely would love to talk to you more about it. I know you have to do something right now, but I love that that's where you're headed. And it's been like that. I mean, when we went to dinner, there were the rumblings of those ideas. I like that you're always thinking outward. And over the last six, seven, eight years, however long it's been since that happened, I haven't always liked you, but I've always respected you. And I think that's what you're saying when you say like, you know, "I might be in debt, but I can make these things happen, and I have the ideas to do it, and I can create these things or these concepts." Like, I'm always going to respect you. And I'm really glad that you had the respect to call me and tell me that as a friend about the song, and it's a really cool thing to do, and a really good show of friendship. So thank you."

Kanye West: "Oh, thank you too."

Taylor Swift: "And you know, if people ask me about it, look, I think it would be great for me to be like, "Look, he called me and told me the line before it came out. Like, the joke's on you guys – we're fine.""

Kanye West: "Yeah. Yeah. Okay. I think that's pretty much the switch right there."

Taylor Swift: "Yeah. Like, you guys want to call this a feud, you want to call this throwing shade, but you know, right after the song comes out, I'm gonna be on a Grammy red carpet, and they're gonna ask me about it and I'll be like, "He called me and sent me the song before it came out." So I think we're good."

Kanye West: "Okay. I'm gonna go lay this verse, and I'm gonna send it to you right now."

Taylor Swift: "[Taken aback.] Oh, you just… you haven't recorded it yet?"

Kanye West: "I recorded it. I'm nuancing the lines – like the last version of it says, "Me and Taylor might still have sex." And then my wife was like, "That doesn't sound as hard!""

Taylor Swift: "Well, I mean, she's saying that honestly because she's your wife, and like, um… So I think whatever one you think is actually better. I mean, obviously do what's best for your relationship, too. I think "owes me sex," it says different things. It says… "Owes me sex" means like "Look, I made her what she is. She actually owes me." Which is going to split people, because people who like me are going to be like, "She doesn't owe him s–." But then people who like thought it was bad-ass and crazy and awesome that you're so outspoken are going to be like, "Yeah, she does. It made her famous." So it's more provocative to say "still have sex," because no one would see that coming. They're both crazy. Do what you want. They're both going to get every single headline in the world. "Owes me sex" is a little bit more like throwing shade, and the other one's more flirtatious. It just depends on what you want to accomplish with it."

Kanye West: "Yeah, I feel like with my wife, that she probably didn't like the "might still have sex" because it would be like, what if she was on a TV show and said "Me and Tom Brady might still have sex" or something?"

Taylor Swift: "You have to protect your relationship. Do what's best. You just had a kid. You're in the best place of your life. I wouldn't ever advise you to f– with that. Just pick whatever… It's cause and effect. One is gonna make people feel a certain way, and it's gonna be a slightly different emotion for the other. But it's not… It doesn't matter to me. There's not one that hurts my feelings and the other doesn't."

Kanye West: "Yeah. It's just, when I'm pointing this gun, what I tried to do differently than two years ago, is like when I shoot a gun, I try to point it away from my face. So one is a little bit more flirtatious and easier… I think, so really, that means the conversation is really: One is like a little bit better for the public and a little bit less good for the relationship. One is a little bit worse for the public and better for the relationship."

Taylor Swift: "Yeah. I can hear it. But it's your goals, really. I mean, you always just go with your gut – obviously. But, um, amazing. Send it to me. I'm excited."

Kanye West: "All right, cool. Thanks so much."

Taylor Swift: "Awesome. I'll talk to you later."

Kany West: "All right, cool. Peace. Bye."

Kanye West: "[To cameraman.] We had to get that on the record."

Cameraman: "[About interruption.] I'm sorry. The battery on this thing died."

Kanye West: "It's just when it dies… You get some s– like Kanye talking to Taylor Swift explaining that line? There's gotta be three cameras on that one. We can't miss one element."[34]

FEBRUARY 11, 2016	
TAYLOR SWIFT	KANYE WEST
-	On February 11, 2016 Kanye West debuted his musical album *The Life of Pablo* at his Yeezy Season 3 show at Madison Square Garden, New York. In one of his songs, 'Famous,' he raps "I feel like me and Taylor might still have sex / Why? I made that bitch famous (God damn) / I made that bitch famous."
FEBRUARY 12, 2016	
TAYLOR SWIFT	KANYE WEST
	Kanye West wrote a few tweets (now deleted) on his Twitter account:

---

[34] Pandoras Box, 'Leaked 2016 Kanye West / Taylor Swift Conversation re: Famous', *Youtube*, March 21, 2020, https://www.youtube.com/watch?v=-OjyJD3pxD4, last accessed: July 1, 2021.

Taylor Swift camp replied:

"Kanye did not call for approval, but to ask Taylor to release his single „Famous' on her Twitter account. She declined and cautioned him about releasing a song with such a strong misogynistic message. Taylor was never made aware of the actual lyric, „I made that bitch famous.""[35]

"I did not diss Taylor Swift and I've never dissed her…
– KANYE WEST (@kanyewest) February 12, 2016"

"First thing is I'm an artist and as an artist I will express how I feel with no censorship
– KANYE WEST (@kanyewest) February 12, 2016"

"2nd thing I asked my wife for her blessings and she was cool with it
– KANYE WEST (@kanyewest) February 12, 2016"

"3rd thing I called Taylor and had a hour long convo with her about the line and she thought it was funny and gave her blessings
– KANYE WEST (@kanyewest) February 12, 2016"

"4th Bitch is an endearing term in hip hop like the word Nigga
– KANYE WEST (@kanyewest) February 12, 2016"

"5th thing I'm not even gone take credit for the idea… it's actually something Taylor came up with …
– KANYE WEST (@kanyewest) February 12, 2016"

"I can't be mad at Kanye because he made me famous! #FACTS
– KANYE WEST (@kanyewest) February 12, 2016"

"6th Stop trying to demonize real artist Stop trying to compromise art

[35] Melody Chiu, Karen Mizoguchi, 'Kanye West Did Not Call Taylor Swift for Approval Over 'B----' Lyric, Singer Cautioned Him Against Releasing 'Strong Misogynistic Message' Rep Says', *People*, February 12, 2016, https://people.com/celebrity/kanye-west-did-not-call-taylor-swift-for-approval-over-bitch-lyric/, last accessed: October 23, 2017.

	— KANYE WEST (@kanyewest) February 12, 2016"
	"That's why music is so fucking watered down right now I miss that DMX feeling — KANYE WEST (@kanyewest) February 12, 2016"
	"7th I miss that feeling so that's what I want to help restore — KANYE WEST (@kanyewest) February 12, 2016"
	"8th They want to control us with money and perception and mute the culture — KANYE WEST (@kanyewest) February 12, 2016."

FEBRUARY 14, 2016	
TAYLOR SWIFT	**KANYE WEST**
-	1. Kanye West said in the backstage of Saturday Night Live on 14 February: "Look at that shit, they took my fucking stage off a 'SNL' without asking me. Now I'm bummed. That and Taylor Swift, fake ass." "Now I ain't gonna do this, we're breaking the motherfucking internet.' 'I went through six years of this fucking shit. Let's get to it, bro. Let's get to it, bro." "Are they fucking crazy, bro? By 50 percent. Stanley Kubrick, Apostle Paul, Picasso... fucking Picasso and Escobar. By 50 percent, more influential than any other human being." "Don't fuck with me. Don't fuck with me. Don't fuck with me. By 50 percent, dead or alive, by 50 percent for the next thousand years. Stanley Kubrick. Ye."[36]

---

[36] ABC News, 'Kanye West 'SNL' Meltdown Leaked', *Youtube*, February 18, 2016, https://www.youtube.com/watch?v=cN4Gnzo9z4c, last accessed: October 23, 2017.

	2. 'The Life of Pablo' and *Famous* song are officially released via Tidal. The song would arrive on Spotify and Apple Music on April 1. 'Famous' is the lead single of his album.[37]

FEBRUARY 15, 2016	
TAYLOR SWIFT	KANYE WEST
While accepting Album of the Year award at the GRAMMYs, Taylor Swift addressed what is believed to be about the infamous Kanye West lyrics about her: "I want to thank the fans for the last 10 years, and the recording academy for giving us this unbelievable honor. I want to thank all of the collaborators that you see on this stage. Mostly, I want to thank my co-executive producer Max Martin, who has deserved to be up here for 25 years. And as the first woman to win album of the year at the Grammy's twice, I want to say to all the young women out there, there are going to be people along the way who, will try to undercut your success or take credit for your accomplishments or your fame. But if you just focus on the work and you don't let those people sidetrack you, someday when you get where you're going, you will know it was you and the people who love you who put you there, and that will be the greatest feeling in the world. Thank you for this moment."[38]	-

FEBRUARY 17, 2016	
TAYLOR SWIFT	KANYE WEST
	1. Two days after Taylor Swift's Grammy win, *Page Six* posted the audio record with Kanye West aventing backstage at SNL on 14 February 2016.[39]

---

[37] Jazz Monroe, 'Kanye West's The Life of Pablo Is Out Now', *Pitchfork*, February 14, 2016, https://pitchfork.com/news/63408-kanye-wests-the-life-of-pablo-is-out-now/, last accessed: October 23, 2017.

[38] Taylor Swift, 'Taylor Swift, Album of the Year Acceptance Speech (Grammys 2016)', *Genius*, February 15, 2016, https://genius.com/Taylor-swift-album-of-the-year-acceptance-speech-grammys-2016-annotated, last accessed: October 23, 2017.

[39] Emily Smith, ''Don't f–k with me': Hear Kanye's uncensored 'SNL' meltdown', *Page Six*, February 17, 2016, https://pagesix.com/2016/02/17/dont-f-k-with-me-hear-kanyes-uncensored-snl-meltdown/, last accessed: October 23, 2017.

2. Paparazzi at *LAX Kanye* questioned Kanye West about his 'Famous' lyric. He answered:

"It's like, I want the best for that person, but there's people going through real issues out here. There's people out of work. There's people in debt that can't make it out of the debt. There's people that's in debt that don't have a shoe. There's people that are in debt that don't have a hit album out also. The media tried to make this an ongoing story and everything for hits and blah blah. I don't think people care about me or her in that way. People care about their families, their kids. If you like my music, listen to it. If you like her music, listen to it."[40]

FEBRUARY 23, 2016	
TAYLOR SWIFT	KANYE WEST
-	Kanye West wrote a few tweets (now deleted) on his Twitter account: "I made Dark Fantasy and Watch the Throne in one year and wasn't nominated for either and you know who has 2 albums of the year." — KANYE WEST (@kanyewest) February 23, 2016

FEBRUARY 24, 2016	
TAYLOR SWIFT	KANYE WEST
-	At Yo Gotti's album release party at the 1OAK nightclub in Hollywood, Kanye West reiterates he told Taylor Swift about the 'Famous' lyric and said "She had two seconds to be cool and she fucked it up!"[41]

APRIL 14, 2016	
TAYLOR SWIFT	KANYE WEST
In an interview with Vogue, Taylor Swift addressed her acceptance speech at Grammy Awards and Kanye West:	

---

[40] Ted Simmons, 'Kanye West Tells Paparazzi He Wants the Best for Taylor Swift', *XXL Magazine*, February 18, 2016, http://www.xxlmag.com/news/2016/02/kanye-west-talks-taylor-swift-to-paparazzi/, last accessed: October, 23,2017.
[41] Complex, *A Timeline of Kanye West and Taylor Swift's Feud Over the 'Famous' Lyric*, July 18, 2016, http://www.complex.com/music/2016/07/kanye-west-taylor-swift-famous-lyric-timeline, last accessed: October 23, 2017.

"I think the world is bored with the saga. I don't want to add anything to it, because then there's just more... I guess what I wanted to call attention to in my speech at the Grammys was how it's going to be difficult if you're a woman who wants to achieve something in her life - no matter what."[42]

JUNE 16, 2016	
TAYLOR SWIFT	KIM KARDASHIAN

In a GQ interview for July new issue, Kim Kardashian spoke about Taylor Swift and her implication in the 'Famous' song:

"She totally approved that.' […] 'She totally knew that that was coming out. She wanted to all of a sudden act like she didn't. I swear, my husband gets so much shit for things he really was doing proper protocol and even called to get it approved.' […] 'What rapper would call a girl that he was rapping a line about to get approval?"

Taylor Swift camp, after Kim Kardashian's interview with GQ, issued a statement to GQ:

"Taylor does not hold anything against Kim Kardashian as she recognizes the pressure Kim must be under and that she is only repeating what she has been told by Kanye West. However, that does not change the fact that much of what Kim is saying is incorrect. Kanye West and Taylor only spoke once on the phone while she was on vacation with her family in January of 2016 and they have never spoken since. Taylor has never denied that conversation took place. It was on that phone call that Kanye West also asked her to release the song on her Twitter account, which she declined to do. Kanye West never told Taylor he was going to use the term 'that bitch' in referencing her. A song cannot be approved if it was never heard. Kanye West never played the song for Taylor Swift. Taylor heard it for the first time when everyone else did and was humiliated. Kim Kardashian's claim that Taylor and her team were aware of being recorded is not true, and Taylor cannot understand why

"I don't know why she just, you know, flipped all of a sudden.… It was funny because said, 'When I get on the Grammy red carpet, all the media is going to think that I'm so against this, and I'll just laugh and say, 'The joke's on you, guys. I was in on it the whole time.' And I'm like, wait, but your Grammy speech, you completely dissed my husband just to play the victim again."

GQ reporter: "Were they in touch after that?"

Kim Kardashian: "No. Maybe an attorney's letter she sent saying, 'Don't ever let that footage come out of me saying that. Destroy it."

GQ reporter: "She sent one?"

Kim Kardashian: "Yeah."

[42] Jason Gay, 'Taylor Swift As You've Never Seen Her Before', *Vogue*, April 14, 2016, https://www.vogue.com/article/taylor-swift-may-cover-maid-of-honor-dating-personal-style, last accessed: October 23, 2017.

Kanye West, and now Kim Kardashian, will not just leave her alone."[43]

Kim Kardashian: "And then they sent an attorney's letter like, 'Don't you dare do anything with that footage,' and asking us to destroy it.' She pauses. 'When you shoot something, you don't stop every two seconds and be like, 'Oh wait, we're shooting this for my documentary.' You just film everything, and whatever makes the edit, then you see, then you send out releases. It's like what we do for our show."[44]

JUNE 24, 2016	
TAYLOR SWIFT	KANYE WEST
-	'Famous' official music video is released exclusive on Tidal and at the event 'The Forum' in Inglewood, California.[45]

JULY 1, 2016	
TAYLOR SWIFT	KANYE WEST
-	'Famous' official music video is released on Kanye West Vevo Youtube account.[46]

JULY 14, 2016	
TAYLOR SWIFT	KIM KARDASHIAN
-	A trailer with Kim Kardashian with a scene from the upcoming episod *Keeping Up with the Kardashians* is released. In it Kim Kardashian speaks again about Taylor Swift and her implication in the 'Famous' song.[47]

JULY 17, 2016	
TAYLOR SWIFT	KIM KARDASHIAN
	1. Kim Kardashian wrote on her Twitter account: "Wait it's legit National Snake Day?!?!? They have holidays for everybody, I mean everything these days!"

[43] Caity Weaver, 'Kanye and Taylor Swift, What's in O.J.'s Bag, and Understanding Caitlyn', *GQ*, June 16, 2016, https://www.gq.com/story/kim-kardashian-west-gq-cover-story, last accessed: October 23, 2017.
[44] *Ibidem*.
[45] Colin Stutz, 'Kanye West Nuzzles Naked Taylor Swift, Donald Trump & Bill Cosby in 'Famous' Video', *Billboard*, June 25, 2016, https://www.billboard.com/articles/columns/hip-hop/7416556/kanye-west-naked-taylor-swift-donald-trump-famous-video-premiere, last accessed: October 23, 2017.
[46] KanyeWestVevo, 'Kanye West Famous', *Youtube*, July 1, 2016, https://www.youtube.com/watch?v=p7FCgw_GlWc, last accessed: October 23, 2017.
[47] E! Entertainment, 'KUWTK, Kim Kardashian Has 'Had It' With Kanye Haters', *Youtube*, July 14, 2016, https://www.youtube.com/watch?v=p7FCgw_GlWc, last accessed: October 23, 2017.

Soon after the post with the phone conversation between Kanye West and Taylor Swift, people posted snakes on Taylor Swift Instagram, Twitter and Facebook account.[49]

2. After the episode from her tv show, *Keeping Up with the Kardashians*, Kim Kardashian posted a series of videos on her Snapchat account. The videos show Kanye West speaking on the phone with Taylor Swift. It is a small part of the conversation they had it in January 2016.

Kanye West: "You still got the Nashville number?"

Taylor Swift: "I still have the Nashville umm area code, but I had to change it."

[video cuts off]

Kanye West: "To all my southside niggas that know me best, I feel like me and Taylor might still have sex."

Taylor Swift: "I'm like this close to overexposure."

Kanye West: "Oh, well this I think this a really cool thing to have."

Taylor Swift: "I know, I mean it's like a compliment, kind of."

[video cuts off]

Taylor Swift responded to Kim Kardashian's Snapchat videos on her Instagram and Twitter account (now the picture with her response is deleted):

"That moment when Kanye West secretly records your phone call, then Kim posts it on the Internet."

"Where is the video of Kanye telling me he was going to call me 'that bitch' in his song? It doesn't exist because it never happened. You don't get to control someone's emotional response to being called 'that bitch' in front of the entire world. Of course I wanted to like the song. I wanted to believe Kanye when he told me that I would love the song. I wanted us to have a friendly relationship. He promised to play the song for me, but he never did. While I wanted to be supportive of Kanye on the

[49] Kim Kardashian West, 'Wait it's legit National Snake Day?!?,' *Twitter*, July 17, 2016, https://twitter.com/kimkardashian/status/754818471465287680?lang=en, last accessed: October 23, 2017.

phone call, you cannot 'approve' a song you haven't heard. Being falsely painted as a liar when I was never given the full story or played any part of the song is character assassination. I would very much like to be excluded from this narrative, one that I have never asked to be a part of, since 2009."[48]

Kanye West: "All I give a fuck about is you as a person and as a friend, I want things that make you feel good."

Taylor Swift: "That's sweet."

Kanye West: "I don't want to do rap that makes people feel bad."

[video cuts off]

Taylor Swift: "Umm, yeah I mean go with whatever line you think is better. It's obviously very tongue in cheek either way. And I really appreciate you telling me about it, that's really nice."

[video cuts off]

Kanye West: "Oh yeah, I just had a responsibility to you as a friend you know, and I mean thanks for being so cool about it."

Taylor Swift: "Aw thanks. Um yeah I really appreciate it, like the heads up is so nice."

[inaudible]

"Even asking or seeing if I would be okay with it and I just really appreciate it. Like I would never expect you to like tell me about a line in one of your songs."

Kanye West: 'It's pretty crazy.'

Taylor Swift: "And then the flowers that you sent me, I like Instagrammed a picture of them and it's like the most Instagram likes I've ever gotten. It was like 2.7 millions."

---

[48] The photo with her reply is now deleted from her Facebook, Twitter and Instagram account. You can find written evidence here: Jemima Skelley, 'Taylor Swift Just Called Out Kanye West On Instagram', BuzzFeed, July 18, 2016, https://www.buzzfeed.com/jemimaskelley/shoulda-chose-the-rose-garden-over-madison-square, last accessed: October 23, 2017.

[video cuts off]

Kanye West: "Relationships are more important than punch lines, ya know?"

Taylor Swift: "I don't think anyone would listen to that and be like that's a real diss she must be crying. You've gotta tell the story the way that it happened to you and the way that you experienced it, like you honestly didn't know who I was before that."

[video cuts off]

Taylor Swift: "It doesn't matter that I sold 7 million of that album before you did that which is what happened, you didn't know who I was before that. It's fine."

[video cuts off]

Taylor Swift: "I might be in debt, but I can make these things happen. I have the ideas to do it and I create these things and concepts. I'm always going to respect you. I'm really glad that you have the respect to call me and tell me that as a friend about the song. It's a really cool thing to do and a really good show of friendship so thank you."

Kanye West: "Thank you, too."

[video cuts off]

Taylor Swift: "And you know, if people ask me about it I think it would be great for me to be like, 'Look, he called me and told me the line before it came out. Jokes on you guys, We're fine.'"

[video cuts off]

"You guys want to call this a feud; you want to call this throwing shade but right after the song comes out I'm going to be on a GRAMMYs red carpet and they're going to ask me about it and I'll be like, 'He called me.'"

[video cuts off]

"It's awesome that you're so outspoken about this and be like, 'Yeah, she does. It made her famous.' It's more provocative to say 'might still have sex…' It's doesn't matter to me. There's not like one [line] that hurts my feelings and one that doesn't."[50]

JULY 24, 2016	
TAYLOR SWIFT	KIM KARDASHIAN
-	Kim Kardashian, during her night at Hakkasan nightclub in the MGM Grand in Las Vegas, shared a video of herself and friend Carla DiBello dancing and singing along to Kanye West's lyric of the song 'Famous,' specifically where Kanye West raps: 'I feel like me and Taylor might still have sex. Why? I made that bitch famous. I made that bitch famous.'[51]

JULY 27, 2016	
TAYLOR SWIFT	KANYE WEST
-	Kanye West makes a guest appearance at Drake's concert in Chicago, and speaks out about Taylor Swift. Kanye West told his fans, "All I gotta say is, I am so glad my wife has Snapchat!", "Now y'all can know the truth and can't nobody talk s–t about 'Ye no more." After his words, he performed the 'Famous' song.[52]

JULY 28, 2016	
TAYLOR SWIFT	KANYE WEST AND KIM KARDASIAN

[50] Kylizzle Snapchizzle, 'Kanye West Phone Call to Taylor Swift about Famous (Full) Via Kim's Snapchat', *Youtube*, July 18, 2016, https://www.youtube.com/watch?v=tlN-2LDGm3A, last accessed: October 23, 2017.

[51] Blake Bakkila, 'Kim Kardashian Raps Along to THAT Kanye Lyric About Taylor Swift After Epic Feud', *People*, July 24, 2016, http://people.com/celebrity/kim-kardashian-sings-along-to-famous-after-taylor-swift-feud/, last accessed: October 23, 2017.

[52] Elias Leight, 'Kanye West on Taylor Swift: 'I'm So Glad My Wife Has Snapchat'', *Rolling Stone*, July 28, 2016, http://www.rollingstone.com/music/news/kanye-west-on-taylor-swift-im-glad-my-wife-has-snapchat-w431395, last accessed: October 23, 2017. D, 'Kanye came and dragged Taylor more', *Twitter*, July 27, 2016, https://twitter.com/holyspearits/status/758516526190321664, last accessed: October 23, 2017.

	Kanye West and Kim Kardashian are on the cover of Harper's Bazaar September issue. When asked by editor Laura Brown about their favourite Taylor Swift song, Kanye West replied, 'For me? I don't have one.' Kim Kardashian replied: 'I was such a fan of hers.'[53]
AUGUST 28, 2016	
TAYLOR SWIFT	**KANYE WEST**
-	Kanye West takes the stage at the 2016 MTV Video Music Awards. He received 6 minutes to do what he wants. He addressed the 'Famous' song and Taylor Swift by saying that he's a 'lover of all,' which is 'why I called her.'[54]
AUGUST 25, 2017	
TAYLOR SWIFT	**KANYE WEST**
Taylor Swift released a new song 'Look What You Made Me Do' with lyrics possible related to Kanye West: "I don't like your little games/ I don't like your tilted stage." Kanye West used an elevated tilted stage during his Saint Pablo tour.[55]	-
AUGUST 27, 2017	
TAYLOR SWIFT	**KANYE WEST AND KIM KARDASHIAN**
Taylor Swift released the music video of 'Look What You Made Me Do' which possibly contains coded references to Kanye West and Kim Kardashian: snake imagery (see page and the table *The New and Complet Timeline* 17 July 2016), imitation of Kim Kardashian and the Paris robbery (Kim Kardashian was caught in a bath tub and threaten with a gun), makes selfies then telling the others that she's 'getting receipts' so that she can 'edit them later,' at the end of the video says: "I would like very much like to be excluded from this narrative" (is the last part of her reply to Kim	-

[53] Carine Roitfeld, 'Icons: In Bed with Kim and Kanye', *Harper Bazaar*, July 28, 2016, http://www.harpersbazaar.com/fashion/photography/a16784/kanye-west-kim-kardashian-interview/, last accessed: October 23, 2017.

[54] MTV, 'Kanye West's Moment, 2016 Video Music Awards', *Youtube*, August 28, 2016, https://www.youtube.com/watch?v=ycnTPgp3DY8, last accessed: October 23, 2017.

[55] Taylor Swift, 'Out Now', *Instagram*, August 25, 2017, https://www.instagram.com/p/BYM6v4FH9Bo/?taken-by=taylorswift, last accessed: 23 October 2017. Taylor Swift, 'Look What You Made Me Do Lyrics', *Genius*, https://genius.com/Taylor-swift-look-what-you-made-me-do-lyrics, last accessed: October 23, 2017.

Kardashian's videos on her Snapchat account with the phone conversation between her and Kanye West).[56]

NOVEMBER 10, 2017	
TAYLOR SWIFT	KANYE WEST AND KIM KARDASHIAN
Taylor Swift released her newest musical album entitled *reputation*, which includes another song, *This Is Why We Can't Have Nice Things*, which is believed to be about Kanye West. The lyrics are: "It was so nice being friends again, there I was giving you a second chance, but you stabbed me in the back without shaking my hand'"; "therein lies the issues, friends don't try to trick you, get you on the phone and mind twist you."[57] Taylor Swift's Team denied the speculation regardin the releasing date of her album and the 10th anniversary of Donda West (Kanye West mother).[58]	People accused Taylor Swift on social media (Twitter, Facebook, Instagram) that the release of *reputation* album on this day is connected to the 10th anniversary of the death of Kanye West's mother, Donda West.[59]

[56] TaylorSwiftVevo, 'Look What You Made Me Do', *Youtube*, August 27, 2017, https://www.youtube.com/watch?v=3tmd-ClpJxA, last accessed: October 23, 2017.
[57] Taylor Swift, 'This Is Why We Can't Have Nice Things', *Genius*, November 10, 2017, https://genius.com/Taylor-swift-this-is-why-we-cant-have-nice-things-lyrics, last accessed: November 10, 2017.
[58] Roisin O'Connor, 'Taylor Swift: Reputation release date coinciding with anniversary of Donda West death is a 'coincidence'', *The Independent*, August 26, 2017, https://www.independent.co.uk/arts-entertainment/music/news/taylor-swift-donda-west-reputation-release-date-kanye-kim-kardashian-album-tour-dates-a7914191.html, last accessed: October 23, 2017.
[59] Eddie Fu, 'Taylor Swift denies Reputation release date is connected to the anniversary of the death of Kanye West's mother', *Consequence of Sound*, August 25, 2017, https://conequenceofsound.net/2017/08/taylor-swift-denies-reputation-release-date-is-connected-to-the-anniversary-of-the-death-of-kanye-wests-mother/ , last accessed: October 23, 2017.

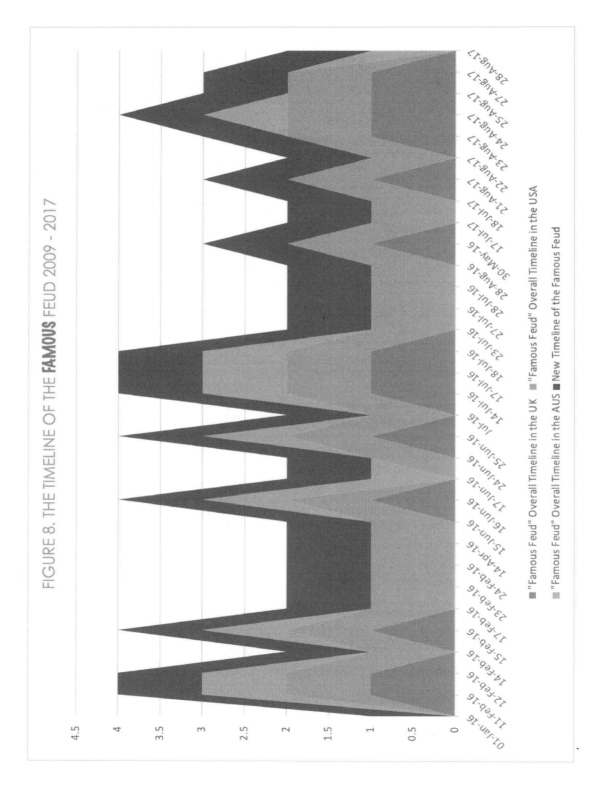

FIGURE 8. THE TIMELINE OF THE **FAMOUS** FEUD 2009 - 2017

■ "Famous Feud" Overall Timeline in the UK   ■ "Famous Feud" Overall Timeline in the USA

■ "Famous Feud" Overall Timeline in the AUS   ■ New Timeline of the Famous Feud

The Conclusions of the *Famous* timeline are based on the evidence available, however, it is possible that in reality, in the full conversation between Kanye West and Taylor Swift) maybe more than 25 minutes as we have today on Youtube) to be more information that either reject, approve or reject and accept different parts of the following conclusions:

Kanye West:

- said the truth about calling Taylor Swift and having a telephone conversation about his song and lyrics: Taylor Swift knew Kanye West's intention to make a song that includes lyrics about her: 'You guys want to call this a feud; you want to call this throwing shade but right after the song comes out I'm going to be on a GRAMMYs red carpet and they're going to ask me about it and I'll be like, 'He called me[60].'
- half presented that Taylor Swift came (as whole) with the idea of the lyrics: Kanye West tweeted in February 2016: I'm not even gone take credit for the idea… it's actually something Taylor came up with[61]); indeed, Kanye West read the lyrics to Taylor Swift to which she replied: ''Yeah, she does. It made her famous.' It's more provocative to say 'might still have sex…' It doesn't matter to me. There's not like one that hurts my feelings and one that doesn't'[62], but it was only *a part* of the lyrics, not *all* the lyrics and the song as Kanye West and Kim Kardashian wanted the world to believe (Kim Kardashian: ‚She totally approved that.' […] She totally knew that that was coming out. She wanted to all of a sudden act like she didn't[63]');
- used the telephone agreement to justify the lyrics about Taylor Swift in his song (Taylor Swift: 'Umm, yeah I mean go with whatever line you think is better. It's obviously very tongue in cheek either way. And I really appreciate you telling me about it, that's really nice. [...] You've gotta tell the story the way that it happened to you and the way that you experienced it[64]') and added a new line in the lyrics of the song, namely ‚I made that bitch famous';
- didn't disclose to the general public that during the telephone conversation he didn't inform Taylor Swift about the word 'bitch' and the full line 'I made that bitch famous' and that it was his only decision to add the word 'bitch' and the line in the lyrics of the song;
- wrongly presented to the world the song's lyrics from the perspective that Taylor Swift knew about it, including the word ‚bitch' and the line ‚I made that bitch famous';

[60] Kylizzle Snapchizzle, idem.
[61] Kanye West, A tweet on Twitter, February 2016.
[62] Kylizzle Snapchizzle, idem.
[63] Caity Weaver, 'Kanye and Taylor Swift, What's in O.J.'s Bag, and Understanding Caitlyn'.
[64] Kylizzle Snapchizzle, idem.

- he might have used the freedom of creativity given by Taylor Swift to add lyrics to the song in the direction he wanted as Taylor Swift said: ‚go with whatever line you think is better' and Kanye West added the line ‚I made that bitch famous';
- the *Famous* song was released in the week that happened to be one of the most important events in Taylor Swift's career: the Grammy Awards (she received the Grammy Award for the *Album of the Year* for the second time, which is a global record);
- presented the telephone conversation:

a. *in pieces* (in February 2016 in news as rumours and possible evidence of a telephone conversation recorded between him and Taylor Swift and later in heavily edited video of the telephone conversation posted on Kim Kardashian's Snapchat account) ***and not the full conversation at the same time in the same day***, so that the general public to know exactly the context of the telephone conversation;

b. *doesn't include the fact that he added the line* ‚I made that bitch famous' *without Taylor Swift's knowledge*;

c. *when are in motion events that are part of the promotion of his album, The Life of Pablo*:

c.1 *on the cover of his album is a picture with* ‚look like a white girl' (there is no evidence to support a clear causal link that the model is definitely a white person) wearing a bath suit and a black family which depicts a matrimony, also it is written on the cover ‚Which/One[65]', the general meaning that readers might have is choosing between the white girl (which is lonely in the picture) or the black family; before the release of the album's cover, Kanye West launched the song with the infamous line ‚I made that bitch famous' about Taylor Swift (she is white and according with her dress style in music videos and private life -where there are pictures published on different websites about her in private life- is in opposition with the picture from Kanye West's album cover; Taylor Swift never pictured herself in the way that the white girl (?) is pictured on Kanye West's album cover; maybe the 'look like a white girl' picture on the album cover is a metaphor and artistic representation of Taylor Swift; maybe it's an alternate reality that exists in Kanye West's mind, meaning, to him, that Taylor Swift is just a 'bitch'; maybe it's Kanye West's way of saying about

---

[65] Google, *The Life of Pablo album cover*,
https://www.google.com/search?q=the+life+of+pablo+album+cover&newwindow=1&safe=active&client=safari&rls=en&source=lnMs.&tbm=isch&sa=X&ved=0ahUKEwjunYH8rpzkAhUFPFAKHQ7-BogQ_AUIESgB&biw=1440&bih=812, last accessed: 23 October 2017.

Taylor Swift that in reality she is different from what she promotes to the general public and he managed to demonstrate her true personality;

c.2 Kim Kardashian, in an interview with GQ magazine, talked about the existence of a telephone conversation between Kanye West and Taylor Swift; Kim Kardashian: 'She totally approved that.' […] 'She totally knew that that was coming out. She wanted to all of a sudden act like she didn't[66]': this interview (June 16, 2016) happened in the week that Kanye West started to sale tickets (June 14 for American Express cardholders and June 16 for Tidal members, June 18 for general public[67]) to his music tour named *Saint Pablo Tour*;

c.3 Kim Kardashian presented a heavily edited video telephone conversation between Kanye West and Taylor Swift at a month after the start of Kanye West's sale of tickets for his music tour and in the video listeners can hear Taylor Swift agreeing with the lyrics, *but not the line* ,I made that bitch famous'; also a month before the start of *Saint Pablo Tour*, Kanye West and Kim Kardashian were on the cover of *Harper's Bazaar* September issue, and when they were asked by editor Laura Brown about the favourite Taylor Swift song, Kanye West replied, 'For me? I don't have one.' Kim Kardashian replied: 'I was such a fan of hers'[68];

- used the song and the lyrics about Taylor Swift in his concerts (from August 2016 to November 2016 and at the MTV VMA Awards 2016) and presented Taylor Swift as being a liar, while he is telling the whole truth;
- Kanye West had (has as of today) lots of opportunities to say that it was his decision to add the line 'I made that bitch famous' in the lyrics of the song and that Taylor Swift didn't know that and found out at the same time as the rest of the world;
- used the lyrics of the song to take credit for Taylor Swift's fame and to justify his actions 'I made that bitch famous', but also in a tweet, 'I can't be mad at Kanye because he made me famous! #FACTS';
- Kanye West during the telephone conversation with Taylor Swift said to her: 'Relationships are more important than punchlines, ya know?', however, the fact that he failed (even today) to recognize that he added a new line in the lyrics that Taylor Swift wasn't aware of, and then saying to the general public that Taylor Swift knew

[66] Caity Weaver, 'Kanye and Taylor Swift, What's in O.J.'s Bag, and Understanding Caitlyn'.
[67] Fionna Agomuoh, 'Kanye West Tour Dates 2016: 'Saint Pablo' Tickets, Prices And Schedule Released', June 14, 2016, https://www.player.one/kanye-west-tour-dates-2016-saint-pablo-tickets-prices-and-schedule-released-540277, last accessed: October 23, 2017.
[68] Carine Roitfeld, 'Icons: In Bed with Kim and Kanye', *Harper Bazaar*, July 28, 2016, http://www.harpersbazaar.com/fashion/photography/a16784/kanye-west-kim-kardashian-interview/, last accessed: October 23, 2017.

the full *Famous* song and the line 'I made that bitch famous', it is a pure 'punch line' and definitely not friendly relationship;

- Kanye West and Kim Kardashian's treatment and behaviour toward Taylor Swift on social media, interviews in magazines and mostly during Kanye West music tour, *Saint Pablo Tour*, in the USA is unfair, mean and wrong: the song and the lyrics encouraged people to send thousands of inappropriate comments on Taylor Swift's social media pages (Facebook, Instagram, Twitter), 'bitch', 'snake' and 'liar' being one of the favourite words in reference to Taylor Swift;

- Kanye West and Kim Kardashian had the opportunity to stop the feud at any moment after the release of the full song along with recognizing what each side knows about the lyrics of the song, but they decided to keep the public attention for at least 5 months on themselves, therefore making people and mass-media extremely curious about the existence or not of the evidence to incriminate Taylor Swift; this decision maybe it was intentional, but it was delivered to the general public under Kim and Kanye's terms;

- Kanye West and Kim Kardashian were fully aware of Taylor Swift's involvement in the lyrics of the song and they continued (and continue as today) to present Taylor Swift in a bad light and that she is to blame for everything bad that followed after; also, Kim Kardashian recorded a snapchat video listening to *Famous* song which intentionally underlined and recorded the part of the song where her husband Kanye West raps the lyrics: 'I made that bitch famous';

- Kanye West is to blame for starting the *Famous* feud and all the reactions from people toward him and Taylor Swift;

- there is evidence to support theories (but not to be considered as genuine true) that Kanye West used Taylor Swift's involvement as source of controversy to spin the public interest around his new musical album, to promote his musical album, *The Life of Pablo* and his music tour *Saint Pablo Tour* (by adding new lyrics; informed the general public that Taylor Swift knew about it, when in fact she did not; the album cover 'looks like a white girl' and Taylor Swift is a white girl; the release of information regarding Taylor Swift's involvement in the song and not all at the same time; when events are in motion which are part of the promotion of the album and his music tour); the contradiction between West's version and Swift's version of the phone conversation resulted in over a thousand articles being written by the Western mass-media and hundreds of thousands (quite possibly over a million) of comments written by the fans on both camps; in the end, a high number of posts about both artists were shared on social media by users around the planet where the main focus was Kanye West's new music album and tour;

- there is evidence to support theories (but not to be considered as genuine true) that West family planned in rich details to use Taylor Swift as scapegoat for their own use (increase and maintain popularity on social media and music genre) and to falsely paint Taylor Swift as a 'liar', not the victim, but the perpetrator and to be blame for the bad things that happens in Kanye and Kim's narrative line;

- it is difficult to agree and prove that Kanye West (even maybe due to a misunderstanding of the freedom of creativity or his intentional interpretation as the phone call as a freedom of creativity from Taylor Swift) took advantage of Taylor Swift's replies in the phone call to present her in a negative light with the aim to destroy Taylor Swift's reputation;
- the behaviour and the press releases by Kanye and Kim regarding Taylor Swift's involvement in the *Famous* song are misleading and biased;
- Kanye West was the first who misled and offered biased information to the general public about Taylor Swift's involvement in the *Famous* song, second was Kim Kardashian;
- there is evidence to suggest that Kanye West created an effective trap against Taylor Swift by creating a negative image, which is being a liar;
- Kanye West said that he made Taylor Swift famous, but he asked her to release his song *Famous* on her Twitter account; he asked Taylor to present the song in a positive view because she 'owns 2 billion people and if she is ok with the song, then the 2 billion people will be ok as well': this is a contradiction of the fame power that Kanye promoted over the years and in his song ('I made that bitch famous') about Taylor Swift and this world; however, from another corner there is the following perspective: Kanye West promoted the idea that Taylor Swift became famous because he interfered in her narrative line during the MTV Awards in 2009 and more people were interested in her songs, and in 2016 maybe he wanted to use Taylor Swift's fame created through his help in his favour, to be rewarded for his interference (this perspective has a weak point because, according to rumours spread by fans on social platforms such as Twitter and Reddit, prior to September 2009 Taylor Swift experienced a strong increase in album sales in countries and places where Kanye West failed to sell as much as Taylor Swift and, because of her, Kanye West managed to enter into the music mind of people who never heard of him before or were not interested);
- Kanye West and Kim Kardashian were the first (and the last) and most interested in keeping their own narrative alive in mass-media and public thoughts through the misleading and biased Taylor Swift's involvement in the creation of the *Famous* song from February 2016 until today;
- accused Taylor Swift of what he did: manipulation, misleading and biased information presented to the general public;
- there is evidence to support the theory that the song *Fade* performed by Teyana Taylor (born a year later than Taylor Swift: December 10, 1990) is a metaphor, but

also a revelation of the effect of his lie: Taylor Swift lost the love of the world and he earned it, the song was released at the MTV VMAs in August 2016.

Taylor Swift:

- said the truth from the following two perspectives: **1.** she heard the full *Famous* song as presented and released by Kanye West at the same time with the general public; **2.** she was not aware of the line 'I made that bitch famous';
- **can be accused of being a liar from the following perspectives:**

  1. she didn't inform the public right after the song release (February 2016) exactly what she knows about it and her involvement in the lyrics: the lack of this information confused people and fans and encouraged Western mass-media to come with their own version of truth in a visible number of negative articles published online;

  2. Taylor Swift failed to bring strong evidence that 'She declined and cautioned him about releasing a song with such a strong misogynistic message' as the evidence (video of the telephone conversation published on Youtube, 25 minutes) doesn't mention anything about the word 'misogynistic'; however, Taylor Swift warned Kanye West about 'feminist' and maybe this is the connection with the misogynistic message:

Taylor Swift: "You know, the thing about me is, anything that I do becomes like a feminist think-piece. And if I launch it, they're going to be like, wow, like, they'll just turn into something that... I think if I launch it, honestly, I think it'll be less cool. Because I think if I launch it, it adds this level of criticism. Because having that many followers and having that many eyeballs on me right now, people are just looking for me to do something dumb or stupid or lame. And I don't know. I kind of feel like people would try to make it negative if it came from me, do you know what I mean? I think I'm very self-aware about where I am, and I feel like right now I'm like this close to overexposure."

Kanye West: "I have this line where I said... And my wife really didn't like this one, because we tried to make it nicer. So I say "For all my Southside [N-word] that know me best, I feel like me and Taylor might still have sex." And my wife was really not with that one. She was way more into the "She owes you sex." But then the "owe" part was like the feminist group-type shit that I was like, ahhhhh."

Taylor Swift: "That's the part that I was kind of... I mean, they 're both really edgy, but that's the only thing about that line is that it's like, then the feminists are going to come out. But I mean, you don't give a f–. So..."

Kanye West: "Yeah, basically. Well, what I give a f— about is just you as a person, as a friend…."

3. Taylor Swift had a poor strategy of communication that couldn't match Kanye and Kim's strategy and that's because they had the evidence of the telephone conversation and they used it how they wanted (edited the video of the recording with parts that they want the public to know) and what time they wanted the public to hear and see it;

4. In her reply from July 2016 she wrote: 'I was never given the full story or **played any part of the song is character assassination'**, however, Taylor did play a part in the song:

Taylor Swift: "Well, I mean, she's saying that honestly because she's your wife, and like, um… So I think whatever one you think is actually better. I mean, obviously do what's best for your relationship, too. I think "owes me sex," it says different things. It says… "Owes me sex" means like "Look, I made her what she is. She actually owes me." Which is going to split people, because people who like me are going to be like, "She doesn't owe him s—." But then people who like thought it was bad-ass and crazy and awesome that you're so outspoken are going to be like, "Yeah, she does. It made her famous." So it's more provocative to say "still have sex," because no one would see that coming. They're both crazy. Do what you want. They're both going to get every single headline in the world. "Owes me sex" is a little bit more like throwing shade, and the other one's more flirtatious. It just depends on what you want to accomplish with it;"

, but still there is no evidence for a dominant argument that Taylor played a part because she *really wanted* or because she was involved in a phone conversation and *wanted to be nice and supportive* with Kanye West; also, Taylor Swift told Kanye West that she would think about the song, Kanye West instead said he would send her the song, but he never did; in the end, Taylor Swift didn't know that Kanye West would use the phone conversation as an implied agreement to her polite advice and suggestion to promote the song without hearing the final version, and then follow through on what she told Kanye West:

Taylor Swift: "And you know, if people ask me about it, look, I think it would be great for me to be like, "Look, he called me and told me the line before it came out. Like, the joke's on you guys – we're fine.""

[…]

Taylor Swift: "Yeah. Like, you guys want to call this a feud, you want to call this throwing shade, but you know, right after the song comes out, I'm gonna be on a Grammy red carpet, and they're gonna ask me about it and I'll be like, "He called me and sent me the song before it came out." So I think we're good."

Kanye West: "Okay. I'm gonna go lay this verse, and I'm gonna send it to you right now."

Taylor Swift: "[Taken aback.] Oh, you just… you haven't recorded it yet?"

Kanye West: "I recorded it. I'm nuancing the lines — like the last version of it says, "Me and Taylor might still have sex." And then my wife was like, "That doesn't sound as hard!""

- ***never denied that a phone conversation took place***[69]: ***February 2016***: Team Taylor replied after the release of the song: 'Kanye did not call for approval, but to ask Taylor to release his single „Famous' on her Twitter account[70]; ***in June 2016***: 'It was on that phone call that Kanye West also asked her to release the song on her Twitter account, which she declined to do[71]'; ***July 2016***: 'Of course I wanted to like the song. I wanted to believe Kanye when he told me that I would love the song. I wanted us to have a friendly relationship. He promised to play the song for me, but he never did. While I wanted to be supportive of Kanye on the phone call, you cannot 'approve' a song you haven't heard[72];'
- disagreed with Kanye West regarding her fame:

Kanye West: "Yeah, exactly. We can't have it like be somebody else's idea that gets in front and they're like… Because if you're like a really true, creative, visceral, vibey type person, it's probably hard for you to work at a corporation. So how can you give a creative ideas and you're working in a house of non-creativity? It's like this weird… So whenever we talk directly… Okay, now what if later in the song I was also to have said, uh… "I made her famous"? Is that a…"

Taylor Swift: "[Apprehensively.] Did you say that?"

Kanye West: "Yes, it might've happened. [Laughs.]"

Taylor Swift: "Well, what am I going to do about it?"

Kanye West: "Uh, like, do the hair flip?"

Taylor Swift: "Yeah. I mean… Um… It's just kind of like, whatever, at this point. But I mean, you've got to tell the story the way that it happened to you and the way that you've experienced it. Like, you honestly didn't know who I was before that. Like, it doesn't matter if I sold 7 million of that album

---

[69] Caity Weaver, 'Kanye and Taylor Swift, What's in O.J.'s Bag, and Understanding Caitlyn'.

[70] Melody Chiu, Karen Mizoguchi, 'Kanye West Did Not Call Taylor Swift for Approval Over 'B----' Lyric, Singer Cautioned Him Against Releasing 'Strong Misogynistic Message' Rep Says'.

[71] Caity Weaver, *idem*.

[72] The photo with Taylor Swift reply is now deleted from her Facebook, Twitter and Instagram account.

["Fearless"] before you did that, which is what happened. You didn't know who I was before that. It's fine. But, um, yeah. I can't wait to hear it."

- Taylor Swift warned Kanye West about her negative thought regarding the content of the lyrics:

Kanye West: "Okay. All right. Wait a second, you sound sad."

Taylor Swift: "Well, is it gonna be mean?"

Kanye West: "No, I don't think it's mean."

Taylor Swift: "Okay, then, let me hear it."

Kanye West: "Okay. It says, um,… and the funny thing is, when I first played it and my wife heard it, she was like, "Huh? What? That's too crazy," blah, blah, blah. And then like when Ninja from Die Atwoord heard it, he was like, "Oh my God, this is the craziest s–. This is why I love Kanye," blah, blah, blah, that kind of thing. And now it's like my wife's favourite f—ing line. I just wanted to give you some premise of that. Right?"

Taylor Swift: "Okay."

Kanye West: "So it says "To all my Southside [N-word] that know me best, I feel like Taylor Swift might owe me sex.""

Taylor Swift: "[Laughs, relieved.] That's not mean."

Taylor Swift: "Oh my God! I mean, I need to think about it, because you know, when you hear something for the first time, you just need to think about it. Because it is absolutely crazy. I'm glad it's not mean, though. It doesn't feel mean. But oh my God, the buildup you gave it, I thought it was going to be like, "That stupid, dumb bitch." But it's not. So I don't know. I mean, the launch thing, I think it would be kind of confusing to people. But I definitely like… I definitely think that when I'm asked about it, of course I'll be like, "Yeah, I love that. I think it's hilarious." But, um, I need to think about it."

- offered space for Kanye and Kim to present their story in the way they wanted and under their terms; Taylor presented a more truthful side of the story in the *Famous* narrative *only after* Kim and Kanye presented new information in regard to her involvement in the making of the song;
- she interfered only to rightfully defend herself from Kanye and Kim's accusations of being a liar and that she knew everything about the song;

- was caught in Kanye West's wrong presentation to the general public of her involvement in the song;
- there is evidence that Taylor Swift is a victim of Kanye and Kim's misleading and biased information about her involvement in the song.

Both artists:

- failed to share all the details of what happened during the telephone conversation from January 2016;
- based on the current evidence: Kanye West misled and presented a biased story of Taylor Swift's involvement in the creation of the song, while Taylor Swift told a more truthful side of her involvement in the creation of the song and the background narrative of the telephone conversation;
- the reaction of the public opinion was excessively huge with hundreds of thousands of comments and distribution of the content with Kanye West, Kim Kardashian and Taylor Swift; overall, the balance of neutrality of the Western mass-media is high, but there are articles in the favour of Kanye and Kim with Taylor Swift being portrayed as the liar while Kanye and Kim as the victims of Taylor Swift;[73]
- the addition of the telephone conversation from January 2016 in the chronological line of January 2016, and then its repetition in July (when the online evidence was released by Kim Kardashian on Snapchat) help to highlight the following facts: Kanye West misinformed the general public about the real contribution of Taylor Swift in the making of the *Famous* song and he is the perpetrator of the feud, while Taylor Swift is the victim who is not being told the whole story, but she is presented by Kanye West and Kim Kardashian as she knows everything; Taylor Swift's refusal to admit the accusations advanced by Kim and Kanye is ignored by them and both refused to accept the negative consequences of the general public toward and in reference to Taylor Swift that followed after they set the path of the negative narrative; Kim and Kanye's negative narrative about Taylor Swift was largely distributed by the Western mass-media online and also through print editions.

---

[73] Nate Jones, 'When Did the Media Turn Against Taylor Swift?', *Vulture*, July 21, 2016, https://www.vulture.com/2016/07/when-did-the-media-turn-against-taylor-swift.html, last accessed: October 23, 2017; The Ringer Staff, 'When Did You First Realize Taylor Swift Was Lying to You?', July 12, 2016, https://www.theringer.com/2016/7/12/16039240/when-did-you-first-realize-taylor-swift-was-lying-to-you-bb5a00a32b65#.paejv7bn2, last accessed: October 23, 2017.

II.2.1 A New Face of the '**Famous** Feud' Timeline

In this subchapter I investigated the narrative line of the relationship between Kanye West and Taylor Swift from September 2009 (MTV Music Awards) to November 2017 (the release of Taylor Swift's album *reputation*) with the aim of finding patterns that could present unknown information, or what we already know can be presented in a new way that could be used for a better and easier understanding of the feud.

To find the existence of patterns:

- I used the key dates of the *Famous* feud (based on the precise date (day, month, year) when the events happened) available in the table with the *Famous* feud timeline; the dates were used to create a figure with a 3D narrative line which exposes the dynamic between the players of the *Famous* feud; the creation of one large figure allowed me to see the whole narrative line.

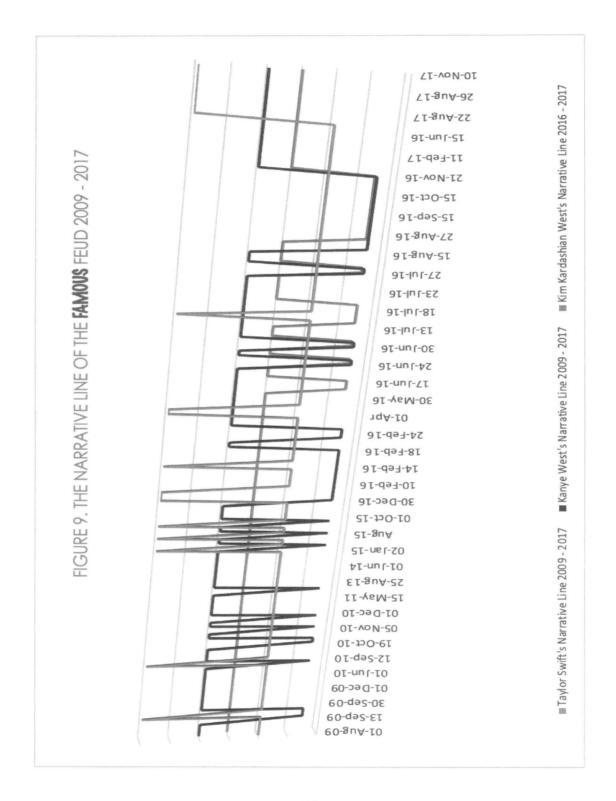

FIGURE 9. THE NARRATIVE LINE OF THE **FAMOUS** FEUD 2009 - 2017

■ Taylor Swift's Narrative Line 2009 - 2017   ■ Kanye West's Narrative Line 2009 - 2017   ■ Kim Kardashian West's Narrative Line 2016 - 2017

II.2.1.1 The Analysis of the **Famous** Feud Timeline 2009 – 2017

Based on Figure 9, I discovered a few patterns of behaviour between Kanye West and Taylor Swift; the starting point of the patterns is in September 2009 with Kanye West and Taylor Swift and continue as of today, even if the figure does not contain information about the feud after November 2017.

The patterns were discovered based on the following method: I linked and compared the events from Kanye West's life with the events from Taylor Swift's life; in other words, what events existed in Taylor Swift's narrative line when Kanye West interfered in her narrative line.

TABLE 5. KANYE WEST'S PATTERNS OF THE **FAMOUS** FEUD TIMELINE 2009 – 2017

PATTERN 1. Interfered in Taylor Swift's key moments from her life: recognition at high level by the music industry and attendance at the awards ceremonies.

Events from Kanye West's Narrative Line	Events from Taylor Swift's Narrative Line
September 13, 2009:	*September 13, 2009:*
Kanye West got onto the stage of the MTV VMA and interrupted Taylor Swift speech for acceptance of the award for the Best Female Video (You Belong with Me).	Taylor Swift was nominated for the first time for the Best Female Video and she won but could not finish her speech because she was interrupted by Kanye West.
February 11, 2016:	*February 15, 2016:*
Kanye West debuted his musical album *The Life of Pablo* at his Yeezy Season 3 show at Madison Square Garden, New York. In one of his songs, 'Famous,' he raps 'I feel like me and Taylor might still have sex / Why? I made that bitch famous (God damn) / I made that bitch famous.' Kanye West told the public that he has the approval from Taylor Swift, in return Taylor Swift's Team replied that she cautioned Kanye West about the song and that Taylor Swift was	It was in the week (four days until the ceremony) before the Grammy Awards (the highest award in the USA music industry) and Taylor Swift presented to the awards with the label 'that bitch' and that her fame is because of Kanye West. Taylor Swift was the winner of the *Album of the Year* for the second time (the first woman in the music industry).

never aware of the line 'I made that bitch
famous'.

PATTERN 2. Interfered in Taylor's narrative line with a negative view about her character and skills while key events from his life are in motion: such as releasing a new album, tickets for sale for a tour and promoting a musical tour.

Before the release of his album My Beautiful Dark Twisted Fantasy in 2010:

October 20, 2010:

Kanye West had an interview with Access Hollywood:

Kanye West: 'Why are the last four Albums of the Year: Taylor Swift, Dixie Chicks, Ray Charles and Herbie Hancock? Like, you know, with all due respect… that's inaccurate.'

November 5, 2010:

Kanye West had an interview with the radio station KDWB:

Kanye West: "My moment with Taylor, 12 years old, eighteen year old girl me um cutting her off it show like a lack of compassion with everything she went to to deserve this one moment that shouldn't you know that [inaudible] have 100 magazine covers and sell a million first week, but um um that shouldn't even categorize with the greatest living artists that we have to date even be put in the same category you know it's it's just it's just disrespectful was retarded and I for me you can see the amount of work that we put into this."

Kanye West: "It's like, what's so arrogant about that moment? If anything, it's selfless. I'm walking around now with half an arm, trying to sell albums and having to walk in rooms and be afraid of my food getting spat in, like people going 'I lost all total respect for you,' and nobody wants to just sit and look at the reality."

Kanye West: "The audacity of it losing anything … I guarantee if it was the other way around, and Taylor Swift was 15, 12, 15 years into the game, and on her 40th video or 50th video, and she made the video of her career, do you think she would have lost to a brand new artist? Hell no!"

During a secret show slash release party at the Bowery Ballroom in New York City last night, 1.00 am, Kanye West continued his rant by expressing his continued issues with singer Taylor Swift and said: "Taylor never came to my defense at any interview. … And rode the waves and rode it and rode it."

Before the release of his album Yeezus in 2013:

Seven days before the release of his album, June 11, 2013: In a *New York Times* interview Kanye West stated about Taylor Swift VMA's moment that he doesn't have any regret about his interruption and that it was a situation where he gave into peer pressure to apologize. When asked if he'd take back the original action or the apology, if given the choice, he answered, "You know what? I can answer that, but I'm – I'm just -- not afraid, but I know that would be such a distraction. It's such a strong thing, and people have such a strong feeling about it. *My Beautiful Dark Twisted Fantasy* was my long, backhanded apology. You know how people give a backhanded compliment? It was a backhanded apology. It was like, all these raps, all these sonic acrobatics. I was like: 'Let me show you guys what I can do, and please accept me back. You want to have me on your shelves."

Before the release of his album The Life of Pablo in 2016:

On February 11, 2016 Kanye West debuted his musical album *The Life of Pablo* at his Yeezy Season 3 show at Madison Square Garden, New York. In one of his songs, 'Famous,' he raps "I feel like me and Taylor might still have sex / Why? I made that bitch famous (God damn) / I made that bitch famous."

In a GQ interview (June 16, 2016) for July new issue, Kim Kardashian spoked about Taylor Swift and her implication in the 'Famous' song. Two days before this interview Kanye West started to sale tickets (June 14 for American Express cardholders and June 16 for Tidal members, June 18 for general public) to his music tour named *Saint Pablo Tour*.

Before Saint Pablo Tour in 2016:

Kanye West and Kim Kardashian are on the cover of Harper's Bazaar September issue. When asked by editor Laura Brown about their favourite Taylor Swift song, Kanye West replied, 'For me? I don't have one.' Kim Kardashian replied: 'I was such a fan of hers.'

PATTERN 3. Disagreed and shared negative views about Taylor Swift's music and achievements.

SEPTEMBER 13, 2009:

While Taylor Swift was giving her acceptance speech for Best Female Video *You Belong with Me* at MTV Video Music Awards, Kanye West got onto the stage and interrupted her; he took her microphone, saying: "Yo, Taylor, I'm really happy for you and I'mma let you finish, but Beyoncé had one of the best videos of all time! One of the best videos of all time!" (Kanye West was referring to the music video for 'Single Ladies (Put a Ring on It)'. He then handed the microphone back to Taylor Swift.

OCTOBER 20, 2010:

Kanye West had an interview with *Access Hollywood*:
Kanye West: 'Why are the last four Albums of the Year: Taylor Swift, Dixie Chicks, Ray Charles and Herbie Hancock? Like, you know, with all due respect… that's inaccurate.'

NOVEMBER 5, 2010:

Kanye West had an interview with the radio station KDWB:

Kanye West: "My moment with Taylor, 12 years old, eighteen year old girl me um cutting her off it show like a lack of compassion with everything she went to to deserve this one moment that shouldn't you know that [inaudible] have 100 magazine covers and sell a million first week, but um um that shouldn't even categorize with the greatest living artists that we have to date even be put in the same category you know it's it's just it's just disrespectful was retarded and I for me you can see the amount of work that we put into this."

Kanye West: "The audacity of it losing anything … I guarantee if it was the other way around, and Taylor Swift was 15, 12, 15 years into the game, and on her 40th video or 50th video, and she made the video of her career, do you think she would have lost to a brand new artist? Hell no!"

FEBRUARY 11, 2016:

On 11 February 2016 Kanye West debuted his musical album *The Life of Pablo* at his Yeezy Season 3 show at Madison Square Garden, New York. In one of his songs, 'Famous,' he raps "I feel like me and Taylor might still have sex / Why? I made that bitch famous (God damn) / I made that bitch famous."

FEBRUARY 23, 2016:

Kanye West wrote a few tweets in now deleted (deactivated?) Twitter account:
"I made Dark Fantasy and Watch the Throne in one year and wasn't nominated for either and you know who has 2 albums of the year."
– KANYE WEST (@kanyewest) February 23, 2016

JULY 28, 2016:

Kanye West and Kim Kardashian are on the cover of Harper's Bazaar September issue. When asked by editor Laura Brown about their favourite Taylor Swift song, Kanye West replied, 'For me? I don't have one.'

PATTERN 4: Refused to take responsibility for his negative and inappropriate behaviour against Taylor Swift.

NOVEMBER 5, 2010:

Kanye West had an interview with the radio station KDWB:
Kanye West: "It's like, what's so arrogant about that moment? If anything, it's selfless. I'm walking around now with half an arm, trying to sell albums and having to walk in rooms and be afraid of my food getting spat in, like people going 'I lost all total respect for you,' and nobody wants to just sit and look at the reality."

JUNE 11, 2013:

In a *New York Times* interview Kanye West stated about Taylor Swift VMA's moment that he doesn't have any regret about his interruption and that it was a situation where he gave into peer pressure to apologize. When asked if he'd take back the original action or the apology, if given the choice, he answered, "You know what? I can answer that, but I'm – I'm just -- not afraid, but I know that would be such a distraction. It's such a strong thing, and people have such a strong feeling about it. *My Beautiful Dark Twisted Fantasy* was my long, backhanded apology. You know how people give a backhanded compliment? It was a backhanded apology. It was like, all these raps, all these sonic acrobatics. I was like: 'Let me show you guys what I can do, and please accept me back. You want to have me on your shelves."

FEBRUARY 24, 2016:

At Yo Gotti's album release party at the 1OAK nightclub in Hollywood, Kanye West reiterates he told Taylor Swift about the 'Famous' lyric and said "She had two seconds to be cool and she fucked it up!"

JULY 27, 2016:

Kanye West makes a guest appearance at Drake's concert in Chicago, and speaks out about Taylor Swift. Kanye West told his fans, "All I gotta say is, I am so glad my wife has Snapchat!", "Now y'all can know the truth and can't nobody talk s–t about 'Ye no more." After his words, he performed the 'Famous' song.

AUGUST 28, 2016:

Kanye West takes the stage at the 2016 MTV Video Music Awards. He received 6 minutes to do what he wants. He addressed the 'Famous' song and Taylor Swift by saying that he's a 'lover of all,' which is 'why I called her.'

During the music concert tour, Saint Pablo Tour, presented the *Famous* song with Taylor Swift as the negative character of the song, and encouraged people to shout 'bitch' when referencing to Taylor Swift.

PATTERN 5. *He does not want to be a truly friend of Taylor Swift.*

Interrupted her speech in 2009, negative views about her music in 2010, 2011, 2013 and 2016; added new lyrics in the *Famous* song and presented those lyrics as Taylor Swift knew about it; encouraged people to shout 'bitch' in referencing Taylor Swift at his concerts in 2016.

PATTERN 6. *Cannot move on and let Taylor Swift alone.*

From 2010 to the present, he refuses to admit his wrongdoing and apologize to Taylor Swift for not sending her the final version of the song and not confirming to the public the truth that Taylor did not know the line she disputed.

PATTERN 7. Created, maintained and supported the Famous feud according with his needs.

From 2009 through various events created and promoted by him while important events (songs and album release, tour tickets available and during the tours across USA, interview).

PATTERN 8. It is solely responsible for the negative opinion of the general public toward and in reference to Taylor Swift.

In 2009 by himself and from 2016 onwards with Kim Kardashian.

PATTERN 9. Presented biased information regarding Taylor Swift's involvement in the Famous song from 2016.

From February 2016, June and July 2016 until today.

PATTERN 10. Created and maintained a negative image about Taylor Swift.

In September 2009 while interrupting her speech with the reason that she did not deserve the award; in 2010 through interviews; in February, June and July 2016: through tweets and Kim Kardashian parts of the telephone conversation; from September until October through the concert Saint Pablo Tour where he encouraged people to shout 'bitch' in referencing Taylor Swift.

In the table above, I wrote the following text: 'During a secret show slash release party at the Bowery Ballroom in New York City last night, 1.00 am, Kanye West continued his rant by expressing his continued issues with singer Taylor Swift and said: "Taylor never came to my defense at any interview. … And rode the waves and rode it and rode it."' However, there is evidence to show that Taylor Swift did not 'rode the waves and rode it and rode it' and that she tried to stop the feud: during an interview on the radio programme MJ's Morning Show, Taylor Swift refused to talk about Kanye West: 'I'm just honestly trying not to make it into a bigger deal than it already is' […] It's kind of become more of a big deal than I ever thought it would be.' […] 'I just, you know, it happened on TV, so everybody saw what happened. I just would like to move on maybe a little bit.' […] 'I really would appreciate it if we could talk about something else, because I've asked you three times now, and I'm trying to be nice about it.' […] 'It just isn't something we need to spend this whole interview talking about.'[74] Overall, Kanye West has talked more negatively about Taylor Swift since September 2009.

If each album represents the life of the artist, then *The Life of Pablo* is the life of a man who sacrificed a life that does not belong to him, does not take responsibility for his negative actions, is against a person who can write and sing her own lyrics and titles of songs.[75]

TABLE 6. TAYLOR SWIFT'S PATTERNS OF THE **FAMOUS** FEUD TIMELINE 2009 – 2017
PATTERN 1. Interfered in the narrative line of the feud to defend herself from Kanye West's negative behaviour about her character and skills.

SEPTEMBER 14, 2009:

The interview with E Online News after the MTV show:

"I was standing on stage and I was really excited because I had just won the award and then I was really excited because Kanye West was on the stage," […] "And then I wasn't so excited anymore after that."

The reporter asked Taylor Swift if she has hard feelings about Kanye West. Taylor responded:

"I don't know him and I've never met him."

The reporter continued asking Taylor if she was a fan before the event from the stage. Taylor responded:

"Yeah, It's Kanye West."

The reporter continued asking Taylor if she is still a fan and 'I take a no?' Taylor responded:

"You know I just… I don't know him and I don't want to start anything because I just, you know, I had a great night tonight."

---

[74] Catriona Wightman, 'Swift 'Refuses to Talk About Kanye'', *Digital Spy*, September 19, 2009, available at: https://www.digitalspy.com/showbiz/a178162/swift-refuses-to-talk-about-kanye/, last accessed: May 25, 2018.
[75] Read Casian Anton, *Black and White Music: A Journey Behind the Musical Notes*, Second Edition, August 2022, Amazon (printed edition) and available on Google Play, Apple Books and Kobo e-book stores.

SEPTEMBER 15, 2009:

Taylor Swift (after The View) told ABC News Radio: "Kanye did call me and he was very sincere in his apology, and I accepted that apology."

SEPTEMBER 12, 2010:

During MTV VMAs, Taylor Swift sang 'Innocent', a song widely believed (mass media and fans of Taylor Swift and Kanye West) to be about Kanye West and her forgiveness for what Kanye West did to her a year later:

"It's alright, just wait and see
Your string of lights is still bright to me
You're still an innocent
Lives change like the weather
It's okay, life is a tough crowd
32 and still growin' up now
I hope you remember
Today is never too late to
Be brand new."

FEBRUARY 12, 2016:

Taylor Swift camp replied:

"Kanye did not call for approval, but to ask Taylor to release his single „Famous' on her Twitter account. She declined and cautioned him about releasing a song with such a strong misogynistic message. Taylor was never made aware of the actual lyric, „I made that bitch famous.""

FEBRUARY 15, 2016:

While accepting Album of the Year award at the GRAMMYs, Taylor Swift addressed what is believed to be about the infamous Kanye West lyrics about her:

"I want to thank the fans for the last 10 years, and the recording academy for giving us this unbelievable honor. I want to thank all of the collaborators that you see on this stage. Mostly, I want to thank my co-executive producer Max Martin, who has deserved to be up here for 25 years. And as the first woman to win album of the year at the Grammy's twice, I want to say to all the young women out there, there are going to be people along the way who, will try to undercut your success or take credit for your accomplishments or your fame. But if you just focus on the work and you don't let those people sidetrack you, someday when you get where you're going, you will know it was you and the people who love you who put you there, and that will be the greatest feeling in the world. Thank you for this moment."

JUNE 16, 2016:

Taylor Swift camp, after Kim Kardashian's interview with GQ, issued a statement to GQ:

"Taylor does not hold anything against Kim Kardashian as she recognizes the pressure Kim must be under and that she is only repeating what she has been told by Kanye West. However, that does not change the fact that much of what Kim is saying is incorrect. Kanye West and Taylor only spoke once on the phone while she was on vacation with her family in January of 2016 and they have never spoken since. Taylor has never denied that conversation took place. It was on that phone call that Kanye West also asked her to release the song on her Twitter account, which she declined to do. Kanye West never told Taylor he was going to use the term 'that bitch' in referencing her. A song cannot be approved if it was never heard. Kanye West never played the song for Taylor Swift. Taylor heard it for the first time when everyone else did and was humiliated. Kim Kardashian's claim that Taylor and her team were aware of being recorded is not true, and Taylor cannot understand why Kanye West, and now Kim Kardashian, will not just leave her alone."

JULY 17, 2016:

Taylor Swift responded to Kim Kardashian's Snapchat videos on her Instagram and Twitter account (now the picture with her response is deleted):

"That moment when Kanye West secretly records your phone call, then Kim posts it on the Internet."

"Where is the video of Kanye telling me he was going to call me 'that bitch' in his song? It doesn't exist because it never happened. You don't get to control someone's emotional response to being called 'that bitch' in front of the entire world. Of course I wanted to like the song. I wanted to believe Kanye when he told me that I would love the song. I wanted us to have a friendly relationship. He promised to play the song for me, but he never did. While I wanted to be supportive of Kanye on the phone call, you cannot 'approve' a song you haven't heard. Being falsely painted as a liar when I was never given the full story or played any part of the song is character assassination. I would very much like to be excluded from this narrative, one that I have never asked to be a part of, since 2009."

AUGUST 25, 2017:

Taylor Swift released a new song 'Look What You Made Me Do' with lyrics possible related to Kanye West: "I don't like your little games/ I don't like your tilted stage." Kanye West used an elevated tilted stage during his Saint Pablo tour.

AUGUST 27, 2017:

Taylor Swift released the music video of 'Look What You Made Me Do' which possibly contains coded references to Kanye West and Kim Kardashian: snake imagery (see page and the table *The New and Complet Timeline* July 17, 2016), imitation of Kim Kardashian and the Paris robbery (Kim Kardashian was caught in a bath tub and threaten with a gun), makes selfies then telling the others that she's 'getting receipts' so that she can 'edit them later,' at the end of the video says: "I would like very much like to be excluded from this narrative" (is the last part of her reply to Kim Kardashian's videos on her Snapchat account with the phone conversation between her and Kanye West).

10 NOVEMBER 2017:

Taylor Swift released her newest musical album entitled *reputation*, which includes another song, *This Is Why We Can't Have Nice Things*, which is believed to be about Kanye West. The lyrics are: "It was so nice being friends again, there I was giving you a second chance, but you stabbed me in the back without shaking my hand'"; "therein lies the issues, friends don't try to trick you, get you on the phone and mind twist you." Taylor Swift's Team denied the speculation regardin the releasing date of her album and the 10th anniversary of Donda West (Kanye West mother).

PATTERN 2. Shared positive views about Kanye West's music and achievements.

SEPTEMBER 14, 2009:

The interview with E Online News after the MTV show:

"I was standing on stage and I was really excited because I had just won the award and then I was really excited because Kanye West was on the stage," […] "And then I wasn't so excited anymore after that."

The reporter asked Taylor Swift if she has hard feelings about Kanye West. Taylor responded:

"I don't know him and I've never met him."

The reporter continued asking Taylor if she was a fan before the event from the stage. Taylor responded:

"Yeah, It's Kanye West."

The reporter continued asking Taylor if she is still a fan and 'I take a no?' Taylor responded:

"You know I just… I don't know him and I don't want to start anything because I just, you know, I had a great night tonight."

APRIL 25, 2015:

In an interview with *Entertainment Tonight*, Cameron Mathison asked Taylor Swift about the rumored collaboration between her and Kanye West. Taylor Swift answered: "He has said that… We're never been in the studio together, but he's got a lot of amazing ideas, he's one of those people who's just like idea, idea, idea, like what you think of this, what you think of that, he's very creative and like I've think we've talked about it but we've also about so many other things, I think I completely respect his vision as a producer, so that's all I know now, I have no idea how the next album is gonna be though."

APRIL 30, 2015:

In an interview with *E! News*, Jason Kennedy asked Taylor Swift about the rumored collaboration between her and Kanye West. Taylor Swift answered: "Everybody is saying that […] He did said that […] We've hung out, gone to dinner, talked and he's one of those people who's always throwing out ideas, so that was one of the ideas that was thrown out. There were lots of other ideas he has, you can imagine. But no creative decision has been made up about the next record."[76]

AUGUST 11, 2015:

During a cover interview with *Vanity Fair*, Taylor Swift said about Kanye West:

"I feel like I wasn't ready to be friends with him until I felt like he had some sort of respect for me, and he wasn't ready to be friends with me until he had some sort of respect for me – so it was the same issue, and we both reached the same place at the same time' […] And then Kanye and I both reached a place where he would say really nice things about my music and what I've accomplished, and I could ask him how his kid doing. … We haven't planned [a collaboration, added by the author] … But hey, I like him as a person. And that's a really good, nice first step, a nice place for us to be."

AUGUST 30, 2015:

[76] Bruna Nessif, 'Is This Taylor Swift and Kanye West Collaboration Happening or What?! Watch Now', *EOnline*, April 30, 2015, https://www.eonline.com/news/652354/is-this-taylor-swift-and-kanye-west-collaboration-happening-or-what-watch-now, last accessed: October 23, 2017.

Taylor Swift accepted Kanye West's request to be the person to give him the Video Vanguard Award at the MTV from 2015 and invoked the original incident in her speech:

'I first met Kanye West six years ago – at this show, actually! [..] *The College Dropout* was the very first album my brother and I bought on iTunes when I was 12 years old…I've been a fan of his for as long as I can remember because Kanye defines what it means to be a creative force in music, fashion and, well, life. So, I guess I have to say to all the other winners tonight: I'm really happy for you, and imma let you finish, but Kanye West has had one of the greatest careers of all time.'

PATTERN 3. Tried to forgive Kanye West and move on.

Taylor wrote the song 'Innocent' for Kanye West; despite the negative views about her by Kanye West in 2010 and 2013, in 2015 she accepted Kanye West's invitation to give him the MTV Vanguard Award; during the telephone conversation from January 2016, she supported Kanye's song and was nice on the phone. In April 2016 she refused to talk about the *Famous* song.

PATTERN 4. Used same methods to reply as Kanye West: through interviews, official statements and music.

September 2009 (interviews); September 2010 though 'Innocent'; October 2010 ('Innocent' song was included on her album *Speak Now*); June and July 2016 through official statement; August 2017, November 2017 through music.

PATTERN 5. She wanted to have a positive relationship with Kanye West.

SEPTEMBER 14, 2009:

The interview with E Online News after the MTV show:

The reporter asked Taylor Swift if she has hard feelings about Kanye West. Taylor responded:

"I don't know him and I've never met him."

The reporter continued asking Taylor if she is still a fan and 'I take a no?' Taylor responded:

"You know I just… I don't know him and I don't want to start anything because I just, you know, I had a great night tonight."

SEPTEMBER 15, 2009:

Taylor Swift (after The View) told ABC News Radio: "Kanye did call me and he was very sincere in his apology, and I accepted that apology."

SEPTEMBER 12, 2010:

During MTV VMAs, Taylor Swift sang 'Innocent', a song widely believed (mass media and fans of Taylor Swift and Kanye West) to be about Kanye West and her forgiveness for what Kanye West did to her a year later:

"It's alright, just wait and see
Your string of lights is still bright to me
You're still an innocent
Lives change like the weather
It's okay, life is a tough crowd
32 and still growin' up now
I hope you remember
Today is never too late to
Be brand new."

APRIL 29, 2015:

In an interview with *Entertainment Tonight*, Cameron Mathison asked Taylor Swift about the rumored collaboration between her and Kanye West. Taylor Swift answered: "He has said that… We're never been in the studio together, but he's got a lot of amazing ideas, he's one of those people who's just like idea, idea, idea, like what you think of this, what you think of that, he's very creative and like I've think we've talked about it but we've also about so many other things, I think I completely respect his vision as a producer, so that's all I know now, I have no idea how the next album is gonna be though."

APRIL 30, 2015:

In an interview with *E! News*, Jason Kennedy asked Taylor Swift about the rumored collaboration between her and Kanye West. Taylor Swift answered: "Everybody is saying that […] He did said that […] We've hung out, gone to dinner, talked and he's one of those people who's always throwing out ideas, so that was one of the ideas that was thrown out. There were lots of other ideas he has, you can imagine. But no creative decision has been made up about the next record."[77]

AUGUST 11, 2015:

During a cover interview with *Vanity Fair*, Taylor Swift said about Kanye West:

"I feel like I wasn't ready to be friends with him until I felt like he had some sort of respect for me, and he wasn't ready to be friends with me until he had some sort of respect for me — so it was the same issue, and we both reached the same place at the same time' […] And then Kanye and I both reached a place where he would say really nice things about my music and what I've accomplished, and I could

---

[77] Bruna Nessif, 'Is This Taylor Swift and Kanye West Collaboration Happening or What?! Watch Now', *EOnline*, April 30, 2015, https://www.eonline.com/news/652354/is-this-taylor-swift-and-kanye-west-collaboration-happening-or-what-watch-now, last accessed: October 23, 2017.

ask him how his kid doing. … We haven't planned [a collaboration, added by the author] … But hey, I like him as a person. And that's a really good, nice first step, a nice place for us to be."

AUGUST 30, 2015:

Taylor Swift accepted Kanye West's request to be the person to give him the Video Vanguard Award at the MTV from 2015 and invoked the original incident in her speech:

'I first met Kanye West six years ago – at this show, actually! [..] *The College Dropout* was the very first album my brother and I bought on iTunes when I was 12 years old…I've been a fan of his for as long as I can remember because Kanye defines what it means to be a creative force in music, fashion and, well, life. So, I guess I have to say to all the other winners tonight: I'm really happy for you, and imma let you finish, but Kanye West has had one of the greatest careers of all time.'

PATTERN 6. Maintained and supported the feud as side effect of her defence mechanism from Kanye West.

September 2009; September 2010; February, June and July 2016; August 2017 to November 2017.

PATTERN 7. Does not want to be a part of the Famous feud since 2009.

SEPTEMBER 14, 2009:

The interview with E Online News after the MTV show:

"I was standing on stage and I was really excited because I had just won the award and then I was really excited because Kanye West was on the stage," […] "And then I wasn't so excited anymore after that."

The reporter asked Taylor Swift if she has hard feelings about Kanye West. Taylor responded:

"I don't know him and I've never met him."

The reporter continued asking Taylor if she was a fan before the event from the stage. Taylor responded:

"Yeah, It's Kanye West."

The reporter continued asking Taylor if she is still a fan and 'I take a no?' Taylor responded:

"You know I just… I don't know him and I don't want to start anything because I just, you know, I had a great night tonight."

SEPTEMBER 19, 2009:

During an interview on the radio programme MJ's Morning Show, the host asked Taylor Swift about Kanye West and she replied:

'I'm just honestly trying not to make it into a bigger deal than it already is' […] It's kind of become more of a big deal than I ever thought it would be.'

'I just, you know, it happened on TV, so everybody saw what happened. I just would like to move on maybe a little bit.'

'I didn't know what to think, but I think that we should maybe talk about something else, because I've talked about this in one interview, and that was going to be it'. […] 'It's not something I feel like we need to keep talking about.'

'I really would appreciate it if we could talk about something else, because I've asked you three times now, and I'm trying to be nice about it.'

'It just isn't something we need to spend this whole interview talking about.'

In the end, the host insisted more about Kanye West, however, Taylor Swift decided to stop the interview[78].

APRIL 14, 2016:

In an interview with Vogue, Taylor Swift addressed her acceptance speech at Grammy Awards and Kanye West:

"I think the world is bored with the saga. I don't want to add anything to it, because then there's just more… I guess what I wanted to call attention to in my speech at the Grammys was how it's going to be difficult if you're a woman who wants to achieve something in her life - no matter what."

JUNE 16, 2016:

Taylor Swift camp, after Kim Kardashian's interview with GQ, issued a statement to GQ:

"Taylor does not hold anything against Kim Kardashian as she recognizes the pressure Kim must be under and that she is only repeating what she has been told by Kanye West. However, that does not change the fact that much of what Kim is saying is incorrect. Kanye

---

[78] Catriona Wightman, 'Swift 'Refuses to Talk About Kanye''.

West and Taylor only spoke once on the phone while she was on vacation with her family in January of 2016 and they have never spoken since. Taylor has never denied that conversation took place. It was on that phone call that Kanye West also asked her to release the song on her Twitter account, which she declined to do. Kanye West never told Taylor he was going to use the term 'that bitch' in referencing her. A song cannot be approved if it was never heard. Kanye West never played the song for Taylor Swift. Taylor heard it for the first time when everyone else did and was humiliated. Kim Kardashian's claim that Taylor and her team were aware of being recorded is not true, and Taylor cannot understand why Kanye West, and now Kim Kardashian, will not just leave her alone."

JULY 17, 2016:

Taylor Swift responded to Kim Kardashian's Snapchat videos on her Instagram and Twitter account (now the picture with her response is deleted):

"That moment when Kanye West secretly records your phone call, then Kim posts it on the Internet."

"Where is the video of Kanye telling me he was going to call me 'that bitch' in his song? It doesn't exist because it never happened. You don't get to control someone's emotional response to being called 'that bitch' in front of the entire world. Of course I wanted to like the song. I wanted to believe Kanye when he told me that I would love the song. I wanted us to have a friendly relationship. He promised to play the song for me, but he never did. While I wanted to be supportive of Kanye on the phone call, you cannot 'approve' a song you haven't heard. Being falsely painted as a liar when I was never given the full story or played any part of the song is character assassination. I would very much like to be excluded from this narrative, one that I have never asked to be a part of, since 2009."

PATTERN 8. Promoted a more truthful version of the events.

September 2009 and 2010; February, June and July 2016; August – November 2017; Present day.

Surprisingly, Taylor Swift is not the only artist which had to deal with Kanye West's interference in the narrative line. In the following section I wrote examples of the marketing strategy? of Kanye West from the point of view of one pattern (shortly modified, but the essence is the same):

Pattern: *interference in the narrative line of other people while events from his life are in motion, this time the release of a new album, ye, from 2018.*

Kanye West[79] met with Rick Rubin, the executive producer on Kanye West's previous two albums, *Yeezus* (2013) and *The Life of Pablo* (2016).[80] Later that month, Kanye West met with and previewed the album for radio host Charlamagne Tha God (Mr. Lenard McKelvey as real name).[81]

On April 13, Kanye West was back on social media. Following his return, Kanye West was very active, his first retweet being about the Ferguson Shootings (which involved protests and riots that began the day after the fatal shooting of Michael Brown by the white police officer Darren Wilson on August 9, 2014, in Ferguson, Missouri). Due to lots of tweets and information, I wrote a list with the main topics of Kanye West.

- Saint Pablo (memories and two tattoo designs with the word 'saint');
- philosophical statements;
- new shoes prototypes;
- he is writing a book in real time on Twitter;
- video: Lauren Hill 20 years of relevance;
- announced his new album of 7 songs: June 1st, me and Kudi June 8th and its called Kids See Ghosts, Teyana Taylor June 22, Pusha T May 25;
- he likes the thinking of Candance Owens;
- doesn't subscribe to the term and concept of God fearing;
- David Hammos, Bliz-aard Ball Sale. Elena Filipovic;
- David: Higher Goals;
- Slavery (a sensible topic in the U.S.A.);
- Jospeh Beuys;
- Tesla and Elon Musk;
- retweets videos made a person named Scott Adams about Kanye West and his power to change minds, takes us in the Golden Age, he advocates for african americans, racism and has good credential;
- Donald Glover is a free thinker;
- Prince;

[79] In *April 2018* section, all the information (except where there is a footnote) was collected from Kanye West's Twitter account.
[80] Eddie Fu, 'Kanye West spotted with Rick Rubin at Calabasas office', *Consequence of Sound*, April 3, 2018, https://consequenceofsound.net/2018/04/kanye-west-spotted-at-rick-rubins-recording-studio/, last accessed: May 28, 2018.
[81] Nerisha Penrose, 'Kanye West Previewed His New Album For, *Billboard*, April 19, 2018, https://www.billboard.com/articles/columns/hip-

hop/8350853/kanye-west-previewed-new-album-charlamagne-tha-god, last accessed: May 28, 2018; TMZ, *NEW ALBUM'S OUT But Only for Charlamagne*, April 19, 2018, http://www.tmz.com/2018/04/19/kanye-west-charlamagne-tha-god-new-album/, last accessed: May 25, 2018; Danielle Harling, 'Charlamagne Tha God Details Secret Kanye West Meeting', *Hiphopdx*, April 19, 2018, https://hiphopdx.com/news/id.46551/title.charlamagne-tha-god-details-secret-kanye-west-meeting#, last accessed: May 25, 2018.

- Michael Jackson;
- earns more than Michael Jordan, exposes fake news about Yeezy;
- I'm this generation Ford Hughes Jobs Disney;
- TMZ fake news;
- People magazine fake news;
- Charlamagne interview: 10 million offer for his album;
- Yeezy prices;
- partnership with Adidas;
- Presidency;
- Final tribe album should have won the grammys;
- turn the grammys into yammys;
- Rocky ASAP: album release;
- Mr. Trump: both dragon energy, he is my brother;
- Kids See Ghosts: short film shot by: Dexter Navy;
- Google;
- Wants to meet with Lary from Google;
- we got love: hat MAGA signed;
- Peter Thiel;
- picture Kanye president 2024;
- retweet of president Donal Trump reply to his MAGA tweet;
- Scooter Braun;
- Irving;
- David Joseph Frank Bridgman Oliver Nusse;
- Need Hypes William for Nas movie;
- wants to meet with Tom Cook;
- wants to see a tour with Nici Minaj and Cardi B;
- about what his fans are and should be;
- black people don't need to be democrats;
- Claudio Silverstein;
- Claudio, Chance and Kanye to build new homes in Chicago;
- Obama was in office 8 years and nothing changed in Chicago;
- Cook and Trump: favourite people;
- retweet president Donald Trump retweet of his tweet with signed MAGA;
- dialogue with John Legend;
- retweet with his philosophical statements in cartoon;
- Yeezy pictures behind the backstage;
- Lift Yourself song is released;
- John Legend;
- a conversation with a person named ‚Wes' about his album cover: Kanye West decided to put as cover a picture with plastic surgeon Jan Adams (he performed his mother last surgery); Kanye West asked ‚Wes' for an idea as a cover album, ‚Wes' replied: ‚LOVE EVERYONE', Kanye West replied back: ‚I love that';
- asked people to ‚contact a person with whom you haven't spoken in years, tell them that you love them';
- Ye vs the people song is released;
- Ms. Emma Gonzalez inspired Kanye West with her personality and thinking, he cut his hair as a way to identify himself with Emma Gonzalez (his hair was painted blonde);
- J Cole;
- retweet Ali post about him;
- project Ashley Morgan Hastings;
- retweet John Durant;
- statements about love;
- Disney and Apple designers;
- picture with sketch about new Yeezy products;
- youth and their role in the world;
- Candace Owens:
- Axel Vervoordt the globe;
- Adi Shankar;
- update: I said I was the greatest artist, but we all are great artists;

- open letter from Jan Adams (mother surgeon) to Kanye West and his desire that Kanye West to not use a picture with him as cover for his new musical album.

Due to lots of tweets and information, I wrote a list with the main topics of Kanye West's Twitter content from May 2018[82]:

- wegotlove.com website;
- The interview with Charlamagne is available on his Youtube channel: the key topics are about Mr. Donald Trump and Kanye West support because Mr. Trump proved anything is possible in the USA; his hospitalization; Jay Z; Beyoncé; Taylor Swift; he wants an apology from Barack Obama; Mrs. Kim Kardashian's robbery; Harriet Tubman and his face on the $20 bill, he wants Michael Jordan on the bill; *Yeezy* company, racism and slavery[83];
- he stopped by TMZ to share his thoughts on politics and freedom; there, he said the following controversial quote that shook the world to its core: 'When you hear about slavery for 400 years. For 400 years?! That sounds like a choice'[84];
- TMZ life with Harvey and Candance Owens;
- Retweet an article about the open letter from Jan Adams;

- Tmz article about him and his drugs; http://www.tmz.com/2018/05/01/kanye-west-opioids-liposuction/
- Magic Johnson;
- retweet a message about love with a biblical quotation;
- Learns about love;
- Tesla and Elon Musk;
- shared This is America music video;
- SNL video: Kanye world;
- google search with names;
- Ricki and Morti show;
- UN sustainable development goals in 2015 to transform the world in 2030
- short video with the new music, two tracks from his album;
- we need hugs, Amma Mata had given over 32 millions of hugs;
- Phone addiction and advice how to use it;
- Google dopamine;
- Video youtube: Basically Sigmund Frued's nephew Edward Bernays capitalized off of his uncle's philosophies and created modern day consumerism, the century of self: https://www.youtube.com/watch?v=eJ3RzGoQC4s;
- Daytona Pusha T cover work from Houston bathroom;
- download the app Wav Media to see live from his album release;
- In an interview with Kanye West[85] conducted during the June 1st listening party, Kanye West said he

---

[82] In May 2018 section all the information (except where there is a footnote) was collected from Kanye West's Twitter account.
[83] Kanye West, 'kanye west / charlamagne interview', *Youtube*, May 1, 2018, https://www.youtube.com/watch?v=zxwfDlhJIpw, last accessed: May 2, 2018; Luke Morgan Britton, 'A quest to understand Kanye West: The biggest revelations in Ye's Charlamagne interview', *NME*, May 1, 2018,

http://www.nme.com/blogs/nme-blogs/kanye-west-charlamagne-interview-biggest-revelations-2306236#a4pssa1bPShD2rg4.99, last accessed: May 2, 2018.
[84] Matt Bardon, 'Slavery Is A Choice' Kanye West FULL Interview on TMZ Live', *Youtube*, May 1, 2018, https://www.youtube.com/watch?v=IWJBWU7asEg, last accessed: May 28, 2018.
[85] In *June 2018* section, all the information (except where there is a footnote) was collected from Kanye West's Twitter

„redid the whole album after TMZ', alluding to an interview with TMZ on May 1st and suggesting that the entire album was re-recorded in a month;

- Kanye West explained the album title, which is a diminutive of his own name commonly used in his songs, by stating: „I believe Ye is the most commonly used word in the Bible, and in the Bible it means ,you'. So I'm you, I'm us, it's us. It went from Kanye, which means ,the only one', to just Ye – just being a reflection of our good, our bad, our confused, everything. The album is more of a reflection of who we are.'[86]

As *April 2018* and *May 2018* sections, and due to lots of tweets and information, I wrote a list with the main topics of Kanye West's Twitter content from June 2018:

- the album title: 'ye' not 'Love everyone';
- shop link to his website and the new merchandise;
- links with his album to Apple, Spotify, it was deleted, people reacted negatively;
- picture with the final tracks from 'ye' (it does not include the two tracks showed few days before the album release) and 'Kids See Ghosts';

- 'ye' cover generator[87];
- pictures with his success;
- picture with Kate Spade and her suicide, she was suffering from maniac depression;
- 'Kids See Ghosts' cover work of the album;
- retweets with success of his wife Mrs. Kim Kardashian West battle for the release from the prison of Mrs. Alice Marie Johnson (a first-time nonviolent drug offender who was given a life sentence without parole, plus 25 years); after months of work behind the scenes, the final step was for Mrs. West was a face to face meeting with president Donald Trump in the Oval Office the result being a clemency granted from the president and her release from the prison[88];
- Tyler, the Creator: retweet;
- Nas *Nasir* album;
- retweet of a tweet posted by Billboard and his musical success;
- shared stories about other cases of people who tried to commit suicide;
- thanked to all the people who supported his album for number 1, he says 'our album';
- tweet an article written by CNN: he was not abandoned by his fans, his songs are in top[89];

---

account. Due to a possible (future, past?) intervention of Kanye West, some information from this section could be deleted or changed.
[86] Trupti Rami, 'Kanye West on Being 'Diagnosed With a Mental Condition' and Redoing Ye After Crashing TMZ', *Vulture*, June 3, 2018, https://www.vulture.com/2018/06/kanye-west-on-ye-being-diagnosed-with-a-mental-condition.html, last accessed: June 4, 2018.
[87] Ye Cover generator, https://yenerator.com/, last accessed: June 25, 2018.

[88] Jake Horowit, Kendall Ciesemier, 'President Donald Trump grants clemency to Alice Johnson after Kim Kardashian West involvement', *Mic*, June 6, 2018, https://mic.com/articles/189663/exclusive-president-trump-grants-clemency-to-alice-johnson-after-kim-kardashian-west-involvement#.8s6qxOIuT, last accessed: June 25, 2018.
[89] Lisa Respers France , 'Kanye West's entire album hits the Top 40', *CNN*, June 12, 2018, https://edition.cnn.com/2018/06/12/entertainment/kanye-west-album-charts/index.html, last accessed: June 25, 2018.

- Deadpool soundtrack, tracks that sound like his music; I would have cleared my music for Deadpool;
- Wegotlove.com website and three videos about album release party, his interview with Charlamagne and a conversation about evolution and the song Ye vs. the people[90];
- pictures with his new shoes and clothes;
- tweeted Nas album *Nasir* tracklist, then link to his album;
- retweet of a person who suffers from bipolarity and how his music inspired people;
- Mrs. Kim Kardashian West meeting with president Donald Trump and the release of Alice;
- he killed his ego, is only 'Ye';
- tweets about Ms. Teyana Taylor album release party and link to listen the album.

---

[90] Kanye West, https://wegotlove.com/, last accessed: June 25, 2018.

III. How much Taylor Swift knew about the **FAMOUS** song?

This chapter was written for Kim Kardashian to support her interest in becoming a lawyer. The work in courts requires attention to details and this chapter is all about that. The content of this chapter is a way to check in percentage (details) to see how much Taylor Swift knew about the *Famous* song (still, this is no evidence for a genuine argument that Taylor played a part because *she really wanted* or because she was involved in a phone conversation and *wanted to be nice* and *supportive* with Kanye West). The information presented below is also for lovers of details, numbers and percentages. This chapter is not an analysis to confirm Taylor's genuine intention in the creation of the song and her refusal to accept the final version because she wanted to put Kanye West in a bad light. In this chapter I explored the dynamics of the feud through numbers and statements. For Kim Kardashian this chapter is another source of how to work with information to prove the veracity of a statement.

Now we know that Taylor Swift was aware of a song produced by Kanye West and knew parts of the lyrics, but not the line 'I made that bitch famous'.

In this chapter I investigated, for accuracy of information, the following affirmations to find out how much Taylor Swift 'played any part' in the *Famous* song in percentage before the release to the general public:

a) Kanye West wrote on Twitter: '3rd thing I called Taylor and had a hour long convo with her about the line and she thought it was funny and gave her blessings';
b) Kim Kardashian in the interview with GQ magazine from 16 June 2016 and during her show *Keeping Up With The Kardashians* (season 12, episode 11): 'She totally approved that. […] 'She totally knew that that was coming out;'
c) the affirmation made by Taylor Swift in July 2016: 'Being falsely painted as a liar when I was never given the full story *or played any part of the song* (underline by author) is character assassination';
d) the general knowledge of the *Famous* song in percentage.

a. Kanye West wrote on Twitter: ***'3rd thing I called Taylor and had a hour long convo with her about the line and she thought it was funny and gave her blessings'***: this information is partial true: the leak of the conversation is around 25 minutes (maybe there is more); *the conversation was funny and gave her blessing for the lyrics that she was aware*, but not for the new line, 'I made that bitch famous', added by Kanye West for which Taylor was not aware, but presented as being aware from the beginning; Taylor Swift knew 50% of the title of the song: Kanye West told Taylor Swift the first title of the song: *Hood Famous*, however, the final title was *Famous*, which is half of the first title and converts into 50%;

b. Kim Kardashian in the interview with GQ magazine from June 16, 2016 and during her show *Keeping Up with The Kardashians* (season 12, episode 11): **'She totally approved that. [...] 'She totally knew that was coming out'**: this information is biased and misleading as there is evidence that Taylor Swift was not aware of the full version of the song, lyrics and instrumentals and, therefore, she did not know what was all and exactly coming out; Taylor Swift did not approve *totally* of what Kanye West released to the general public and supported by Kim Kardashian's affirmation during her interview and TV show: Taylor Swift thanked Kanye West for letting her know about his intention, parts of the lyrics, and *she will think about it* which it is not approval;

c. the affirmation made by Taylor Swift in July 2016: *'Being falsely painted as a liar when I was never given the full story or played any part of the song (underline by author) is character assassination'*: this information is mostly true and based on the new recordings of the conversation leaked on Youtube in March 2020; **Taylor Swift was never given the full story of the song, *but did played a part of the song***: she knew some lyrics and even suggested a change of the lyrics, but still there is no evidence for a genuine argument that Taylor played a part because she *really wanted* or because she was involved in a phone conversation and *wanted to be nice* and *supportive* with Kanye West; based on Taylor Swift's statement she wasn't aware that Kanye West is going to use the telephone conversation as implicit agreement of her polite advice and suggestion; the last part: **'character assassination'** is true: Kanye West and Kim Kardashian presented to the general public biased, misleading and partial information about Taylor's involvement in the song that suited their agenda of blaming Taylor Swift for the song's evolution and the reaction of the general public; the character assassination is true as today because Kim and Kanye refuse to take responsibility and to acknowledge that they did not presented the information from the telephone conversation as it happened, while blaming Taylor Swift for being the perpetrator, and she is to blame for everything that happened after the release of the song;

ON THE **FAMOUS** FEUD

d. general knowledge of the Famous song in percentage: I decided to explore the truth in numbers and percentage as a method to show, as accurate as possible, Taylor Swift's knowledge of the *Famous* song.

As research method, I divided the *Famous* song in independent elements according with the Credits of the *Famous* song found on Kanye West and Genius's website[91]: production, co-production, additional production, engineering, recording vocals, mix, songwriters, name of the song, lyrics, publishing rights, sample, the complete *Famous* song[92].

For each author/participant in the song I gave 1 point. In the end, the points for each participant/author were added and the total number was divided between the numbers of the authors/participants in the creation of the song; the results of this maths were converted into percentage, then the percentage for Kanye West (because Taylor Swift spoke only with Kanye West, where is the case and according with each independent elements of the song) was considered for how much Taylor Swift knew.

III.1 Production

TABLE 7. PRODUCTION

Author/Participant	Kanye West	Havoc
Points	1	1
Taylor Swift Knows	1	0
Taylor Swift Knows in Percentage	50%	

---

[91] Kanye West, 'Famous Credits', *The Life of Pablo*, https://www.kanyewest.com/credits/, last accessed: September 24, 2017; Kanye West, 'The Life of Pablo [Credits]', *Genius*, https://genius.com/Kanye-west-the-life-of-pablo-credits-annotated, last accessed: October 23, 2017.
[92] This element was proposed by myself in this report and it is not found on Credits.

FIGURE 10. THE PRODUCTION OF THE **FAMOUS** SONG

■ Kanye West   ■ Havoc

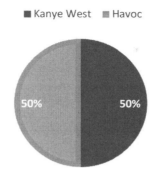

50%   50%

III.2 Co-Production

TABLE 8. CO-PRODUCTION

Author/Participant	Noah Goldstein for ARK Productions, INC	Charlie Heat for Very GOOD Beats, INC	Andrew Dawson
Points	1	1	1
Taylor Swift Knows	0	0	0
Taylor Swift Knows in Percentage	0%		

III.3 Additional Production

TABLE 9. ADDITIONAL PRODUCTION

Participant	Husdon Mohawke	Mike Dean #MWA for Dean's List Productions	Plain Pat
Points	1	1	1
Taylor Swift Knows	0	0	0
Taylor Swift Knows in Percentage	0%		

III.4 Engineering

TABLE 10. ENGINEERING

Author/Participant	Noah Goldstein	Andrew Dawson	Anthony Kilhoffer	Mike Dean
Points	1	1	1	1
Taylor Swift Knows	0	0	0	0
Taylor Swift Knows in Percentage	0%			

III.5 Rihanna Vocals Recording

TABLE 11. RIHANNA VOCALS RECORDING

Author/Participant	Marcos Tovar
Points	1
Taylor Swift Knows	0
Taylor Swift Knows in Percentage	0%

III.6 Rihanna Vocals Assistance

TABLE 12. RIHANNA VOCALS ASSISTANCE

Author/Participant	Jose Balaguer
Points	1
Taylor Swift Knows	0
Taylor Swift Knows in Percentage	0%

III.7 Rihanna Vocal Production

TABLE 13. RIHANNA VOCAL PRODUCTION

Author/Participant	Kuk Harrel
Points	1
Taylor Swift Knows	0
Taylor Swift Knows in Percentage	0%

III.8 Swizz Vocals Recording

TABLE 14. SWIZZ VOCALS RECORDING

Author/Participant	Zeke Mishanec
Points	1
Taylor Swift Knows	0
Taylor Swift Knows in Percentage	0%

III.9 Mix

TABLE 15. MIX

Author/Participant	Manny Marroquin
Points	1
Taylor Swift Knows	0
Taylor Swift Knows in Percentage	0%

III.10 Mix Assisted

TABLE 16. MIX ASSISTED

Author/Participant	Chris Galland	Ike Schultz	Jeff Jackson
Points	1	1	1
Taylor Swift Knows	0	0	0
Taylor Swift Knows in Percentage		0%	

III.11 Vocals

TABLE 17. VOCALS

Author/Participant	Kanye West	Rihanna	Swizz
Points	1	1	1
Taylor Swift Knows	1	0	0
Taylor Swift Knows in Percentage		34%	

FIGURE 11. THE VOCALS OF
THE **FAMOUS** SONG

■ Kanye West   ■ Rihanna   ■ Swizz

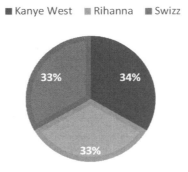

III.12 Lyricists

TABLE 18. THE **FAMOUS** LYRICISTS AS CREDITS FROM WIKIPEDIA[93]

AUTHOR/PARTICIPANT	POINTS	TAYLOR SWIFT KNOWS	TAYLOR SWIFT KNOWS IN PERCENTAGE
Kanye West	1	1	
Cydel Young	1	0	
Kejuan Muchita	1	0	
Noah Goldstein	1	0	
Andrew Dawson	1	0	
Mike Dean	1	0	
Chancelor Bennett	1	0	
Kasseem Dean	1	0	6%
Ernest Brown	1	0	
Ross Birchard	1	0	
Pat Reynolds	1	0	
Jimmy Webb	1	0	
Winston Riley	1	0	
Luis Enriquez Bacalov	1	0	
Enzo Vita	1	0	
Sergio Bardotti	1	0	

[93] This list was made based on Credit page of the *Famous* song from Wikipedia, 'Famous (Kanye West song)', https://en.wikipedia.org/wiki/Famous_(Kanye_West_song), last accessed: October 23, 2017; Kanye West website: *The Life of Pablo, Credits*, https://www.kanyewest.com/credits/, last accessed: October 23, 2017; Tidal, *The Life of Pablo, Credits*, https://listen.tidal.com/album/57273408, last accessed: October 23, 2017.

Giampiero Scalamogna	1	0

FIGURE 12. THE LYRICISTS OF THE **FAMOUS** SONG

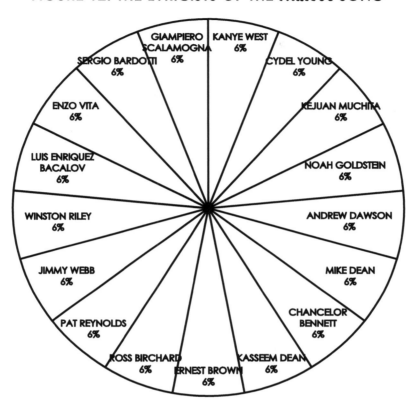

III.13 Name of the Song

TABLE 19. NAME OF THE SONG (HOOD **FAMOUS**)

Author/Participant	Kanye West
Points	1
Taylor Swift Knows	0.5
Taylor Swift Knows in Percentage	50%

III.14 The Lyrics of the **FAMOUS** Song[94]

For this section I used the following mathematical formulas:

Subtraction (any combination of the following information):

- total lyrics without the chorus and outro (Rihanna and Swizz)
- total lyrics without the chorus (Rihanna and Swizz)
- total lyrics as the song is played
- lyrics known by Taylor Swift
- "bam"
- "dilla"
- "ey"
- "I just wanted you to know".

Percentage conversion: the results were converted in percentage; it was used for all the independent elements of the song.

Average: the percentage result from each independent element of the song was calculated using the average method understood as: dividing the total numbers of lyrics (taken as 6 types of lyrics described in *Subtraction*) by the total number of independent elements of the lyrics (6 for total, but was also used as 1 or 2 depending on the purpose of each section of the calculation for lyrics known by Taylor Swift) or the song (18 independent elements available in the last section of this chapter). The results from the *Famous Song* and *Lyrics* section were used to find out how much in percentage Taylor Swift knew from the full version of the song *Famous*.

TABLE 20. THE LYRICS OF THE **FAMOUS** SONG

Total lyrics as the song is played	471
Lyrics known by Taylor Swift	19
Bam (repeats many times)	72
'I wanted you to know'	6 (as full line numbers of words for each line) and 36 words
Intro	39
Outro	35
Chrous 1	42

---

[94] This section is based on the lyrics of the *Famous* song as published and the format used by Genius website.

Chorus 2	8
'Ey'	56
'Dilla'	8
Lyrics known by Kanye West	471 (100%)

III.14.1 The **FAMOUS** Lyrics as the Song is Played

TABLE 21. THE **FAMOUS** LYRICS AS THE SONG IS PLAYED

Lyrics as the song is played	471
Taylor Swift	19
Taylor Swift Knows in Percentage	4%

FIGURE 13. THE **FAMOUS** LYRICS AS THE SONG IS PLAYED

■ Taylor Swift   ▨ Lyrics as Played in the Full Song

III.14.2 The **FAMOUS** Lyrics Without 'Bam'

TABLE 22. THE **FAMOUS** LYRICS WITHOUT 'BAM'

Lyrics as the song is played	471
Taylor Swift	19
Bam	72
Taylor Swift Knows in Percentage	5%

FIGURE 14. THE **FAMOUS** LYRICS WITHOUT USING THE WORD 'BAM'

■ Taylor Swift   ■ Lyrics Without Using the Word Bam

III.14.3 The **FAMOUS** Lyrics Without 'Ey'

TABLE 23. THE **FAMOUS** LYRICS WITHOUT 'EY'

Lyrics as the song is played	471
Taylor Swift	19
Ey	56
Taylor Swift Knows in Percentage	5%

FIGURE 15. THE **FAMOUS** LYRICS WITHOUT 'EY'

■ Lyrircs without 'ey'   ■ Taylor Swift

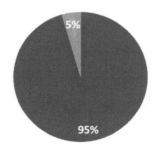

III.14.4 The **FAMOUS** Lyrics Without the Line 'I Just Wanted You To Know'

TABLE 24. THE **FAMOUS** LYRICS WITHOUT 'I JUST WANTED YOU TO KNOW'

Lyrics without 'I just wanted you to know'	420
I just Wanted you to know	36
Taylor Swift	19
Taylor Swift Knows in Percentage	4%

FIGURE 16. THE **FAMOUS** LYRICS WITHOUT 'I JUST WANTED YOU TO KNOW'

■ Taylor Swift ■ Lyrics Without the Line 'I just wanted you to know'

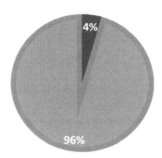

III.14.5 The **FAMOUS** Lyrics Without 'Dilla'

TABLE 25. THE **FAMOUS** LYRICS WITHOUT 'DILLA'

Lyrics as the song is played	471
Lyrics Without 'dilla'	8
Taylor Swift	19
Taylor Swift Knows in Percentage	4%

FIGURE 17. THE **FAMOUS** LYRICS WITHOUT 'DILLA'

■ Taylor Swift   ■ Lyrics Without 'Dilla'

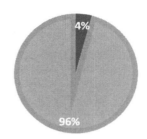

III.14.6 The **FAMOUS** Lyrics Without 'Bam', 'Ey' 'Dilla', 'I Just Wanted You To Know'

TABLE 26. THE **FAMOUS** LYRICS WITHOUT 'BAM', 'DILLA', 'I JUST WANTED YOU TO KNOW'

Lyrics as the song is played	471
Bam	72
Ey	56
I just wanted you to know	36
Dilla	8
Taylor Swift	19
Taylor Swift Knows in Percentage	6%

FIGURE 18. THE **FAMOUS** LYRICS WITHOUT
'BAM', 'EY', 'DILLA' AND 'I JUST WANTED
YOU TO KNOW'

■ Taylor Swift

■ Lyrics Without 'Bam', 'Ey', 'Dilla' and 'I just wanted you to know'

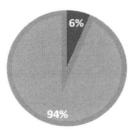

III.14.7 The **FAMOUS** Lyrics Without Intro and Outro

TABLE 27. THE **FAMOUS** LYRICS WITHOUT 'INTRO' AND 'OUTRO'

Lyrics as the song is played	471
Intro	39
Outro	35
Taylor Swift	19
Taylor Swift Knows in Percentage	5%

FIGURE 19. THE **FAMOUS** LYRICS
WITHOUT 'INTRO' AND 'OUTRO'

■ Lyrics without 'Intro' and 'Outro'   ■ Taylor Swift

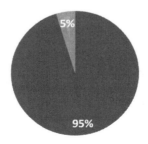

III.14.8 The **FAMOUS** Lyrics Without Chorus (Rihanna & Swizz 1&2)

TABLE 28. THE **FAMOUS** LYRICS WITHOUT CHORUS (RIHANNA & SWIZZ 1&2)

Lyrics as the song is played	471
Chorus 1	42
Chorus 2	8
Taylor Swift	19
Taylor Swift Knows in Percentage	5%

FIGURE 20. THE **FAMOUS** LYRICS WITHOUT CHORUS (RIHANNA & SWIZZ 1&2)

■ Lyrics without 'Intro' and 'Outro'   ■ Taylor Swift

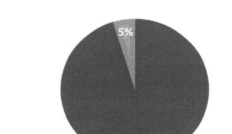

III.14.9 The **FAMOUS** Lyrics Without Repeating Same Words

The repeated words taken into account are: to, be, the, they, try, you, free, in, see, just, air, her, we, I, just, wanted, know, made, that, bitch, famous, this, for, that, us, best, goddam, Kanye, West, all, but, hood, don't, blame, much, wanting, free, up!, whoo!, never, gonna, die, bam, dilla, ey, let, me, motherfucker, how, feelin, can't, do, is, man, too, late, it's, way.[95] I decided to keep Taylor Swift numbers of known lyrics because Kanye West shared them with her during the telephone conversation.

---

[95] It is possible to omit words, which is unintended.

TABLE 29. THE **FAMOUS** LYRICS WITHOUT REPEATING SAME WORDS

Lyrics without repeating same words	210
Taylor Swift	19
Taylor Swift Knows in Percentage	9%

FIGURE 21. THE **FAMOUS** LYRICS WITHOUT REPEATING SAME WORDS

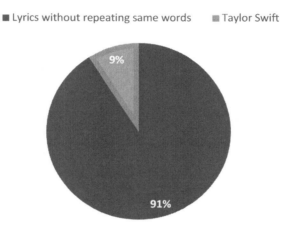

TABLE 30. THE MATHS OF THE **FAMOUS** LYRICS

Independent methods of calculations of the lyrics	Taylor Swift knew about each independent element of the lyrics in percentage
Lyrics as the song is played	4%
Lyrics without 'Bam'	5%
Lyrics without 'ey'	5%
Lyrics without the line 'I just wanted you to know'	4%
Lyrics without 'dilla'	4%
Lyrics without 'Bam', 'Ey', 'Dilla', 'I just wanted you to know'	6%
Lyrics without 'Intro' and 'Outro'	5%
Lyrics without chorus (Rihanna & Swizz 1&2)	5%
Lyrics without repeating same words	9%

The Average Method:

In total, there are 9 independent methods of calculations of the lyrics and I have the following maths calculation:

first: I added the percentage of each independent methods of calculations of the lyrics:

4% + 5% + 5% + 4% + 4% + 6% + 5% + 5% + 9% = 47%

second: I divided with the total number of independent methods of calculations of the lyrics (9):
47% / 9 = 5,22(22)%.

Conclusion:

Overall, based on the mathematical formulas used above, Taylor Swift knew an average of 5.22(22)% lyrics of the *Famous* song.

III.15 Publishing Rights

TABLE 31. PUBLISHING RIGHTS

Author/Participant	Publishing Rights
Points	1
Taylor Swift Knows	0%
Taylor Swift Knows in Percentage	0%

III.16 Sample 1

TABLE 32. SAMPLE 1

Author/Participant	Sample 1: 'Do what you gotta do', Performed by Nina Simon
Points	1
Taylor Swift Knows	0
Taylor Swift Knows in Percentage	0%

III.17 Sample 2

TABLE 33. SAMPLE 2

Author/Participant	Sample 2: 'Bam Bam' Performed by Sister Nancy
Points	1
Taylor Swift Knows	0
Taylor Swift Knows in Percentage	0%

III.18 Sample 3

TABLE 34. SAMPLE 3

Author/Participant	Sample 3: 'Mi Sono Svegliato E.. Ho Chiuso Gli Occhi' Performed by Il Rovescio Della Medgalia
Points	1
Taylor Swift Knows	0
Taylor Swift Knows in Percentage	0%

III.19 The '**FAMOUS**' Song

TABLE 35. HOW MUCH TAYLOR SWFIT KNEW ABOUT THE **FAMOUS** SONG?

Independent elements of the *Famous* song	Taylor Swift knew about each independent element of the *Famous* song in percentage
Production	50%
Co-Production	0%
Additional Production	0%
Engineering	0%
Vocals	34%
Songwriters	6%
Name Of The Song	50%
Rihanna Vocals Recording	0%
Rihanna Vocal Assistance	0%
Rihanna Vocal Production	0%
Swizz Vocals Recording	0%
Mix	0%

	Mix Assisted	0%
	Publishing Rights	0%
	Sample 1	0%
	Sample 2	0%
	Sample 3	0%
Lyrics	1. Lyrics as the song is played	4%
	2. Lyrics without repeating same words	9%

I selected these methods for calculating the lyrics because option *1* has the lowest percentage and *2* has the highest percentage. Below I used two different methods of calculation to see, as accurately as possible, if there are any differences and similarities that can provide a different picture of Taylor Swift's level of knowledge about the *Famous* song.

The Average Method:

In total, there are 18 independent elements of the song and I have the following maths calculation:

- If I use **1.** *Lyrics as the song is played (4%) and Taylor Swift knew the name of the song (50%):*

first. I added each independent element of the song:

50% + 0% + 0% + 0% + 34% + 6% + 50% + 0% + 0% + 0% + 0% + 0% + 0% + 0% + 0% + 0% + 0% + 4% = 144%

second: I divided 194% with the total number of independent elements of the song (18):
144% / 18 =8%.

- If I use **2.** *Lyrics without repeating same words (9%) and Taylor Swift knew the name of the song (50%):*

first. I added each independent element of the song:

50% + 0% + 0% + 0% + 34% + 6% + 50% + 0% + 0% + 0% + 0% + 0% +
0% + 0% + 0% + 0% + 0% + 9% = 149%

second: I divided 149% with the total number of independent elements of
the song (18):
149% / 18 = 8.27%.

CONCLUSIONS:

- due to multiple calculation Taylor Swift knew between 8% to 8.27% about the *Famous* song;
- however, despite this evidence, Taylor Swift said to Kanye West that she will think about it; Taylor Swift did not receive the final song and she found out the final version of the song at the same time with the world; Kanye West did not give Taylor the chance to hear the final version of the song and, therefore, to receive her final approval.

IV. The impact of the **FAMOUS** feud

In this chapter I created a comparative analysis of

1. the impact of the *Famous* feud on music album sales: the first week in the USA between Taylor Swift and Kanye West;
2. the global sales of the songs that are the cause of the feud: *Famous* for Kanye West, *Look What You Made Me Do* for Taylor Swift and *Swish, Swish* for Katy Perry;
3. the impact of the *Bad Blood – Swish, Swish* feud on global album sales between Taylor Swift and Katy Perry;
4. the number of producers and songwriters of the songs involved in the *Famous* feud: *Famous* for Kanye West, *Look What You Made Me Do* for Taylor Swift;
5. the sources of inspiration and originality of the albums released after the MTV VMA event in 2009: Taylor Swift's album: *Speak Now, 2010*, and Kanye West's album: *My Beautiful Dark Twisted Fantasy, 2010*;
6. the rating available on Metacritic;
7. the connection between the *Famous* feud and the *Bad Blood – Swish, Swish* feud, Taylor Swift versus Katy Perry.

IV.1 Kanye West versus Taylor Swift

IV.1.1 First Week Sales in the USA (Solo Album)

TABLE 36. TAYLOR SWIFT AND KANYE WEST FIRST WEEK SALES IN THE USA (SOLO ALBUM)

YEAR / ARTIST	TAYLOR SWIFT	KANYE WEST

2004	-	441.000[96]
2005	-	860.000[97]
2006	40.000[98]	-
2007	-	957.000[99]
2008	592.000[100]	450.455[101]
2010	1.047.000[102]	496.000[103]
2012	1.208.000[104]	-
2013	-	327.000[105]
2014	1.287.000[106]	-
2016	-	28.000[107]
2017	1.216.000[108]	-
2018	-	85.000[109]

[96] Hao Nguyen, 'Can't Tell Me Nothing: Ranking Kanye West First Week Album Sales', *Stop The Breaks*, December 15, 2013, https://www.stopthebreaks.com/first-week-album-sales/kanye-west-first-week-album-sales/, last accessed: October 23, 2017.
[97] Ibidem,
[98] Billboard, *'Hannah Montana' Trumps My Chem, Legend At No. 1*, November 1, 2006, https://www.billboard.com/articles/news/56784/hannah-montana-trumps-my-chem-legend-at-no-1, last accessed: October 23, 2017.
[99] Hao Nguyen, idem.
[100] Jonathan Cohen, 'Taylor Swift Soars To No. 1 Debut', *Billboard*, November 19, 2008, https://www.billboard.com/articles/news/1043458/taylor-swift-soars-to-no-1-debut, last accessed: October 23, 2017.
[101] Hao Nguyen, idem.
[102] Ed Christmas, 'What Taylor Swift's Million-Selling Album Means for Music', *Billboard*, November 5, 2010, https://www.billboard.com/articles/news/951633/what-taylor-swifts-million-selling-album-means-for-music, last accessed: October 23, 2017.
[103] Hao Nguyen, idem.
[104] Keith Caulfield, 'Taylor Swift's 'Red' Sells 1.21 Million; Biggest Sales Week for an Album Since 2002', *Billboard*, October 30, 2012, https://www.billboard.com/articles/news/474400/taylor-swifts-red-sells-121-million-biggest-sales-week-for-an-album-since-2002, last accessed: October 23, 2017.
[105] Hao Nguyen, idem.
[106] Keith Caulfield, 'Official: Taylor Swift's '1989' Debuts With 1.287 Million Sold In First Week', *Billboard*, November 4, 2014, https://www.billboard.com/articles/columns/chart-beat/6304536/official-taylor-swifts-1989-debuts-with-1287-million-sold-in, last accessed: October 23, 2017.
[107] Keith Caulfield, 'Kanye West's 'The Life of Pablo' Debuts at No. 1 on Billboard 200 Chart', *Billboard*, April 10, 2016, https://www.billboard.com/articles/columns/chart-beat/7326493/kanye-wests-the-life-of-pablo-debuts-at-no-1-on-billboard-200, last accessed: October 23, 2017.
[108] Keith Caulfield, 'Taylor Swift's 'Reputation' Debuts at No. 1 on Billboard 200 Albums Chart', *Billboard*, November 20, 2017, https://www.billboard.com/articles/columns/chart-beat/8039679/taylor-swift-reputation-debuts-no-1-billboard-200-albums, last accessed: August 25, 2019.
[109] Keith Caulfield, 'Kanye West Earns Eighth No. 1 Album on Billboard 200 Chart With 'Ye'', *Billboard*, June 10, 2018, https://www.billboard.com/articles/columns/chart-beat/8460189/kanye-west-eighth-no-1-album-billboard-200-ye, last accessed: October 23, 2018.

2019	679.000[110] 715.000[111]	109,000[112]
2020	615.000[113] 627.000[114]	-

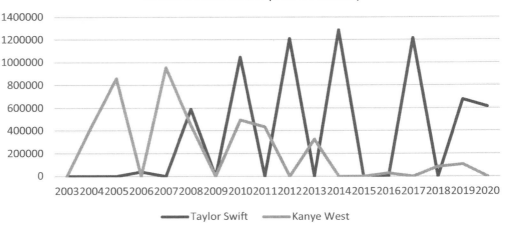

FIGURE 22. TAYLOR SWIFT AND KANYE WEST FIRST WEEK PURE SALES IN THE U.S.A. (SOLO ALBUM)

CONCLUSIONS:

- by 2009, for Taylor Swift there was a strong increase in popularity and it is shown by the increase of the sales of her musical albums; overall, Taylor Swift was a global phenomenon before she met Kanye West which is also confirmed in the telephone conversation with Kanye West, Taylor Swift said 'I sold 7 million of that album before you did that which is what happened';
- after September 2009 Taylor Swift's presence continued to increase achieving world records until 2014 (album *1989*), then to decrease in 2017 (album *reputation*) with

[110] Keith Caulfield, 'Official: Taylor Swift's 'Lover' Debuts at No. 1 on Billboard 200 Chart With 867,000 Units Earned in First Week in U.S.', *Billboard*, September 1, 2019, https://www.billboard.com/articles/business/chart-beat/8528870/taylor-swift-lover-album-debuts-at-no-1-on-billboard-200-chart, last accessed: September 1, 2019.

[111] RS Charts, RS Charts: Taylor Swift's 'Lover' Takes Number One By a Landslide, *Rolling Stone*, September 4, 2019, https://www.rollingstone.com/music/music-news/charts-taylor-swift-lover-albums-879502/, last accessed: November 6, 2019.

[112] Keith Caulfield, 'Kanye West's 'Jesus Is King' Arrives as His Record-Tying Ninth Consecutive No. 1 Debut on Billboard 200 Chart', *Billboard*, November 3, 2019, https://www.billboard.com/articles/business/chart-beat/8542364/kanye-west-jesus-is-king-billboard-200-debut-no-1, last accessed: November 6, 2019.

[113] Kevin Rutherford, 'Taylor Swift's 'Folklore' Debuts at No. 1 on Alternative Albums, 'Cardigan' Starts Atop Hot Rock & Alternative Songs', *Billboard*, https://www.billboard.com/articles/business/chart-beat/9428748/taylor-swift-folklore-alternative-albums-cardigan-hot-rock-alternative-songs, last accessed: August 7, 2020.

[114] RS Charts, *Taylor Swift's 'Folklore' Sees the Biggest Debut of 2020, and It Isn't Even Close*, August 2, 2020, available at: https://www.rollingstone.com/music/music-news/taylor-swift-folklore-debut-charts-1037919/, last accessed: August 7, 2020.

around 6% (by using *Billboard* numbers) and more decrease in 2019 when the sales in the first week were around 44% (by using Billboard numbers) less than the last album (*reputation*, 2017); with Rolling Stone Charts the decrease of the album sales from 2017 to 2019 is around 41%; from the point of view of album-equivalent sales in the first week (Billboard reported 867.000[115] while Rolling Stone Charts 998.100[116]) the decrease is lower: around 18% from Rolling Stone and around 29% from Billboard; overall, it took 10 years for Taylor Swift to know a high decrease of lower sales in the first week;

- Kanye West's popularity and album sales decreased around 53% a year before he met Taylor Swift at MTV Awards in September 2009: in 2007 he sold 957.000 copies in the first week, while in 2008 he sold 450.455 copies in the first week; this decrease is still valid as today, the lowest one being the album *The Life of Pablo* with 28.000 copies;

- Kanye West lost half of his popularity in first week pure sales in 1 year (from 2007 to 2008 and after three successful albums and high increase) and remained low (in comparison with the first three albums) as today, while Taylor Swift lost 44% (from Billboard) and 41% (from Rolling Stone Charts) in two years (*reputation* in 2017 and *Lover* in 2019); from the point of view of a combination of pure sales and album-equivalent sales, Taylor Swift lost 27.5%[117] of her popularity in first week sales in 5 years (from album *1989*- the highest number of sales in the first week- to album *Lover* in 2019);

- Kanye West has the highest decrease in selling albums in the first week, however, he also had an increase of sales in the last 2 years: in 2016 he sold 28.000 copies, in 2018 sold 85.000 copies and in 2019 sold 109.000 copies; it is possible that behind this increase of fans to be the effect of an 'consumed feud' by the general public and a return of the lost fans (forgiveness?), perhaps even new fans (Christians? because of the album *Jesus is King*?);

- it is hard to say that the decrease of Taylor Swift's *Lover* album could be related only to loss of fans (around 41% - 44% and only in the first week) as the album was her first to be available on digital platforms such as Spotify and Youtube in the same time where fans and users can listen her music for free, therefore selling less albums;

---

[115] Keith Caulfield, *Official: Taylor Swift's 'Lover' Debuts at No. 1 on Billboard 200 Chart With 867,000 Units Earned in First Week in U.S.*
[116] RS Charts, *RS Charts: Taylor Swift's 'Lover' Takes Number One By a Landslide.*
[117] The average result is based on the Billboard and Rolling Stone Chart for the first week sales: Billboard: 6% + 44% and 29% + Rolling Stone: 41% + 18% = 132 divided by 5 charts results (three from Billboard and two from Rolling Stone) = 27.5% average decrease. If we calculate: 6% + 44% + 41+ = 91 divided by 3 = 30.33(3)% decrease from the point of view of pure sales. If we calculate 6% + 18% + 29% = 53 divided by 3 = 17.66(6)% decrease from the point of view of pure sales (album 1989) and album-equivalent sales (*reputation* and *Lover*).

- due to different methods of calculation of the final charts, it is highly possible, that despite the decrease of pure album sales in the first week, Taylor Swift to still have one million fans and this is based on pure sales and streaming (paid and free) as released by Billboard (867.000) and Rolling Stone numbers (991.800);
- on long term, Kanye West successfully managed to maintain a good number of fans on various digital platforms which helped his albums to remain popular in charts (with other even to achieve and stay in top 10, in the US Top Gospel Albums Jesus in King (2019) became number 1), however, Taylor Swift has a definitely a higher number of fans and it is more popular in charts than Kanye West;
- in 2017 (*reputation*, an album considered by the wider audience to be a response to Kanye West song *Famous* and his musical album *The Life of Pablo*) Taylor Swift sold in the first week a little bit over 43 more pure albums (1.216.000) than Kanye West' album, *The Life of Pablo* (28.000);
- the decrease in the album sales is not something that happens only to Kanye West and Taylor Swift, but with other artists as well, such as Beyoncé, Rihanna, Lady Gaga, Rihanna, Katy Perry and many others; however, Kanye West's decrease is the lowest amongst all the artists written above; based on the above evidence, Kanye West's decrease (and other artists) followed a natural pattern: most artists (95-99%) have a high increase in popularity, fame and albums sales in the first two-three-four (rarely) albums of their career, then a decrease as they are in competition with other new artists with new songs, other strategies of promotion and themes of the music, but also because people lose interest (one reason can be linked to the public behaviour of the artist, and the perception of the general public of the consequences of that behaviour) for the same artist; in the case of Taylor Swift, it seems that she makes a different sort of music and promotion that keep fans closed and albums sales higher than many other artists (99%?);
- during September 2009 (the start of the feud) Taylor Swift was on the natural path of increasing as global pop artist, while Kanye West was decreasing as global rap artist, therefore it is wrong to say that Taylor Swift became famous because Kanye West rudely interrupted her speech for an award that people voted in favour of Taylor Swift, not Beyoncé;
- despite Kanye West's strategy of promotion of the *Famous* song, *The Life of Pablo* musical album, Saint Pablo Tour and Taylor Swift intentional implication by Kanye West in his song, Taylor Swift kept her position in top of the music industry, while Kanye West highly decreased with a slow increase, but still below Taylor Swift;
- based on the above evidence (first week pure album sales) there is a higher negative impact on the long term for Kanye West than for Taylor Swift.

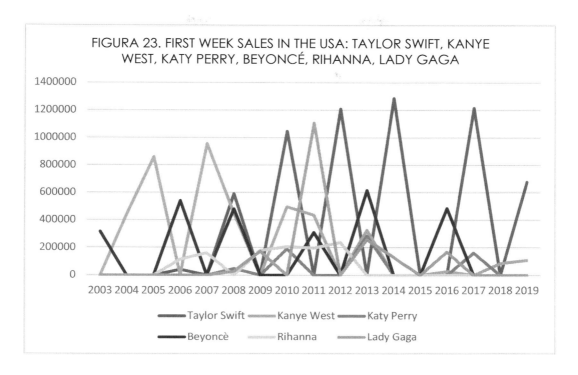

FIGURA 23. FIRST WEEK SALES IN THE USA: TAYLOR SWIFT, KANYE WEST, KATY PERRY, BEYONCÉ, RIHANNA, LADY GAGA

IV.1.2 Worldwide Sales of Songs from **Famous** Feud

TABLE 37. WORLDWIDE SALES OF SONGS FROM **FAMOUS** FEUD

TAYLOR SWIFT	KANYE WEST
Look What You Made Me Do (August 2017): 6.026.666.[118]	*Famous (February 2016):* 2.585.000.[119]

CONCLUSIONS:

- Taylor Swift's song sold with 64% more copies than Kanye West in a time where her reputation was the one of a 'bitch' (from the lyrics of *Famous* song, the fans singing with Kanye West on his concerts 'I made that bitch famous', on Facebook and Twitter there was a visible number of posts with the caption 'rePUTAtion' highlighting the word 'puta' which translated from Spanish into English means 'bitch'), 'snake' and

[118] The numbers are based on certification of sales from various countries, see Taylor Swift, *Look What You Made Me Do*, https://en.wikipedia.org/wiki/Look_What_You_Made_Me_Do#Commercial_performance, last accessed: February 21, 2020.
[119] The numbers are based on certification of sales from various countries, see Kanye West, *Famous*, https://en.wikipedia.org/wiki/Famous_(Kanye_West_song)#Certifications, last accessed: February 21, 2020.

'liar' highly promoted on social media (Twitter, Facebook, Instagram and so forth); the reputation of a 'liar' was spread even in mass-media through various articles though there was not enough evidence to accuse her of genuine wrongdoing and intentional manipulation of the feud in her favour; apparently, at least one million fans disagreed with the negative narrative of Kanye West and the Western mass-media, and decided to trust Taylor's story by buying and listening to her albums;

- the high sales show a high interest of the fans for petty songs, the love for drama between artists, which artist is more famous after a scandal and which artist has a strong and genuine fanbase.

IV.1.3 Producers or Songs from **Famous** Feud

TABLE 38. PRODUCERS OF SONGS FROM **FAMOUS** FEUD

TAYLOR SWIFT	KANYE WEST
Look What You Made Me Do:	*Famous*:
Producers *(2):* Jack Antonoff, Taylor Swift,	**Producers** (6): Andrew Dawson, Charlie Heat, Havoc, Kanye West, Kuk Harrell, Noah Goldstein,
Lyricists *(5):* Fred Fairbrass, Jack Antonoff, Richard Fairbrass, Rob Manzoli, Taylor Swift.[120]	**Lyricists** *(17)*: Andrew Dawson, Chancelor Bennett, Cydel Young, Enzo Vita, Ernest Brown, Giampiero Scalamogna, Jimmy Webb, Kanye West, Kasseem Dean, Kejuan Muchita, Luis Enriquez Bacalov, Mike Dean, Noah Goldstein, Patrick Reynolds, Ross Birchard, Sergio Bardotti, Winston Riley.[121]

Conclusion:

Taylor Swift used less producers and lyricists and her song was more popular in sales than Kanye West's army of lyricists and producers.

---

[120] Taylor Swift,'reputation Credits', *Tidal*, https://listen.tidal.com/artist/3557299, last accessed: August 25, 2019.
[121] Kanye West, 'The Life of Pablo Credits', *Tidal*, https://listen.tidal.com/album/57273408, last accessed: October 23, 2017.

IV.1.4 The Rabbit Hat: Fame, Originality and Creativity After VMA 2009[122]

In this chapter I investigated the roots of the new album released a year after the MTV scene, that is the music released by both artists in the autumn of 2010, first Taylor Swift then Kanye West.

TABLE 39. THE RABBIT'S HAT: TAYLOR SWIFT AND KANYE WEST

CATEGORY	TAYLOR SWIFT: *SPEAK NOW* (DELUXE, 2010)	KANYE WEST: *MY BEAUTIFUL DARK TWISTED FANTASY* (2010)
FIRST WEEK SALES	HIGH INCREASE	HIGH DECREASE
OVERALL ALBUM SALES	HIGH NUMBER OF SALES ON LONG TERM	MODERATE NUMBER OF SALES WITH TRACKS OF SLOW SALES ON LONG TERM
USE OF SAMPLE	0%	10 OUT OF 14 SONGS
ORIGINAL SONGS WITH NO SAMPLE	17 SONGS (100%)	4 OUT OF 14 SONGS
ORIGINAL SONG AS SOLE LYRICIST	16 OUT OF 17 SONGS	0 SONGS (0%)
ORIGINAL SONG WITH TWO LYRICISTS	1 OUT OF 17 SONGS	0 OUT OF 14 SONGS (0%)
ORIGINAL SONG WITH THREE LYRICISTS	0 SONGS	1 OUT OF 14 SONGS
ORIGINAL SONG WITH AT LEAST FOUR LYRICICTS	0 SONGS	13 OUT OF 14 SONGS
DIRECT INSPIRATION FROM OTHER SONGS	NO	YES
TOP CHARTS & AWARDS OF THE SONG SAMPLED	NO	YES
DIRECT WHITE MALE INSPIRATION	N/A	21 OUT OF 25
DIRECT WHITE FEMALE INSPIRATION	N/A	1 OUT OF 1
DIRECT BLACK MALE INSPIRATION	N/A	4 out of 25
DIRECT BLACK FEMALE INSPIRATION	N/A	
METACRITIC RATING	77	94
LENGTH OF SONG AS SOLE LYRICIST	75:29 MINUTES	0 MINUTES
LENGTH OF SONG WITH TWO LYRICISTS	3:54	0 MINUTES (THERE IS A HIGHER NUMBER OF MINUTES ONLY TO SONGS WITH AT LEAST 4 SONGWRITERS)
LYRICS	OWN LYRICS	LYRICS FROM OTHER ARTISTS

---

[122] This section was also included in Casian Anton, *Black and White Music*.

THE ORIGINS OF TITLE SONGS	OWN TITLES	FROM OTHER TITLE SONGS AND LYRICS OF SONGS SAMPLED IN HIS MUSIC
	2006: October 24 2008: November 11 2010: October 25	2004: February 10 2005: August 30 2007: September 11 2008: November 24 2010: November 22
PATTERN OF MUSIC RELEASE	The following date are written to observe the full pattern of music release of both artists.	
	2012: October 22 2014: October 27 2017: November 10 2019: August 23 2020: July 24 2020: December 11	2013: June 18 2016: February 14 2018: June 1 2019: October 25

CONCLUSIONS:

- *Taylor Swift*:

    o came with traces of global success;
    o came with her own lyrics;
    o released an album with original songs never heard in the music industry;
    o the length of the music written by her for *Standard Edition* is 100% of the album, for *Deluxe Edition* she has one song written in partnership with another lyricist;
    o released the music following October – November pattern;

- *Kanye West*:

    o came with lyrics written by other artists and instruments already created and used by other artists in the music industry;
    o Kanye West has 0% as sole lyricist on his album;
    o 13 out of 14 songs were written by at least 4 lyricists, compared to Taylor Swift who wrote all the songs on her own (Standard Edition) and sold at least 50% more albums in one week than Kanye West;
    o it is inspired by the music written by white male artists, 21 out of 25 male artists;
    o overall, his album was rated on Metacritic with higher grade than Taylor Swift, 94, while for Taylor Swift is 77;

- changed the pattern of music release and interfered for a second time in Taylor Swift's pattern of album release: one album in each year for two years and in total for four albums: the first two albums: 2004 and 2005, the next two albums: 2007 and 2008; since 2008 Kanye West changed the season and released his album in the same month as Taylor Swift, but two weeks later: Taylor Swift on November 11, 2008 and Kanye West on November 24; in 2010: Taylor Swift released the album on October 25 (she released her first album in October 24, 2006), then Kanye West later in November 22, keeping the release date connected with the last release, which is the first and last time when Kanye West follows this release pattern; the following albums will be released in different seasons, only to change it to October 25, 2019 with *Jesus is King*, the same date that Taylor Swift released *Speak Now* in 2010;

- **Album reviews**: Kanye West received higher reviews and grades than Taylor Swift, but given the sources of his songs, the following questions arise: do the reviews also include an analysis of his voice? Online critics argue that his singing skills are either weak or he does not know how to sing[123], did the reviewers perform a genuine analysis of his voice? If this argument is true, how did he manage to get such a high score? Moreover, Kanye West used samples (title, lyrics, instrumental music) from other artists, basically what is Kanye West's original contribution in his album? Are the reviews and grades received based only on his work or the final song that contains samples? Are reviewers able to make the difference between Kanye West's original part and the samples part? If we take the samples from Kanye's album, what remains written and produced by him alone is worth grades 9 and 10? Taylor Swift got the grades based on her own lyrics and 50% participation as producer of her album, and were 7 and 8 in the eyes of the reviewers, Kanye got the grades 9 and 10 with the help of more lyricists and producers than Taylor Swift, but we do not know for sure how much is Kanye's contribution in the lyrics of the songs and production. Are the reviews real or have they been exaggerated to the detriment of the music industry, but also of the white artist Taylor Swift to prove that black artists have better music than white artists, and Kanye West was right to point out that Taylor Swift did not deserve the award from 2009?

[123] *Quora*, 'How Well Does Kanye West Really Sing', available at: https://www.quora.com/How-well-does-Kanye-West-really-sing, last accessed: February 25, 2020; 'Why is Kanye West considered to be a great artist? I have listened to his music, and it sounds like every other song on the radio. Am I missing something?', available at: https://www.quora.com/Why-is-Kanye-West-considered-to-be-a-great-artist-I-have-listened-to-his-music-and-it-sounds-like-every-other-song-on-the-radio-Am-I-missing-something, last accessed: February 25, 2020; 'David Crosby: Kanye West can neither sing, nor write, nor play', *The Guardian*, October 28, 2016, available at: https://www.theguardian.com/music/2016/oct/28/david-crosby-kanye-west, last accessed: February 25, 2020.

IV.1.5 The Rating on Metacritic[124]

TABLE 40. THE ALBUM RATINGS ON METACRITIC

TAYLOR SWIFT[125]	KANYE WEST[126]
Taylor Swift (Deluxe, 2006): not on Metacritic	The College Dropout (2004): 87
Fearless (Platinum, 2008): 73	Late Registration (2005): 85
Speak Now (Deluxe, 2010): 77	Graduation (2007): 79
RED (Deluxe, 2012): 77	88s & Heartbreak (2008): 75
1989 (Deluxe, 2014): 76	My Beautiful Dark Twisted Fantasy (2010): 94
reputation (2017): 71	Yeezus (2013): 84
Lover (2019): 79	The Life of Pablo (2016): 75
folklore (Deluxe, 2020): 88	Ye (2018): 64
Evermore (Deluxe, 2020): 85	Jesus is King (2019): 53
Fearless (Taylor's Version, 2021): 82	Donda (2021): 53
Red (Taylor's Version, 2021): 91	
Total average by albums in this table: 79.99	Total average by albums in this table: 74.9
Total average by Metacritic: 80	Total average by Metacritic: 74

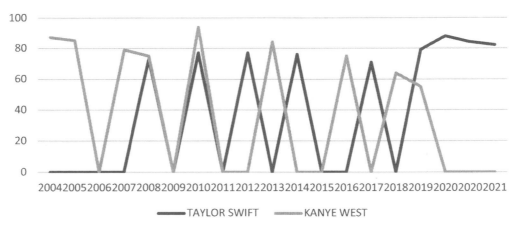

FIGURE 24. RATING ON METACRITIC: TAYLOR SWIFT AND KANYE WEST

CONCLUSIONS:

- *Taylor Swift*:

  - the notes received for each album are based on the work and ideas of the artist, but also to a considerable extent of other artists and producers she worked with (see the producers of *folklore* and *Evermore*, most of them is one producer, Aaron Dessner);
  - male producers are the constant base of her musical career;
  - compared to Kanye West and Metacritic, the grades received is close to 8, where they increase and decrease over the years;
  - a significant percentage of the grade received is based purely on her ability to write and compose unheard songs; in her music catalogue there are lots of songs that were written shortly after she heard the instruments and were hits on the radio and charts;
  - Metacritic does not include all the reviews written about her albums, there are reviews with higher and lower grades which are not included; it is highly possible that the final grade to be over 80.

- *Kanye West*:

  - the notes received for each album are based on the work and ideas of the artist, but also to a considerable extent of other artists from whom he abundantly sampled; also, for lyricists and producers who contributed to his songs;
  - compared to Taylor Swift (the grades increased and before the age 30 she has one of the highest reviewed album in her life, *folklore*), he received a high grade, 87 and then decreased (for 3 albums), then raised to the highest grade (94) and since then is continuously decreasing, the last album receiving grade 55;
  - Metacritic does not include all the reviews written about his albums, there are reviews with higher and lower grades which are not included; it is highly possible that the final grade to be over 80.

IV.2 **Bad Blood – Swish, Swish** Feud

Although being presented as a feud of Taylor Swift with Katy Perry, actually this feud is linked with the *Famous* feud. In this section I explored and set the narrative line of the feud between Taylor Swift and Katy Perry. I also showed the connection of this feud with the *Famous* feud and Kanye West.

IV.2.1 **Bad Blood – Swish, Swish** Feud Narrative Line[127]

FIGURE 25. BAD BLOOD - SWISH, SWISH FEUD NARRATIVE LINE

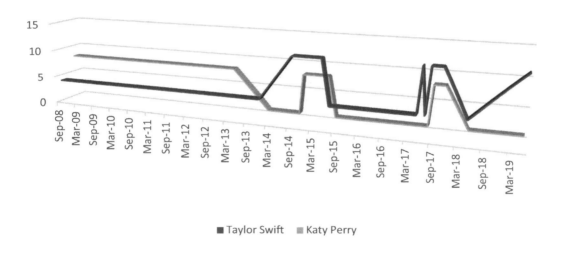

CONCLUSIONS:

- during the *Carpool Karaoke Primetime Special*, Katy Perry discussed the *Bad Blood – Swish, Swish* feud with James Corden by saying: *"Honestly, it's really like she started it and it's time for her to finish it,'* however, this affirmation is not true as the narrative line indicates that Katy Perry started the feud, and she is the perpetrator of the feud

---

[127] Eliza Thompson, 'Why Were Katy Perry and Taylor Swift Even Fighting in the First Place?' *Cosmopolitan*, July 10, 2020, https://www.cosmopolitan.com/entertainment/celebs/news/a61450/taylor-swift-katy-perry-feud-timeline/, last accessed: August 6, 2020.

when she decided to interfere in the music business of Taylor Swift: two dancers of Katy Perry got a job with Taylor Swift's *Red Tour*, however, Katy Perry wanted them back to join her *Prismatic Tour*, which the dancers agreed, and she tried to hire them without telling Taylor Swift; *'She basically tried to sabotage an entire arena tour. She tried to hire a bunch of people out from under me,'* answered Taylor Swift[128];

- it is considered that Taylor Swift got involved in the feud only to reply to Katy Perry's idea with the thing that she decided to mess with: her music tour; maybe Taylor Swift wrote the song *Bad Blood* as a reply mechanism to answer back to Katy Perry: the attempt to sabotage her music tour = wrote a song from her musical mind; *Bad Blood's* lyric 'If you live like that, you live with ghosts' and 'Ghost' is a song from Katy Perry's album called *Prism* (released in 2013); *Bad Blood* was awarded with the *Video of the Year* and the *Best Collaboration* at the MTV Video Music Awards in 2015, won the Best Music Video at the 58th Grammy Awards and was certified 6× Platinum by the Recording Industry Association of America (RIAA) in March 2020;
- Taylor Swift interfered negatively in the narrative line of Katy Perry *only after* Katy interfered first negatively in her narrative line;

IV.2.2 The Link with the **Famous** Feud and Kanye West

TABLE 41. THE LINK OF KATY PERRY WITH THE **FAMOUS** FEUD AND KANYE WEST

KANYE WEST	KATY PERRY
NAME OF THE ALBUM	*SONG & VIDEO*
	Swish, Swish (featuring Nicki Minaj)
	Katy Perry released a song with the same title as Kanye West's album. In 2016, Kanye West included the word 'bitch' in the lyrics of the song *Famous;* in the song Katy Perry also uses the words 'bish' and 'bitch': 'Swish, swish, bish'. 'Swish' is a word close to pronunciation and writing with the artist's name: Taylor Swift; 'Bish' is a word close to pronunciation and writing with the term 'bitch'.
	Maybe for Katy Perry the idea for the song released is a version of truth; however, the title of her song has a visible connection with Kanye West's title of an album entitled *SWISH*. Through the title of the song and the lyrics, there is a possibility that Katy Perry sided with

---

[128] Ibidem.

Kanye West's story about the involvement of Taylor Swift in the *Famous* song.

Nicki Minaj joined Katy Perry because she was also involved in a small feud with Taylor Swift. Although it seemed that everything was resolved in 2015 with Taylor Swift sending an apology through Twitter, Nicki Minaj maybe decided to be on Katy Perry's side and sang negative lyrics possibly about Taylor Swift:

'Initially Kanye West announced a new album entitled *So Help Me God* slated for a 2014 release; in March 2015 Kanye West announced that the album would instead be tentatively called *SWISH*.
Later in January 2016, Kanye West announced that *SWISH* would be released on February 11. On January 26, 2016, Kanye West revealed he had renamed the album from *SWISH* to *Waves*[129]. Several days ahead of its release, Kanye West again changed the title for the last time: *The Life of Pablo*.'[130]

'I already despise you (yeah)
All that fake love you showin'
Couldn't even disguise you, yo, yo
Ran? When? Nicki gettin' tan
Mirror mirror who's the fairest bitch in all the land?'
'I only rock with queens, so I'm makin' hits with Katy'.

In 2015 Taylor Swift and Nicki Minaj were on the MTV stage where she performed along with Taylor Swift. It is possible that these lyrics to be a reference that Nicki Minaj considers Katy Perry to be a queen (like her and the name of her album *Queen, 2018*), and decided to diss Taylor Swift. She also used the word 'bitch' to address a woman. Also, these lyrics can be related to Taylor Swift's *Bad Blood* music video: in her video she invited friends which happens to be famous people in the music, fashion and tv industry; therefore, Katy Perry decided to sing along with a famous female rapper, which happens to have already a small feud with Taylor Swift.

Another common element between Taylor Swift and Katy Perry is the involvement of a rap artist in songs dedicated to the feud: Taylor Swift released the music video *Bad Blood* (2015) with Kendrick Lamar (black artist), and Katy Perry

[129] Matthew Strauss, 'Kanye West Announces New Album Title, Shares Final Tracklist', *Pitchfork*, February 10, 2016, https://pitchfork.com/news/63468-kanye-west-announces-new-album-title-shares-final-tracklist/, last accessed: October 25, 2017.
[130] Mitchell Peters, 'Kanye West Announces Name Change of His New Album on Twitter', *Billboard*, March 5, 2015, https://www.billboard.com/articles/columns/the-juice/6553812/kanye-west-announces-name-change-of-his-new-album-on-twitter-swish-so-help-me-god, last accessed: October 25, 2017.

released the song *Swish, swish* with Nicki Minaj (black artist, 2017).

Katy Perry said her song is an anti-bullying anthem. During a performance, Katy Perry made a slight change to the song switching out the line 'Don't you come for me' with 'God bless you on your journey, oh baby girl'. This is another example to support the idea that *Swish, swish* song is about Taylor Swift.

Despite the evidence that Kanye West did not inform Taylor Swift about the line 'I made that bitch famous', Katy Perry decided to name her song *Swish, swish*, and to include the words 'bish' and 'bitch', allegedly to criticise negatively Taylor Swift's abilities as a pop artist.

The reply mechanism of Taylor Swift:

1. on the day of Katy Perry's album release, named Witness, the world witnessed Taylor Swift's decision to release her entire music catalogue on streaming services for the first time: 'In celebration of 1989 selling over 10 million albums worldwide and the RIAA's 100 million song certification announcement, Taylor wants to thank her fans by making her entire catalogue available to all streaming services tonight at midnight';

overall, Taylor Swift's music outperformed Katy Perry's music despite releasing a new musical album;[131] it seems that Taylor Swift refused to listen to Katy Perry's lyric 'Don't you come for me', 'No, not today (woah)' and she did came on the big day album release, sort of, after Katy Perry, and it seems that Taylor Swift is as Katy Perry said in the lyric: 'You're calculated';

regarding the evolution of both artists, it seems that the outperformance of Taylor Swift's music, (and few month later the *reputation* album) on Spotify and other streaming services over Katy Perry, is a strong evidence that Taylor Swift is not a joker and *she is a killer queen*, as Katy Perry sings in *Swish, swish*: 'And I'm a courtside killer queen', 'Cause I stay winning', 'Your game is tired', 'You should retire'; Taylor Swift's music outperformed Katy Perry's music on the

---

[131] Rihan Daly, 'Taylor Swift's back catalogue is currently outperforming Katy Perry's 'Witness' on Spotify', *NME*, June 11, 2017, available at: https://www.nme.com/news/music/taylor-swifts-back-catalogue-currently-outperforming-katy-perrys-witness-spotify-2087235, last accessed: August 6, 2020.

streaming services and each album makes more history on charts than Katy Perry's music, therefore Katy Perry has more reasons to retire than Taylor Swift;

Katy Perry on *Swish, swish's* lyrics: 'And you will kiss the ring, You best believe': in the end it was the other way around: Katy Perry decided to stop speaking negatively about Taylor Swift: 'I'm ready to let it go' […] 'Absolutely, 100 percent. I forgive her and I'm sorry for anything I ever did, and I hope the same from her and I think it's actually… I think it's time' […] There are bigger fish to fry and there are bigger problems in the world. I love her and I want the best for her, and I think she's a fantastic songwriter and, like, I think that if we both, her and I, can be representatives of strong women that come together despite their differences, I think the whole world is going to go, like 'Yeah we can do this'';[132] Taylor Swift, despite the decision of Katy Perry to forgive and leave her alone, decided to go on with the release of *Look What You Made Me Do* with possible references to Katy Perry.

Taylor Swift did not speak publicly about Katy Perry and, while touring in 2018, she received from Katy Perry an olive tree (a symbol of peace) and she posted a picture with it and a text on Instagram: 'Thank you, Katy.'

2. *she released the song 'Look What You Made Me Do' in August 2017 which might contain possible references to Katy Perry and Kanye West, but not about Nicki Minaj, or perhaps I did not watch the video too many times to discover any possible references.*

IV.2.3 The Impact of the '**Bad Blood – Swish, Swish**' Feud

In the following table I investigated the impact of the *Bad Blood – Swish, Swish* feud between Taylor Swift and Katy Perry.

TABLE 42. THE IMPACT OF THE **FAMOUS** FEUD ON WORLDWIDE ALBUM SALES

YEAR	TAYLOR SWIFT	KATY PERRY
2006	Taylor Swift: 7.000.000 albums as December 2017.	-

---

[132] Ibidem.

2008	*Fearless*: 10.000.000 albums as December 2017.[133]	*One of the Boys:* 7.000.000 as August 2010.[134]
2010	*Speak Now*: 6.000.000 albums as December 2017.[135]	*Teenage Dreams:* 6.000.000 as July 2013.[136]
2012	*RED*: 7.000.000 albums as July 2018.[137]	-
2013	-	*Prism*: more than 4.000.000 album as August 2015.[138]
2014	*1989:* 11.300.000 as of December 2019.[139]	-
2017	*reputation*: 5.100.000 as of December 2019[140].	*Witness*: over 840.000 album as of January 2018.[141]
2019	*Lover (2019)*: more than 5.000.000 as of January 2020.[142]	-
2020	*folklore (2020)*: over 2.000.000 as August 6, 2020.[143]	*Smile (2020)*: 402.000 as March 21, 2021.[144]

FIGURE 26. ALBUM WORLDWIDE SALE KATY PERRY, TAYLOR SWIFT AND KANYE WEST

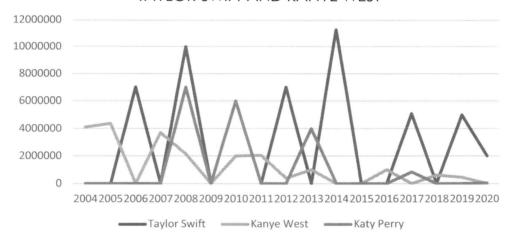

TABLE 43. WORLDWIDE SALES OF SONGS SWIFT & PERRY FEUD

TAYLOR SWIFT	KATY PERRY
Bad Blood: 6.057.500.[145]	*Swish, swish*: 1.000.000 as January 2018[147]
Look What You Made Me Do: 6.026.666.[146]	

---

[145] The numbers are based on certification of sales from different countries, see Taylor Swift, *Bad Blood*, https://en.wikipedia.org/wiki/Bad_Blood_(Taylor_Swift_song)#Chart_performance, last accessed: February 21, 2020 and Taylor Swift, 'Bad Blood', *RIAA*, February 21, 2017, https://www.riaa.com/gold-platinum/?tab_active=default-award&se=bad+blood+Taylor+swift#search_section, last accessed: February 21, 2020.

CONCLUSIONS:

- on long term Taylor Swift sold more albums than Katy Perry;
- the feud does not seem to stop Taylor Swift selling more songs and albums than Katy Perry and that is due to loyal fans that Taylor Swift earned in the last years;
- Taylor Swift's power sale seems to not know the end: *Bad Blood* from 2014 sold at least 6 times more copies than Katy Perry's *Swish, Swish from 2017*; even after Katy Perry confessed that the *Bad Blood* song is about her, Taylor Swift' song, *Look What You Made Me Do* from 2017 sold also at least 6 times more copies than Katy Perry's song; making a full maths of both songs: Taylor Swift sold 12 times more songs than Katy Perry;
- Taylor Swift has definitely more loyal fans than Katy Perry, and not just thousands, but at least a million.

---

[134] Gil Kaufman, 'Katy Perry, Fantasia Look to Unseat Eminem on Charts', *MTV*, August 26, 2010, http://www.mtv.com/news/1646527/katy-perry-fantasia-look-to-unseat-eminem-on-charts/, last accessed: November 6, 2019.

[135] Taylor Swift, 'Speak Now', *RIAA*, December 11, 2017, https://www.riaa.com/gold-platinum/?tab_active=default-award&ar=Taylor+Swift&ti=Speak+Now#search_section, last accessed: December 21, 2019.

[136] Sean Michaels, 'Katy Perry announces new album, Prism, on side of golden lorry', *The Guardian*, July 30., 2013, https://www.theguardian.com/music/2013/jul/30/katy-perry-new-album-prism-lorry, last accessed: November 6, 2019.

[137] Taylor Swift, 'RED', *RIAA*, July 23, 2019, https://www.riaa.com/gold-platinum/?tab_active=default-award&se=taylor+swift#search_section, last accessed: December 21, 2019.

[138] All Access, 'Third Annual Capitol Congress Presents New Projects', Media Notables, August 6, 2015, https://www.allaccess.com/net-news/archive/story/144283/third-annual-capitol-congress-presents-new-project, last accessed: November 6, 2019.

[139] United World Charts, 'Decade Album Chart', *Media Traffic*, http://www.mediatraffic.de/2010-2019-album-chart.htm, last accessed: January 6, 2020. RIAA certified 9.000.000 albums in December 11, 2017, https://www.riaa.com/gold-platinum/?tab_active=default-award&se=taylor+swift#search_section, last accessed: December 21, 2019.

[140] United World Charts, *Decade Album Chart*.

[141] Shirley Halperin, 'Capitol's Steve Barnett on Five Years at the Tower, 'Plan' for Katy Perry, 'Beloved' Niall Horan', *Variety*, January 12, 2018, https://variety.com/2018/music/news/steve-barnett-capitol-interview-katy-perry-niall-horan-1202660297/, last accessed: August 25, 2019.

[142] Chris Willman, 'Taylor Swift Moves to Universal Music Publishing Group with New Pact', *Variety*, February 6, 2020, https://variety.com/2020/music/news/taylor-swift-signs-umpg-publishing-deal-1203484798/, last accessed: February 18, 2020.

[143] Eli Countryman, 'Taylor Swift's 'Folklore' Sells Over 2 Million Copies in First Week', *Variety*, July 31, 2020, available at: https://variety.com/2020/music/news/taylor-swift-folklore-first-week-sales-worldwide-1234722530/, last accessed: August 6, 2020.

[144] Colin Stutz, 'Katy Perry Planning Las Vegas Residency at Brand-New Casino', *Billboard*, March 19, 2021, available at: https://www.billboard.com/articles/business/touring/9543635/katy-perry-las-vegas-residency-aeg-resorts-world, last accessed: July 25, 2021.

[145] The numbers are based on certification of sales from different countries, see Taylor Swift, *Bad Blood*, https://en.wikipedia.org/wiki/Bad_Blood_(Taylor_Swift_song)#Chart_performance, last accessed: February 21, 2020 and Taylor Swift, 'Bad Blood', *RIAA*, February 21, 2017, https://www.riaa.com/gold-platinum/?tab_active=default-award&se=bad+blood+Taylor+swift#search_section, last accessed: February 21, 2020.

[146] The numbers are based on certification of sales from different countries, see Taylor Swift, 'Look What You Made Me Do', *Wikipedia,* https://en.wikipedia.org/wiki/Look_What_You_Made_Me_Do#Commercial_performance, last accessed: February 21, 2020.

[147] Katy Perry, 'Swish, Swish', *RIAA*, January 19, 2018, https://www.riaa.com/gold-platinum/?tab_active=default-award&se=swish+swish#search_section, last accessed: August 25, 2019.

V. The **FAMOUS** feud: strategies of interpretation and communication

During the events from the *Famous* feud, the Western mass-media was the main source of the narrative for the outsiders. After reading about 10 articles, I noticed that the explanations offered by journalists are absurd and mean to Taylor Swift, for example Amy Zimmerman in her article published in *The Daily Beast*: 'has been tapping into virginal white victim tropes her entire career'. For Amy Zimmerman a phone call in which you are not told the whole story, but you are accused of knowing everything from the beginning, small and edited parts of the conversation are published online, was enough to conclude that *all her life* Taylor Swift played the role of virginal white victim. Following this conclusion, I decided to look for more articles to see if there are more journalists with the thinking skills of Amy Zimmerman.

Following the research, I gathered in a word document 1175 articles; the articles were arranged in two big categories: USA and UK with the name of the news agency and link to the website sources, so I can access it anytime. I gathered links about the *Famous* feud from the following news agencies (available in the USA, UK and Australia): Slate Magazine, People, Vanity Fair, Cosmopolitan, Glamour Magazine, Elle, Vulture, Marie Claire, Forbes, Ok! UK, Radar Online, GQ, The Sun, Metro, Evening Standard, Telegraph, Daily Star, The Guardian, The Independent, Express, AOL.co.uk, Mirror, Huffington Post, Daily Mail, Pagesix, Billboard, CBS News, Business Insider, Harpers Bazaar, New York Daily, Gossip Cop (the best source for accuracy, I gathered 33 links about the feud; the articles are not available anymore because they were deleted from the website), Rolling Stone, People, E Online, Lifestyle, The Atlantic, TMZ, W Magazine, Latinpost, Daily Beast, Buzzfeed, Los Angeles Time, US Magazine, TIME.

I managed to read over 500 articles, then I got bored and sick of everything about the feud, so I decided to stop reading; being in this state of mind, I decided to delete the articles and, while deleting some of them, I had another idea: to use the articles and see if the timeline of the feud is correct in all the newspapers that were not deleted. Western mass-media (used in this report) and their role in spreading the *Famous* feud was mostly neutral toward the narrative of the events, even if the timeline is written and presented in short, long and complex articles. In the next pages of this chapter, I created an analysis of Taylor Swift's statements, and I extracted and presented general negative views about Taylor Swift written and published in news agencies from the USA and the UK.

In the table below I analysed the statements released by Taylor Swift and her management team regarding her involvement in the *Famous* song released by Kanye West. This text analysis is done with the purpose to expose the inability of journalists and bloggers to follow and understand the logical flow of Taylor Swift's statements and reach logical conclusions regarding this feud, because Taylor Swift was criticised negatively based on the statements below. In other words, the news articles written about Taylor Swift from February 2016 until March 2020 (before the leak of the phone conversation), and available in this report, were used to analyse her involvement in the *Famous* feud. After the text analysis, I presented the list of the negative content written by various journalists and published in popular and highly acclaimed news agencies in the Western mass-media.

TABLE 44. THE STATEMENTS OF TAYLOR SWIFT FOR THE INVOLVEMENT IN THE **FAMOUS** SONG

STATEMENTS	CONCLUSIONS
1. February 2016: after the release of the song Famous: Taylor Swift camp replied: "Kanye did not call for approval, but to ask Taylor to release his single 'Famous' on her Twitter account. She declined and cautioned him about releasing a song with such a strong misogynistic message. Taylor was never made aware of the actual lyric, "I made that bitch famous.""[148]	In February 2016 Taylor Swift admitted that there was a phone call between her and Kanye West regarding the *Famous* song since the beginning of the feud. I extracted the keywords from her statement to prove she did not lie about the phone call: "Kanye […] call […] to ask Taylor to release his single 'Famous' on her Twitter account." "She declined and cautioned him about releasing a song": Taylor Swift declined (could) him only during the phone conversation.
2. February 2016: during the Grammy Awards ceremony:	

[148] Melody Chiu, Karen Mizoguchi, 'Kanye West Did Not Call Taylor Swift for Approval Over 'B----' Lyric, Singer Cautioned Him Against Releasing 'Strong Misogynistic Message' Rep Says', *People*, February 12, 2016, https://people.com/celebrity/kanye-west-did-not-call-taylor-swift-for-approval-over-bitch-lyric/, last accessed: October 23, 2017.

While accepting Album of the Year award at the GRAMMYs, Taylor Swift addressed what is believed to be about the infamous Kanye West lyrics about her:

"I want to thank the fans for the last 10 years, and the recording academy for giving us this unbelievable honor. I want to thank all of the collaborators that you see on this stage. Mostly, I want to thank my co-executive producer Max Martin, who has deserved to be up here for 25 years. And as the first woman to win album of the year at the Grammy's twice, I want to say to all the young women out there, there are going to be people along the way who, will try to undercut your success or take credit for your accomplishments or your fame. But if you just focus on the work and you don't let those people sidetrack you, someday when you get where you're going, you will know it was you and the people who love you who put you there, and that will be the greatest feeling in the world. Thank you for this moment."[149]

---

3. In an interview with Vogue in April 2016, Taylor Swift addressed her acceptance speech at Grammy Awards and Kanye West:

"I think the world is bored with the saga. I don't want to add anything to it, because then there's just more... I guess what I wanted to call attention to in my speech at the Grammys was how it's going to be difficult if you're a woman who wants to achieve something in her life - no matter what."[150]

---

4. Taylor Swift camp (June 2016), after Kim Kardashian's interview with GQ, issued a statement to GQ:

---

[149] Taylor Swift, 'Taylor Swift, Album of the Year Acceptance Speech (Grammys 2016)', *Genius*, February 15, 2016, https://genius.com/Taylor-swift-album-of-the-year-acceptance-speech-grammys-2016-annotated, last accessed: October 23, 2017.
[150] Jason Gay, 'Taylor Swift As You've Never Seen Her Before', *Vogue*, April 14, 2016, https://www.vogue.com/article/taylor-swift-may-cover-maid-of-honor-dating-personal-style, last accessed: October 23, 2017.

'Taylor does not hold anything against Kim Kardashian as she recognizes the pressure Kim must be under and that she is only repeating what she has been told by Kanye West. However, that does not change the fact that much of what Kim is saying is incorrect. Kanye West and Taylor only spoke once on the phone while she was on vacation with her family in January of 2016 and they have never spoken since. Taylor has never denied that conversation took place. It was on that phone call that Kanye West also asked her to release the song on her Twitter account, which she declined to do. Kanye West never told Taylor he was going to use the term 'that bitch' in referencing her. A song cannot be approved if it was never heard. Kanye West never played the song for Taylor Swift. Taylor heard it for the first time when everyone else did and was humiliated. Kim Kardashian's claim that Taylor and her team were aware of being recorded is not true, and Taylor cannot understand why Kanye West, and now Kim Kardashian, will not just leave her alone.'[151]

For a second time in June 2016, before the release of the edited videos by Kim Kardashian on Snapchat in July 2016, Taylor Swift admitted that indeed she talked with Kanye West about the *Famous* song:

"Kanye West and Taylor only spoke once on the phone while she was on vacation with her family in January of 2016 and they have never spoken since. Taylor has never denied that conversation took place. It was on that phone call that Kanye West also asked her to release the song on her Twitter account, which she declined to do."

---

5. Taylor Swift (July 2016) responded to Kim Kardashian's Snapchat videos on her Instagram and Twitter account (now the picture with her response is deleted on both platforms):

'That moment when Kanye West secretly records your phone call, then Kim posts it on the Internet.'

'Where is the video of Kanye telling me he was going to call me 'that bitch' in his song? It doesn't exist because it never happened. You don't get to control someone's emotional response to being called 'that bitch' in front of the entire world. Of course I wanted to like the song. I wanted to believe Kanye when he told me that I would love the song. I wanted us to have a friendly relationship. He promised to play the song for me, but he never did. While I

For a third time in July 2016, after the release of the edited videos by Kim Kardashian on Snapchat, Taylor Swift admitted that indeed she talked with Kanye West about the *Famous* song:

"I wanted to believe Kanye when he told me that I would love the song."

"While I wanted to be supportive of Kanye on the phone call [...]"

---

[151] Caity Weaver, 'Kanye and Taylor Swift, What's in O.J.'s Bag, and Understanding Caitlyn', *GQ*, June 16, 2016, https://www.gq.com/story/kim-kardashian-west-gq-cover-story, last accessed: October 23, 2017.

wanted to be supportive of Kanye on the phone
call, you cannot 'approve' a song you haven't
heard. Being falsely painted as a liar when I was
never given the full story or played any part of
the song is character assassination. I would very
much like to be excluded from this narrative,
one that I have never asked to be a part of,
since 2009.'[152]

Final conclusions:

Taylor Swift admitted twice that she spoke on the phone with Kanye West, in
February and June 2016, therefore before the videos posted by Kim Kardashian
on her Snapchat account in July 2016.
Taylor Swift cautioned Kanye West about feminists (linked with the misogynist).
Taylor Swift told him that she was famous before the event from September
2009.

In March 2020, after the leak of the full conversation between Kanye West and Taylor Swift,
the only new element was: the full conversation, which does not change anything about
Taylor Swift's side of the story: she told the truth since February 2016, repeated in June and
July 2016: was not aware of the line 'I made that bitch famous', she talked and warned
Kanye West about feminists coming after him (linked with the misogynistic message of her
reply), she was supportive with Kanye West over the phone for the lyrics she knew about it
(and her reply for making her famous: 'I sold 7 million albums before' the events from
September 2009); she did not approve the song as Kanye promised her to send it over for a
final consideration, which never happened; Taylor heard the *Famous* song at the same time
with the general public.

Back in 2020, Kim Kardashian replied on March 24 to the leak with the following statement:

'@taylorswift13 has chosen to reignite an old exchange - that at this point in time feels very
self-serving given the suffering millions of real victims are facing right now. I didn't feel the
need to comment a few days ago, and I'm actually really embarrassed and mortified to be
doing it right now, but because she continues to speak on it, I feel I'm left without a choice
but to respond **because she is actually lying. To be clear, the only issue I ever had**

---

[152] The photo with her reply is now deleted from her Facebook, Twitter and Instagram account. You can find written evidence here:
Jemima Skelley, 'Taylor Swift Just Called Out Kanye West On Instagram', *BuzzFee*d, July 18, 2016,
https://www.buzzfeed.com/jemimaskelley/shoulda-chose-the-rose-garden-over-madison-square, last accessed: October 23, 2017.

around the situation was that Taylor lied through her publicist who stated that "Kanye never called to ask for permission..." They clearly spoke so I let you all see that. Nobody ever denied the word "bitch" was used without her permission. At the time when they spoke the song had not been fully written yet, but as everyone can see in the video, **she manipulated the truth of their actual conversation in her statement when her team said she "declined and cautioned him about releasing a song with such a strong misogynistic message." The lie was** never about the word bitch, It was **always whether there was a call or not and the tone of the conversation**. To add, Kanye as an artist has every right to document his musical journey and process, just like she recently did through her documentary. Kanye has documented the making of all of his albums for his personal archive, however has never released any of it for public consumption & **the call between the two of them would have remained private or would have gone in the trash had she not lied & forced me to defend him**. This will be the last time I speak on this because honestly, nobody cares. Sorry to bore you all with this. I know you are all dealing with more serious and important matters'.[153]

Conclusions based on Kim Kardashian reply after the leak:

- failed to follow the logic flow of the statements released by Taylor Swift from February to July 2016: she did not deny the phone conversation, cautioned Kanye West about feminists (linked with the misogynistic message), told him that she was already famous when they met to MTV ceremony in September 2009; was not aware of the full song; Kanye promised her to send the song which he never did; Taylor Swift told Kanye West that she will think about the song and waited for him to send her the *Famous* song;
- either she is not capable of understanding a statement and to analyse a statement and follow the logic flow of it, or she is playing the role of a silly character (based on my research, watching online videos about her, she is capable of logical reasoning) to get away with the unfamous role she played in June and July 2016, and the biased information she presented in those months, and she continued in 2020 through her statement; maybe the end of playing the role of a silly character is (her fans and Taylor Swift's fans saw her lacking of logic and understanding of Taylor Swift's statements and the full conversation between Taylor Swift and Kanye West and posted thousands of comments on Twitter) to stop fans and haters going after her (such as unfollow her on social media, refusal to buy her products, which means

---

[153] Tatiana Tenreyro, 'Kim Kardashian Responded To Taylor Swift's Statement About The Leaked Kanye West Phone Call', *Buzzfeed*, March 24, 2020, available at: https://www.buzzfeed.com/tatianatenreyrowhitlock/kim-kardashian-speaks-about-kanye-west-phone-call-with, last accessed: July 1, 2021.

losing popularity and profit) as she was exposed as a person who is presenting biased and misleading information where we need to follow logic; in the end, maybe she got the wrong advice: to continue her side of the story in order to prove she was right since June and July 2016, and that Taylor Swift is lying since February 2016 until today and forever (however, this strategy does not help her to earn power or the sympathy of the general public and be the final and right winner of the feud, but it is a deceitful strategy as Taylor Swift said the truth since February 2016); the statements released by anyone must be either true or more intelligent than the general public, because there are people more intelligent than us, and able to see and understand everything we say and do, even if we try to hide it;

- **'tone of the conversation'**: the tone was friendly on both sides, however, Kanye added a new line which Taylor disagreed and told the world that she knew everything about it; also he failed to keep his side of the bargain: to send the final version of the song to Taylor; **Taylor's tone of the conversation changed because Kanye's tone *changed first* after he released the final version of the song with new lyrics that Taylor did not know, but accused by him and Kim that she knew everything about what was coming out**; Kanye West and Kim Kardashian tone of the conversation in front to the general public was negative about Taylor Swift despite having the full video with the conversation; let's see how the tone of the conversation was changed by Kanye West:

January 2016:

'Kanye West: "So it says… and the song is so, so dope. And I've literally sat with my wife, with my whole management team, with everything and tried to rework this line. I've thought about this line for eight months. I've had this line and I've tried to rework it every which way. And the original way that I thought about it is the best way, but it's the most controversial way. So it's gonna go Eminem a little bit, so can you brace yourself for a second?"

Taylor Swift: "[Sounding resigned.] Yeah."

Kanye West: "Okay. All right. Wait a second, you sound sad."

Taylor Swift: "Well, is it gonna be mean?"

Kanye West: "No, I don't think it's mean."

Taylor Swift: "Okay, then, let me hear it."

Kanye West: "Okay. It says, um,… and the funny thing is, when I first played it and my wife heard it, she was like, "Huh? What? That's too crazy," blah, blah, blah. And then like when Ninja from Die

143

Atwoord heard it, he was like, "Oh my God, this is the craziest s—. This is why I love Kanye," blah, blah, blah, that kind of thing. And now it's like my wife's favourite f—ing line. I just wanted to give you some premise of that. Right?"

Taylor Swift: "Okay."

Kanye West: "So it says "To all my Southside [N-word] that know me best, I feel like Taylor Swift might owe me sex."

Taylor Swift: "[Laughs, relieved.] That's not mean."'

February 2016:

On February 11, 2016 Kanye West debuted his musical album The Life of Pablo at his Yeezy Season 3 show at Madison Square Garden, New York. In one of his songs, 'Famous,' he raps "I feel like me and Taylor might still have sex / Why? I made that bitch famous (God damn) / I made that bitch famous."

Kanye West wrote a few tweets on his Twitter account:

"I did not diss Taylor Swift and I've never dissed her…
— KANYE WEST (@kanyewest) February 12, 2016"

"First thing is I'm an artist and as an artist I will express how I feel with no censorship
— KANYE WEST (@kanyewest) February 12, 2016"

"2nd thing I asked my wife for her blessings and she was cool with it
— KANYE WEST (@kanyewest) February 12, 2016"

"3rd thing I called Taylor and had a hour long convo with her about the line and she thought it was funny and gave her blessings
— KANYE WEST (@kanyewest) February 12, 2016"

"4th Bitch is an endearing term in hip hop like the word Nigga
— KANYE WEST (@kanyewest) February 12, 2016"

"5th thing I'm not even gone take credit for the idea… it's actually something Taylor came up with …
— KANYE WEST (@kanyewest) February 12, 2016"

At Yo Gotti's album release party at the 1OAK nightclub in Hollywood, Kanye West reiterates he told Taylor Swift about the 'Famous' lyric and said "She had two seconds to be cool and she fucked it up!"

Kanye West makes a guest appearance at Drake's concert in Chicago, and speaks out about Taylor Swift. Kanye West told his fans, "All I gotta say is, I am so glad my wife has Snapchat!", "Now y'all can know the truth and can't nobody talk s–t about 'Ye no more." After his words, he performed the 'Famous' song.

Kanye West and Kim Kardashian are on the cover of Harper's Bazaar September issue. When asked by editor Laura Brown about their favourite Taylor Swift song, Kanye West replied, 'For me? I don't have one.' Kim Kardashian replied: 'I was such a fan of hers.'

Kanye West takes the stage at the 2016 MTV Video Music Awards. He received 6 minutes to do what he wants. He addressed the 'Famous' song and Taylor Swift by saying that he's a 'lover of all,' which is 'why I called her.'

- **'the call between the two of them would have remained private or would have gone in the trash':** then why was Kanye desperate to record the phone conversation with Taylor without her knowledge? and, after the release of the final version of the song in February 2016, he refused to publicly acknowledge that Taylor didn't know the new line he added, that Taylor has the right to challenge the line 'I made that bitch famous'? Why didn't he come up with an explanation where he writes the exact parts that he discussed with Taylor, so that the general public can understand, *because Kanye West told them*, that Taylor was not aware of the line 'I made that bitch famous'?

    Kanye West: "It's just when it dies… You get some s– like Kanye talking to Taylor Swift explaining that line? There's gotta be three cameras on that one. We can't miss one element."

If Kanye and Kim wanted the world to know about what Taylor Swift knew, why did Kim posted only parts of the recording in which there is a visible lack of the context regarding Taylor's answers? Why did Kanye and Kim refused to show everything they had about Taylor Swift if their intention was good from the beginning? Why go to interviews with bits of information in which they incriminate Taylor while keeping the whole video hidden? Why was there a leak instead of Kanye and Kim showing the whole video? Why having concerts made in good faith for the truth in which Kanye, Kim and fans shouted multiple times and locations (included Nashville, the city where Taylor's career began) 'bitch' in reference to Taylor if you have the whole video showing that Taylor was not aware of the line 'I made that bitch famous' for which she publicly challenged? Why these half-truths, biased and misleading information about Taylor Swift when you have the video showing a different picture of the phone call and the conversation?

The theories advanced by Taylor Swift's fans might be true: there is no video in which Taylor agreed with the final lyrics and the song, otherwise Kanye and Kim would have used it on the next minute after Taylor's statement in February 2016.

- the best strategy for Kim Kardashian to get out clean was to say: 'I was given only the edited parts that I posted on Snapchat in 2016 and I was convinced that they were true and I was angry about it and felt the need to defend my husband, which I did. However, after the leak of the conversation (I watched it at the same time with the world as I did not have access to it because I'm not part of the filming team) I was able to see the truth and Taylor Swift was right about the line 'I made that bitch famous'. I'm sorry for the mess I made.' Kim Kardashian had the chance to make it right for her, in the first place, then for Taylor Swift, her fans and Taylor Swift's fans. Of course, her image has not changed since the leak of the phone conversation and the fans still love her and she is still famous. However, in the present and future conversations about the *Famous* feud, Kim Kardashian is seen as a liar and guilty by association and complicity with Kanye West (he dragged her first in his dark narrative about Taylor Swift); in the end, mass media wrote about the vindication of Taylor Swift after the leak[154]; this is a logic exercise for Kim Kardashian as a future lawyer: if Taylor Swift is vindicated about her implication in the *Famous* song, then who are the perpetrators?

In the following table I have the names of the news agencies, journalists and titles with negative content about Taylor Swift's involvement in the *Famous* song; remember: the articles are based on Taylor Swift's statements from February to July 2016.

---

[154] Jordan Hoffman, 'Vindication for Taylor Swift With Newly Leaked Kanye West Call Video', *Vanity Fair*, March 21, 2020, https://www.vanityfair.com/style/2020/03/vindication-for-taylor-swift-with-newly-leaked-kayne-west-call-video, last accessed: July 1, 2021; Lucy Buckland, 'Vindicated Taylor Swift refuses to break silence over Kanye West phone call leak', *Mirror*, March 22, 2020, https://www.mirror.co.uk/3am/celebrity-news/vindicated-taylor-swift-refuses-break-21733388, last accessed: July 1, 2021; Rachel Kiley, 'Taylor Swift Vindicated After Full 2016 Kanye West Phone Call Leaks', *Pride*, March 21, 2020, https://www.pride.com/celebrities/2020/3/21/taylor-swift-vindicated-after-full-2016-kanye-west-phone-call-leaks, last accessed: July 1, 2021; Nate Jones, 'Now That No One Cares Anymore, Who Was Right in the Kanye-Taylor Feud?', *Vulture*, March 28, 2020, https://www.vulture.com/2020/03/taylor-swift-kanye-west-who-was-right.html, last accessed: July 1, 2021; Verity Sulway, 'Kim Kardashian and Kanye West's lies in full as Taylor Swift is vindicated at last', *Mirror*, March 23, 2020, https://www.irishmirror.ie/showbiz/celebrity-news/kim-kardashian-kanye-wests-lies-21739005#comments-wrapper, last accessed: July 1, 2021; Bryan Rolli, 'Kanye West Needs Taylor Swift', *Forbes*, March 24, 2020, https://www.forbes.com/sites/bryanrolli/2020/03/24/kanye-west-needs-taylor-swift/, last accessed: July 1, 2021; Jen McDonnell, 'Taylor Swift Vindicated as Leaked Kanye West Tape Surfaces', *Dose*, March 22, 2020, http://dose.ca/2020/03/22/taylor-swift-kanye-west-leak-phone/, last accessed: July 1, 2021; Alex Clark, '4 Years Later Swifties Are Finally Vindicated: Taylor Swift Did Tell The Truth About Kanye West', *Evie Magazine*, March 23, 2020, https://www.eviemagazine.com/post/4-years-later-swifties-are-finally-vindicated-taylor-swift-did-tell-the, last accessed: July 1, 2021.

V.1 The **FAMOUS** Feud in Western Mass-Media

TABLE 45. LIST OF NEWS SOURCE WITH NEGATIVE/SHADDY VIEWS ABOUT TAYLOR SWIFT IN THE **FAMOUS** FEUD

SOURCE	AUTHOR	TITLE	DATE OF PUBLICATION	LAST ACCESSED
ROLLING STONE	BRITANNY SPANOS	Hear Taylor Swift Approve Kanye West's 'Famous' Lyrics	JULY 18, 2016	SEPTEMBER 2, 2019
ROLLING STONE	ELISABETH SHERMAN	Why Taylor Swift's 'Famous' Objection Still Rings True	JULY 18, 2016	SEPTEMBER 2, 2019
SEVENTEEN	HANNAH ORENSTEIN	People Are Celebrating the Anniversary of Kim Kardashian and Taylor Swift's Drama Today'	JULY 17, 2017	SEPTEMBER 2, 2019
BUZZFEED	ELLIE WOODWARD	How Taylor Swift Played The Victim For A Decade And Made Her Entire Career	JANUARY 31, 2017	SEPTEMBER 2, 2019
THE DAILY BEAST	AMY ZIMMERMAN	How Kim Kardashian Beat Taylor Swift at Her Own Game	JULY 18, 2016	SEPTEMBER 2, 2019
THE DAILY BEAST	AMY ZIMMERMAN	Taylor Swift's History of Suing Friends, Fans, and Foes—and Now Kimye?	JULY 23, 2016	SEPTEMBER 2, 2019
THE DAILY BEAST	AMY ZIMMERMAN	Kim Kardashian and Kanye West Are Rich, in Love, and Mourning Taylor Swift: 'I Was Such a Fan of Hers'	JULY 28, 2016	SEPTEMBER 2, 2019
THE DAILY BEAST	KEVIN FALLON	Can Taylor Swift Survive Kim Kardashian's Snapchat Burial?	JULY 18, 2016	SEPTEMBER 2, 2019
THE DAILY BEAST	AMY ZIMMERMAN	Taylor Swift Hasn't Shed Her Old Skin. She's Still Playing the Victim	AUGUST 25, 2017	SEPTEMBER 2, 2019
NEW STATESMAN	ANNA LESZKIEWICZ	Kim Kardashian vs Taylor Swift: a battle of two PR styles	JULY 18, 2016	SEPTEMBER 2, 2019
NEW STATESMAN	ANNA LESZKIEWICZ	Taylor Swift's troubled relationship with revenge	SEPTEMBER 1, 2017	SEPTEMBER 2, 2019
BILLBOARD	ASHLEY MONAE	Kanye & Kim or Taylor Swift: Who Won the Feud? Media Critics Weigh In	JULY 19, 2016	SEPTEMBER 2, 2019
POPFRONT	ADMIN8	Swiftly to the alt-right: Taylor subtly gets the lower case kkk in formation	SEPTEMBER 5, 2017	SEPTEMBER 2, 2019
POPFRONT	ADMIN8	Taylor Swift tries to silence Popfront with cease and desist letter	NOVEMBER 6, 2017	SEPTEMBER 2, 2019
COMPLEX	NOLAOJOMU	Taylor Swift Has a Long History of Omitting Facts to Fit Her Own Narrative	JULY 2, 2019	SEPTEMBER 2, 2019
COMPLEX	LAUREN M. JACKSON	The Delicious, Blinkered Hypocrisy of Taylor Swift's "Look What You Made Me Do"	AUGUST 30, 2017	SEPTEMBER 2, 2019
MADAME NOIRE	VERONICA WELLS	Taylor Swift, Kanye West And The Perpetuation Of The "Intimidating Black Man" Myth	JULY 18, 2016	SEPTEMBER 2, 2019

TENNESSEAN	BEAU DAVIDSON	It's time to call out Taylor Swift's hypocrisy and privilege | Opinion	DECEMBER 28, 2019	JULY 25, 2021
THE DAILY BEAST	AMY ZIMMERMAN	It's Time for Taylor Swift to Denounce Her Neo-Nazi Admirers	AUGUST 6, 2017	SEPTEMBER 2, 2019
SEVENTEEN	HANNAH ORENSTEIN	People Are Celebrating the Anniversary of Kim Kardashian and Taylor Swift's Drama Today	JULY 17, 2017	SEPTEMBER 2, 2019
NEW YORK TIMES	JON CARAMANICA	Kim Kardashian West and Kanye West Reignite Feud With Taylor Swift	JULY 18, 2016	SEPTEMBER 2, 2019
JUNKEE	JARED RICHARDS	Taylor Swift, You Need To Calm Down, Because Pride Isn't About Straight People	JUNE 18, 2019	SEPTEMBER 2, 2019
TELL TALES	NO NAME	https://www.telltalesonline.com/20889/taylor-swift-liar-kanye-west-famous: the link does not work, it was replaced with the link of the articles written in the next column. However, I saved the context of the article and it was used in this report.	DUE TO LACK OF ACCESS TO THIS ARTICLE, THERE IS NO DATE AVAILABLE	SEPTEMBER 2, 2019
TELL TALES	ANGELA STEPHANOU	Kanye West and Taylor Swift: A Timeline of Their Feud	FEBRUARY 24, 2016, Updated later with information about the feud until August 25, 2017	SEPTEMBER 2, 2019
THE WASHINGTON POST	EMILY YAHR	Is Taylor Swift a hypocrite or just a really savvy songwriter?	JULY 20, 2016	SEPTEMBER 2, 2019
FSUNEWS	MACKENZIE JAMIESON	Look what you made me write, Taylor Swift	NO DATE AVAILABLE IN THE ARTICLE, HOWEVER THE CONTENT SHOWS THAT THE ARTICLE MIGHT HAVE BEEN PUBLISHED AT THE END OF AUGUST 2017	SEPTEMBER 2, 2019
ELLE	ANGELICA JADE BASTIÉN	In Kimye Vs. Taylor, No One Wins	JULY 22, 2016	SEPTEMBER 2, 2019
VICE	GRACE MEDFORD	Criticizing Taylor Swift Isn't About Negativity Towards Successful Women, It's About Vindication	JULY 20, 2016	SEPTEMBER 2, 2019
		Taylor Swift Isn't Like Other Celebrities, She's Worse: this title at some points was not		

VICE	RICHARD S. HE	available on their page, however, I saved the article. You can find the original article ere. I do not know if the new link and page is the original article that I read in 2016.	JULY 2016	SEPTEMBER 2, 2019
VICE	SADY DOYLE	The Depressingly Predictable Downfall Of Taylor Swift	AUGUST 31, 2017	SEPTEMBER 2, 2019
NEWS.COM. AU	JAMES WEIR	Taylor Swifts reign comes crashing down: Has she caught a case of the Anne Hathaways?	JULY 15, 2016	SEPTEMBER 2, 2019
THE GUARDIAN	BRIDIE JABOUR	Taylor Swift's 'downfall': what the online celebrations really say	JULY 18, 2016	SEPTEMBER 2, 2019
VULTURE	NATE JONES	When Did the Media Turn Against Taylor Swift?	JULY 21, 2016	SEPTEMBER 2, 2019
THE CUT	FRANK GUAN	Now That Taylor Swift Is Definitely Less Innocent Than She Pretends to Be, What's Next?	JULY 19, 2016	SEPTEMBER 2, 2019
NEW YORK POST	HARDEEP PHULL	Why Taylor Swift needs to disappear for her own good	JULY 18, 2016	SEPTEMBER 2, 2019
NEW YORK POST	HARDEEP PHULL	Why is Taylor Swift ghosting the world?	NOVEMBER 9, 2017	SEPTEMBER 2, 2019
THE ATLANTIC	SPENCER KORNHABER	The War Over 'That Bitch'	JULY 18, 2016	SEPTEMBER 2, 2019
SLATE	HEATHER SCHWEDEL	What Do Kim Kardashian's Snapchat "Receipts" Actually Prove About Taylor Swift and Kanye?	JULY 18, 2016	SEPTEMBER 2, 2019
SLATE	KATHRYN VANARENDONK	How Keeping Up With the Kardashians Helps Kim Tell a Better Story Than Taylor	JULY 20, 2016	SEPTEMBER 2, 2019
FORBES	DANI DI PLACIDO	Taylor Swift's Carefully Cultivated Image Is Starting To Crack	JULY 18, 2016	SEPTEMBER 2, 2019
VOX	CONSTANCE GRADY	Taylor Swift is cold-blooded and calculating. That's what makes her a great pop star.	JULY 19, 2016	SEPTEMBER 2, 2019
VOX	CONSTANCE GRADY	A unified theory of Taylor Swift's reputation	MAY 7, 2018	SEPTEMBER 2, 2019
THE VERGE	KAITLYN TIFFANY	Taylor Swift's internet rulebook	AUGUST 27, 2017	SEPTEMBER 2, 2019
MICHIGAN DAILY	CHRISTIAN KENNEDY	The danger of Taylor Swift's privileged pop	AUGUST 27, 2017	SEPTEMBER 2, 2019
THE DAILY FREE PRESS	NASHID FULCHER	FULCHER: Taylor Swift is creating trash, and we're letting it happen	SEPTEMBER 28, 2017	SEPTEMBER 2, 2019
CNET	DANIEL VAN BOOM	How Taylor Swift carefully manipulates her 'Reputation' online	SEPTEMBER 1, 2017	SEPTEMBER 2, 2019
CONSEQUENCE OF SOUND	ALEX YOUNG	Taylor Swift won't stop talking about Kanye West	NOVEMBER 10, 2017	SEPTEMBER 2, 2019

HIP HOP DX	KYLE EUSTICE	Why is Taylor Swift still obsessed with Kanye West?	NOVEMBER 11, 2017	SEPTEMBER 2, 2019
NYLON	HAYDEN MANDERS	What is Taylor Swift's reputation anyway?	NO DATE FOUND IN THE ARTICLE, MOST PROBABLY IT WAS WRITTEN AFTER THE ANNOUNCEMENT OF REPUTATION ALBUM IN AUGUST 2017.	SEPTEMBER 2, 2019
LOYOLA PHOENIX	GIANNI KULLE	Taylor Swift's New "Reputation" Feels Manufactured	NOVEMBER 15, 2017	SEPTEMBER 2, 2019
THE REBEL HEART	NO AUTHOR	Taylor Swift is not done taking shots at Kanye West	NOVEMBER 10, 2017	SEPTEMBER 2, 2019
THE STANDFORD DAILY	UGUR DURSUN	The business of Taylor Swift's 'Reputation'	NOVEMBER 17, 2017	SEPTEMBER 2, 2019
THE IRISH TIMES	JENNIFER GANNON	Taylor Swift: Why is it so difficult to support her?	JUNE 9, 2018	SEPTEMBER 2, 2019
MEDIUM	DEVON MALONEY	Just Like Us: The Rise, Fall, and Future of Taylor Swift, America's Relatable Sweetheart	OCTOBER 6, 2017	SEPTEMBER 2, 2019

In the table below I have extracted, from the articles published above, the most negative, biased and misleading information in explaining the truth of the events of the *Famous* feud. There are also positive parts in these articles, but I selected the negative parts because they were part of the article and can support this investigation to create a better view of the role played by few journalists and experts in spreading the narrative of the *Famous* feud.

The conclusions I have reached are set out below. The journalists from the articles used in this report:

- exaggerated with absurd, manipulative and sleazy interpretations that portrayed the wrong role of Taylor Swift in the *Famous* feud;
- don't bother to explain why Kanye West and Kim Kardashian would not publish the part where the word 'bitch' was mentioned;
- are not a source of accuracy of events and rational conclusions;
- omitted facts and created a narrative where Taylor Swift is presented as a false victim of the feud;

- sided with the perpetrators, Kanye West and Kim Kardashian, and forgot the mission of a genuine journalist: neutrality;
- show superficial thinking and reasoning;
- wrote the articles from the perspective of an invisible witness that saw and listened to everything, like they were there holding the candle;
- failed to follow the exact moments of the narrative and a neutral presentation of the conclusions based on the available information from the players of the feud;
- presented and played the race card where the white woman (Taylor) is trying to harm a black man (Kanye);
- promoted Kanye and Kim's narrative as the only truth;
- draw final conclusions while the feud was in motion and with big gaps in the narrative where all the main players failed to say exactly (the details that mass media was waiting, for other people Taylor Swift's statements were enough) what happened;
- played the judge and executioner of Taylor Swift;
- passionate haters of Taylor Swift?
- failed to hold Kanye and Kim accountable rightly at the same level they did wrongly with Taylor Swift; there are no articles calling Kanye and Kim liars for good reasons as they did with Taylor Swift for the wrong reasons;
- acted and presented the feud as self-entitled to know everything Taylor Swift knows and, in the absence of this information directly from her, justified the negative views written about her;
- the journalists/bloggers forgot or did not want to consider the following option: Taylor Swift has the right to decide what information is out on her own terms, just because she does not confirm all the theories online does not mean she is guilty, the journalists from this report is not the supreme court to decide that lack of information from a feud give them the right to decide who is the perpetrator and the victim.

Despite the negative, misled and biased articles from Western mass-media, this mess can be solved easy: while reading the parts where the negative, misleading and bias is happening, to replace the name of Taylor Swift with Kanye West and Kim Kardashian and vice versa, also switch white with black; this method of reading will allow readers to reach a closer truth about the feud than what the journalists from this report were capable.

It is highly possible to exist more negative and positive articles about the feud which I have not used in this report.

The information you are about to read on the following pages was extracted only with the purpose to research the feud from the perspective of the logical mind of a few journalists from various news agencies. Remember: the articles are based on Taylor Swift's statements from February to July 2016.

TABLE 46. LIST OF NEWS SOURCE WITH BIASED AND MISLEADING INFORMATION ABOUT TAYLOR SWIFT IN THE **FAMOUS** FEUD

SOURCE	TITLE OF THE ARTICLE AND SPECIFIC CONTENT
ROLLING STONE ELISABETH SHERMAN	*Hear Taylor Swift Approve Kanye West's 'Famous' Lyrics* 'Taylor Swift has denied any knowledge of the lyrics prior to the song's official release.'
SEVENTEEN HANNAH ORENSTEIN	*People Are Celebrating the Anniversary of Kim Kardashian and Taylor Swift's Drama Today* 'In case you need a refresher, Kim proved that Kanye asked for Taylor's blessing before including a vulgar lyric about her in his song "Famous." The news dropped like a bombshell — previously, Taylor had acted as if she was upset by the line. And the Snapchats proved that Taylor had planned to act surprised by the lyric the entire time. In one swift Snapchat — pun intended — Kim exposed Taylor's lie and played the trump card in the old Kanye/Taylor feud'. [...] 'Or to quote Taylor's other rival, swish, swish, bish.'
	How Taylor Swift Played The Victim For A Decade And Made Her Entire Career 'Swift had witnessed the negative reaction to "Famous." Her spokesperson said she was never made aware of the lyric: "I made that bitch famous." She reverted back to a well-practised posture: that of victim.' 'Swift's speech at the Grammys was arguably the catalyst for West's wife, Kim Kardashian, stepping in. Three months after the awards ceremony, she told GQ that she believed the speech was a deliberate attempt to "diss" West after he'd done nothing but "follow protocol". She went on to claim that not only had Swift "totally approved" the lyrics in "Famous", but that there was also video footage to prove it.' 'The dominant reaction, however, was a reflection of what the world has been conditioned to see: the "threat" of an "angry" black man terrorising the "innocent" white woman. Even their clothes reflected the racially fuelled victim/villain framework that would define the incident: The image of West,

wearing dark shades and an entirely black outfit, accosting sweet Swift in her white and silver party dress, remains an iconic one.'

'Swift, on the other hand, was able to capitalise on the stereotype of the "angry black man", an archetype that has been described as a "figment of the white imagination", used to incarcerate and oppress black men. For Swift, it was PR gold.'

'It may seem that Swift's posture of victimhood is founded on her relationship with West. But it can, in fact, be traced back to the very beginning of her decade-long career.'

BUZZFEED
ELLIE WOODWARD

'But by the time 1989 came to fruition, Swift had arguably overplayed her hand. In repeating the same narrative with each relationship, she had failed to tread the line between fascination and overexposure. So, ahead of the album's release, she assigned responsibility for the fascination with her love life to the media. By presenting herself as a victim of their coverage, Swift provided a competing and more compelling narrative to counter the increasingly negative rhetoric surrounding her love life.'

'A similar result arose from what became a second strand of PR strategy – the publicity from befriending vulnerable fans online. She gave advice to teens being bullied, thoughtful words and a playlist to a fan experiencing a breakup, a cheque for $1,989 to help pay back a student's loan. But at the heart of this was a shared sense of victimhood, exemplified in a comment she left for a bullied fan: "We go through life with a list of names we've been called. (I have a feeling mine is longer than yours ;)) But it doesn't mean those things are true and it doesn't mean we have to let those terrible names define us in any way, you lovely, BEAUTIFUL girl."'

'The result was twofold: In giving fans advice and inserting herself into their narrative, she encouraged them to connect with the messages she proffered, to buy her albums and pay for her tour tickets, fuelling the Taylor Swift brand. And each time Swift bonded with fans through victimhood, it also resulted in a wealth of positive press attention.'

'In fact, her fragile white femininity is merely a reflection of her privilege. That she felt so acutely victimised by Minaj's tweets and West calling her "that bitch" is proof of her never having experienced oppression.'

'Yet, the image that provoked Kardashian to expose Swift was the one of her standing onstage at the Grammys, using her white feminine fragility to compound the well-worn narrative of her as victim and West as villain, while simultaneously imploring young women to work hard. But, as she stood, flanked by all the people who helped create her Grammy award-winning album, there was not a single other woman onstage.'

'The question is, however, after being exposed playing the victim in plain sight for over a decade, will anyone believe it?'

How Kim Kardashian Beat Taylor Swift at Her Own Game

'In what many are calling the second Lemonade of 2016, Kim Kardashian and Kanye West have totally turned on Taylor Swift. It only took three platforms—print media, reality TV, and Snapchat—to out Swift as two-faced.'

'The final nail in Swift's "Famous" coffin came via Kim Kardashian's Sunday night Snapstory, where she finally leaked the much-hyped footage of hubby Kanye West running his "Famous" lyrics ("I feel like me and Taylor might still have sex / Why? I made that bitch famous") by Swift, who voices her approval. These clips are pretty damning, since Swift has packaged herself as a victim of the explicit track, even referencing it in her Grammys acceptance speech and releasing a statement that she "heard it for the first time when everyone else did and was humiliated."'

THE DAILY BEAST
AMY ZIMMERMAN

'It's a pretty convincing argument—until you remember Swift's first public reaction to "Famous," in which she basically called Kanye out for undercutting her success and taking credit for her accomplishments. Her current insistence that being called a "bitch" was the difference between her recorded consent and her public disapproval is undermined by that initial speech, where she's clearly chastising Kanye based on the concept of his lyrics, not his cuss words.'

'Swift had to search for this note among the many on her phone, giving the impression that she knew the truth would eventually come out and had already worked overtime to craft the most convincing spin.'

'Take her Katy Perry feud; just like with Kanye, Swift publicly painted Perry as the instigator, all but outing the pop star in interviews as the shady friend who inspired her song "Bad Blood."'

Taylor Swift's History of Suing Friends, Fans, and Foes—and Now Kimye?

'Swift, who low-key (but maybe high-key?) has been tapping into virginal white victim tropes her entire career, allegedly threw Kanye under the bus for favorable press.'

'Thank you, Chloë, Miranda, Katy, Calvin, and miscellaneous squad members. It truly takes a village.'

THE DAILY BEAST
AMY ZIMMERMAN

'If Taylor was truly unaware of being on speakerphone—which many think is an outright lie, given Rick Rubin's presence in the room.'

'Back in 2015, Swift was first outed by her own childhood guitar teacher. … Ronnie worked with her for six hours a week, at $32 an hour. Still, he understands why that story never gets told: ‚It's just that their publicity team, that doesn't sell as good> a 36-year-old bald guy taught her. That ain't gonna work."

'But while Ronnie waited years to share his side of the story, Swift's team didn't waste any time taking him to task. About a month after his testimony went public, Cremer received a letter from T(aylor) A(lison) S(wift) Rights Management, threatening to sue him for purchasing the domain name itaughttaylorswift.com. Given the proliferation of Taylor Swift fan sites, it's clear that what Swift was really protecting was her brand as a self-taught songwriting whiz kid. Shockingly, going after the man who taught her her first guitar chords isn't Swift's legal team at its most heartless.'

Can Taylor Swift Survive Kim Kardashian's Snapchat Burial?

'So reads the meme tombstone memorializing the music industry's Empress With No Clothes, stripped naked of her self-victimizing media manipulations by reality TV's Mad Queen.'

THE DAILY BEAST
KEVIN FALLON

'The wife of Kanye West provided video proof that her husband had, indeed, called Swift for her approval to refer to her in the "I feel like me and Taylor might still have sex / Why? I made that bitch famous" lyric in his song "Famous," though Swift's publicist had claimed he never did.'

'Kardashian's videos, however, shone a spotlight—albeit a grainy and at times questionably edited one—on how Swift and her camp manipulate the press and the public, going so far as to even fabricate narratives (cough, Hiddleswift, cough).'

'As The Daily Beast's Amy Zimmerman wrote, Kardashian beat Swift at her own game. Using celebrity power, a PR machine, immeasurable cultural influence, and media masterminding she refocused a spinning, potentially damaging narrative to not just "set the record straight"—once the singular concern in a celebrity controversy, now second to public perception and goodwill—but recast herself as the victimized hero. Swift? Now she's the mean girl.'

Taylor Swift Hasn't Shed Her Old Skin. She's Still Playing the Victim

'While TayTay tried to do damage control, her subsequent statement was fairly unconvincing.'

'Like Donald Trump before her, Swift is clearly trying to turn negative press coverage to her own advantage, placing the blame for her own bad reputation on a third party.'

THE DAILY BEAST
AMY ZIMMERMAN

'The real scandal was the way in which Swift, despite having the heard the song prior to its release, proceeded to play the victim, publicly shaming the rapper for trying to take credit for a young woman's success. Whether or not you agree with Kanye's claim that he made Taylor famous, it's clear Swift only took objection to the sentiment when she saw an opportunity to manipulate the storyline, reframing the entire controversy around her performative feminist agenda. And when you're Taylor Swift, a star who refuses to protest or express an actual political opinion, triumphant displays of girl power are crucial to convincing the world that you're actually a feminist.'

'Since Taylor's machinations have been so widely criticized in the past, it's strange that she would want to double down on her victimhood narrative, further portraying herself as maligned and misunderstood.'

'The problem with "Look What You Made Me Do," leaving aside its questionable musical merits, is that it continues to shift the blame. The very title implies that Swift's reinvention was forced on her by a cruel, conniving world.'

'The old Taylor Swift isn't dead and gone—she's just exploring new revenue streams.'

Kim Kardashian vs Taylor Swift: a battle of two PR styles

'West apologised.'

'During her transformation from underdog to top dog, Swift became representative of everything America privileges: thinness, wealth, a particular brand of blonde, white beauty. Simultaneously, she capitalised on the popularity of social justice movements by incorporating feminism into her appeal – calling herself a feminist in interviews, heavily publicising her female friendships online.'

NEW STATESMAN
ANNA LESZKIEWICZ

'Now, instead, we get overly posed shots of her birthday and 4 July parties, crowded with famous faces. It feels colder, more try-hard, and more fake – to the extent that people are wondering if her current relationship is, in fact, an elaborate prank. (If it was intended as a distraction from this oncoming storm, it hasn't worked.)'

'Her latest Instagram post is a real case in point: a screenshot of the Notes app has, "um, and seventh of all…" quality of someone who is rambling because they lack an obvious response, like a bad lie. The "back to search" option also reveals that she has searched for the post in her phone, suggesting it was written a long time ago in preparation for this day, and revealing the PR machine whirring in the background. "I would very much like to be excluded from this narrative." Like any celebrity, Taylor Swift has long tried to control the media narrative surrounding her life. Now, she has lost some of that control. And she wants out.'

Kanye & Kim or Taylor Swift: Who Won the Feud? Media Critics Weigh In

'However, Swift denied approving the song and specified she was not made aware of the "I made that bitch famous line," which she deemed offensive and derogatory.'

Iyana Robertson, music editor, BET:

'and Taylor Swift got caught in a conversation she claims she didn't have.'

'Much can be said about where this all leaves artistic license, but the victim buck stops here. Sorry, Taylor Swift.'

Sylvia Obell, pop culture writer, BuzzFeed:

'But like, girl, those who have been paying close attention haven't forgotten your rep's statement saying that Ye "did not call for approval" and that you cautioned him about releasing a song with "such a strong misogynistic message." Last I checked, saying you take something as compliment isn't very cautionary. And her attempt to play victim is a cheap shot because none of this would have happened if she hadn't lied about being blindsided by all of this in the first place. Kim did not start this, she just finished it. Taylor just needs to take her first big L like a G (the way Beyoncé, Kendrick, and all the other artists who didn't deserve to lose to her at various award shows did) and move on. People bounce back from bad videos everyday, just look at Kim.'

Sowmya Krishnamurthy, freelance music & pop culture contributor:

BILLBOARD
ASHLEY MONAE

'Taylor Swift's doe-eyed, good girl facade has been effectively stripped. She lied about her approval of "Famous" and Kanye West has been vindicated.'

Stacy-Ann Ellis, assistant editor, Vibe:

'So it (ashamedly) thrilled me to see Kimberly Kardashian-West pull all the receipts from the bottom of her Balenciaga bag to silence Taylor's nagging, victim-y ways. It made me admire Kim in a whole new way. Not only did she make the journalist in me smile by having all her sources handy, credible and downright undeniable, but she doled out a valuable lesson in patience.'

'...the footage was shared silently but widely via Kim's Snapchat after an episode of KUWTK—also made me tip my hat to Kimye in regards to their unwavering loyalty to each other. Even when no one believed 'Ye's claims that he received Swift's blessing, Kim stood by her husband's words and stepped out on a limb to clear his name in the pettiest, most public (but perfect) way possible. Salute, Kim.'

Michael Lewittes, founder, GossipCop.com

'From a perception standpoint, the win goes to Kim Kardashian and Kanye West because the public seems to believe Taylor Swift lied about ever having a conversation with West. But from a factual standpoint, Swift never denied they spoke. In fact, her rep very carefully told Gossip Cop back in February, "Taylor was never made aware of the actual lyric, 'I made that bitch famous.'" There was no denying — or her lying — about talking to West. Swift is the proper winner, while Kardashian is the more popular winner.'

Stephanie "Eleven8" Ogbogu, editor, Baller Alert:

'The faux tears and Grammy speeches become null and void because now the truth is out, Taylor was totally in on it. She even thanked Yeezy for having the decency to reach out to her before dropping the song. Do you know what this means? It means Taylor Swift will forever be known as a liar. It means that Calvin Harris, Katy Perry, and whoever else has beefed with her in the past, were right. It means that every time Taylor Swift pretended to be shocked that she won an award, she really wasn't shocked at all. If I can't trust Taylor Swift, who can I trust?'

'Now I'm torn because as much as I couldn't stand Kim Kardashian before, Taylor Swift made me like her. For that reason, I'll never forgive Taylor Swift."'

Swiftly to the alt-right: Taylor subtly gets the lower case kkk in formation

'But the most notable moment of the Taylor-as-an-innocent-victim narrative may have come when Kanye West interrupted her Best Female Video acceptance speech at the 2009 Video Music Awards to drunkenly ramble about how Beyoncé should have won.'

'... it also looked like the personification of many a long-standing white fear: a black man taking away a white woman's power. And Taylor has been playing off that narrative ever since, while America has embraced the notion of white victimhood — despite the reality.'

'Taylor's lyrics in "Look What You Made Me Do" seem to play to the same subtle, quiet white support of a racial hierarchy.'

'At one point in the accompanying music video, Taylor lords over an army of models from a podium, akin to what Hitler had in Nazis Germany. The similarities are uncanny and unsettling.'

POPFRONT
ADMIN8

'Later in the song, there is another telling line: "I don't like your kingdom keys. They once belonged to me. You asked me for a place to sleep. Locked me out and threw a feast (what?)." These lyrics are the most explicit in speaking to white anger and affirming white supremacy. The lyrics speak to the white people resentful of any non-white person having a position of power and privilege.'

'And considering Taylor's fan base is mostly young girls, does the song also serve as indoctrination into white supremacy?'

'It is hard to believe that Taylor had no idea that the lyrics of her latest single read like a defense of white privilege and white anger — specifically, white people who feel that they are being left behind as other races and groups start to receive dignity and legally recognized rights. "We will not be replaced" and "I don't like your kingdom keys" are not different in tone or message. Both are saying that whites feel threatened and don't want to share their privilege.'

'Quiet racism only needs subtle encouragement, and it seems that 'look what you made me do' fits the criteria perfectly.'

'Taylor is giving support to the white nationalist movements through lyrics that speak to their anger, entitlement, and selfishness.'

'it befits the movement to have a white, blonde, conservative pop star that has no doubt been "bullied" by people of color in the media, singing their feelings out loud'

'So Taylor's silence is not innocent, it is calculated.'

'silence in the face of injustice means support for the oppressor.'

Taylor Swift tries to silence Popfront with cease and desist letter

POPFRONT
ADMIN8

'At a time when the press is under constant attack from the highest branches of government, this cease and desist letter is far more insidious than Swift and her lawyer may understand. The press should not be bullied by legal action nor frightened into submission from covering any subject it chooses. Swift's scare tactics may have worked in the past, but PopFront refuses to back down because we believe the First Amendment is more important than preserving a celebrity's public image.'

Taylor Swift Has a Long History of Omitting Facts to Fit Her Own Narrative

'But for some Taylor Swift fans, like myself: fake friend who wants to destroy your image in the name of being nice and honest.'

'Swift has a habit of omitting details during these public disputes, in an attempt to frame a narrative of herself as a victim, even when she doesn't need to.'

'Swift then made a dig at her frenemy during the acceptance speech for Album of the Year at the Grammys later that month.'

COMPLEX
NOLAOJOMU

'Proving that West and Swift did talk about her name being mention in the song, the video revealed that Taylor even gave her approval for him to rap about them having sex one day.'

'But the question remains: Why didn't she just say West had called, but he hadn't played her the full track? Or perhaps tell fans that he had failed to run the final version by her before release? Why lie entirely and claim he never contacted her when she knew he had? Why was she continuing to omit certain details from these disputes to fit her narrative?'

'Admitting the conversation took place wouldn't have stopped people from supporting her with regards to West's choice of lyrics, or for the music video he made for the song. But in her attempt to play the victim, Swift changed the narrative and allowed herself to get caught in a lie.'

'It's time for Taylor Swift to stop clinging to the victim narrative.'

The Delicious, Blinkered Hypocrisy of Taylor Swift's "Look What You Made Me Do"

COMPLEX
LAUREN M. JACKSON

'She's greedy. She's a mean girl. She runs through Hollywood boyfriends like toilet paper. She's anti-feminist, reinforcing dated gender norms and "playing the victim" whenever it suits her agenda. She embodies white womanhood in all its convoluted phases. Or, as The Read's Kid Fury puts it, "a physical embodiment of white lies... walking around in beautiful gowns."'

'Swift "continues to shift the blame," says The Daily Beast's Amy Zimmerman on the single. Despite the social media cleanse, snake metaphors, and lyrics ("I'm sorry, the old Taylor can't come to the phone right now. Why? Oh, 'cause she's dead") that suggest schlepping off her old selves, "Look What You Made Me Do" "double[s] down on her victimhood narrative, further portraying herself as maligned and misunderstood."'

Taylor Swift, Kanye West And The Perpetuation Of The "Intimidating Black Man" Myth

'But for whatever reason, Taylor Swift seems to be hellbent on perpetuating this narrative that Kanye West is the villain in her story. While I think Taylor is an exceptionally talented songwriter and artist, I can't stand the way she behaves in public. I shake my head when the camera insists on panning to her dancing awkwardly at award shows. I roll my eyes and kiss my teeth every time she acts shocked and stunned when she wins an award at these shows. And when she took the stage at this year's Grammys to accept and award of Album of the Year and slam Kanye for a lyric in his song, "Famous," I almost vomited.'

'Though she tried to play the victim in the incident, all of it came back to bite her in the butt when Kim Kardashian uploaded a few SnapChat videos of Kanye speaking to Taylor specifically about the line.'

MADAME NOIRE
VERONICA WELLS

'"Taylor does not hold anything against Kim Kardashian as she recognizes the pressure Kim must be under and that she is only repeating what she has been told by Kanye West. However, that does not change the fact that much of what Kim is saying is incorrect. Kanye West and Taylor only spoke once on the phone while she was on vacation with her family in January of 2016 and they have never spoken since. Taylor has never denied that conversation took place. It was on that phone call that Kanye West also asked her to release the song on her Twitter account, which she declined to do. Kanye West never told Taylor he was going to use the term 'that bitch' in referencing her. A song cannot be approved if it was never heard. Kanye West never played the song for Taylor Swift. Taylor heard it for the first time when everyone else did and was humiliated. Kim Kardashian's claim that Taylor and her team were aware of being recorded is not true, and Taylor cannot understand why Kanye West, and now Kim Kardashian, will not just leave her alone."'

'One minute she's about love and light and forgiveness, taking pictures with Kanye, singing songs dedicated to him, ki-ki-ing on the phone and the next she's playing victim in the public eye.'

'She and her people could have easily said that while Taylor thought the "have sex" or "made her famous" line was tongue in cheek, she didn't appreciate being called "that bitch." It's still a valid concern. But it's the lies and half truths she tells that make me sick.'

'The narrative of the beautiful, frail, helpless White woman being bullied, attacked, or intimidated by the strong, overpowering Black man is one this country knows all too well. In fact, it's this narrative of the "threatening" Black man that we're fighting against today.'

'but she's made it clear that she has been emotionally threatened by his words and thoughts.'

'But don't make it more than it really is to gain sympathy. Don't one minute call Kanye your friend, saying that you'll always respect him and then the next, when you're speaking to the public, wonder why Kanye and his wife won't leave you alone. They won't leave you alone because they thought y'all were cool. They won't leave you alone because you gassed him all the way up on the phone. Kim, specifically, won't leave you alone because you keep trying to make her husband the big, Black, bad guy because it suits your career.'

'And it's this narrative of the inherently threatening, intimidating, bullying, dangerous Black man that is causing so many innocent ones to lose their lives at the hands of police officers who, like Taylor, benefit from perpetuating such a story.'

'I'm never here for that. But at this time, when this narrative is causing us to literally lose our lives, Taylor can miss me with her sob stories.'

It's time to call out Taylor Swift's hypocrisy and privilege | Opinion

'It's time someone spoke out against Taylor Swift.'

'Media are afraid to do it;'

'the industry is afraid to do it'

'and even those artists who have feuded with her have never really questioned her motives'

'Because Swift has a large online presence'

'rabid fans and a big bank account'

'she has remained relatively immune to criticism'.

'No one even dares to criticize her lacking vocal talent'

TENNESSEAN
BEAU DAVIDSON

'Big Machine Label Group, the label that gave Swift her start and, truly, her entire career'

'yet her own father negotiated her original label deal because he was filthy rich. How many singers get that luxury?'

'Taylor's true privilege'

'Swift forgot where she came from and the people who made her a star'

'Her dad bought her way in, Borchetta got her on radio, and now, the label is the bad guy?'

'Notice that Swift never appears at the CMAs or any country events anymore. Ever wonder why?'

'She has bitten the hands that fed her'

'It's highly hypocritical for her to rally against bullying when that is precisely what she just did to her former label, resulting in death threats, using conflated, false information to do so.'

'Rarely does anyone speak out against Taylor Swift, but the time has come'

'She is a pandering phony and an even bigger bully who needs to mature rather quickly.'

It's Time for Taylor Swift to Denounce Her Neo-Nazi Admirers

THE DAILY BEAST
AMY ZIMMERMAN

'Swift condemned Kanye's lyrics, harnessed this victimhood for her public image, was thwarted by leaked footage of Kanye running the track by her in the studio and then reduced to a Notes app statement—are already the stuff of legend.'

'Not only did she refuse to endorse a presidential candidate—she wouldn't even denounce the candidate who was accused of serial sexual assault. Given Swift's history of failing to do the bare minimum.'

Kim Kardashian West and Kanye West Reignite Feud With Taylor Swift

NEW YORK TIMES
JON CARAMANICA

'Throughout this battle, each has accused the other of dishonesty'

'But her stern response to the song's release served as a reassertion of the old order. It also extended a narrative in which Kanye West, who is black, is painted as the predator and Taylor Swift, who is white, as the prey, a story with uncomfortable racial overtones.'

---

https://www.telltalesonline.com/20889/taylor-swift-liar-kanye-west-famous:
(the link does not work, it was replaced with the link of the articles written in the next column; however, I saved the context of the article and it was used in this report)

'1. In her original statement, Taylor claimed – "Kanye did not call for approval". – LIE!
'We clearly heard Kanye seek approval for the song in the recording, and we heard Taylor give her full consent.'

'2. "She cautioned him about releasing a song with such a strong misogynistic message. Taylor was never made aware of the actual lyric, "I made that bitch famous." – LIE!
If Taylor wasn't aware of the "bitch" lyric in question, what "misogynistic message" did she warn Kanye about, specifically? She'd already approved the line about "Kanye having sex" with her, calling it a "compliment", so what other line could it be? This ultimately proves that she was indeed knowledgeable of the "bitch" lyric. It's also strange that Taylor approved the "sex" line but not the "bitch" line. We'd assume the former was more offensive.'

TELL TALES
NO NAME

'3. In her latest statement, Taylor said, "Where is the video of Kanye telling me he was going to call me 'that bitch' in his song? It doesn't exist because it never happened." – LIE!
Once again, it couldn't be more obvious that Taylor was WELL aware of this lyric. The proof lies in the phone call when she tells Kanye, "Like, you obviously didn't know who I was before [the 2009 VMAs]. It doesn't matter if I sold 7 million of that album before you did that, which is what happened. You didn't know who I

was before that…It's awesome that you're so outspoken and it's gonna be like, "Yeah, she does, it made her famous."" In what other context would this comment make sense, except in regards to a line about him making her famous?'

'4. At the Grammy Awards, Taylor said she was upset with Kanye for trying to "take credit for her accomplishments and her fame" – LIE!
If Taylor hates people taking credit for her accomplishments and fame, why then, in the phone call, did she agree that the 2009 VMAs incident helped make her famous? Why then, did she say her album sales were insignificant before Kanye stormed the stage that night? Taylor even admitted in the recording that she doesn't think anyone would find the song offensive. Her acceptance speech was based on nothing but lies, in an attempt to defame Kanye.'

'5. Taylor was upset with Kanye for calling her a "bitch in front of the entire world" – LIE!
Like Kanye said, "Bitch is an endearing term in hip hop". Why is Taylor suddenly a stranger to the word "bitch" when she claims to listen to rap and says that Kanye West's College Dropout was the "first album she ever bought"? You'd think she was accustomed to hearing that word! Taylor Swift isn't just a liar, but a hypocrite, too.'

Kanye West and Taylor Swift: A Timeline of Their Feud

'Maybe Kanye had a right to call Taylor a "fake ass".'

'Remember when she denied ever approving Kanye's Famous lyrics? Well, in July 2016, Kim Kardashian published a recording of a telephone call between Kanye and Taylor, where she was HEARD fully approving the lyrics in question. Here is part of that conversation:

TELL TALES
ANGELA
STEPHANOU

Taylor Swift: Yeah. I mean, go with whatever line you think is better. It's obviously very tongue-in-cheek either way. And I really appreciate you telling me about it, that's really nice!

Kanye West: Yeah. I just felt I had a responsibility to you as a friend. I mean, thanks for being so cool about it.'

'After being exposed as a liar, Taylor took to Twitter to defend herself, insisting that she never knew Kanye would call her "that bitch" in his song.'

'After dissecting her statement, however, we discovered that Taylor might indeed be a liar. It seems she was very much aware of all the lyrics in Kanye's song.'

Is Taylor Swift a hypocrite or just a really savvy songwriter?

THE WASHINGTON POST
EMILY YAHR

'Swift, who at first gave the impression that she condemned the song, is now heard in a phone call with West (one that went viral when Kardashian leaked it on Snapchat Sunday) telling the rapper she knows he's being "tongue-in-cheek" and that she appreciated him giving her a heads-up. "I never would have expected you to tell me about a line in one of your songs," she said. "It's a really cool thing to do — and a really good show of friendship."'

'It is a rare thing for an artist to do. As everyone knows, Swift's empire was fueled by her extremely successful songs that are — in part — so popular because she hints that they're written about real-life people, which generally sparks a media frenzy and more publicity. Yet there's no indication that she's given a warning to these subjects. So is Swift a hypocrite? Or is she just a really savvy songwriter who knows the best way to help sell millions of albums is to get fans invested in your personal life?

Look what you made me write, Taylor Swift

'Unfortunately, this single plays right into these claims with the title of the song itself literally discarding any sense of responsibility. Not to mention how cringy the lyrics are, with "The role you made me play/Of the fool, no, I don't like you" and "I'm sorry, the old Taylor can't come to the phone right now"/"Why?"/"Oh, 'cause she's dead!"' being by far the most infantile.'

'Also, it's been over a year since her beef with Kanye West and Kim Kardashian was blasted all over social media. This seems too late for a diss track, let alone a whole album dedicated to making Kanye West just roll his eyes once, probably.'

FSUNEWS
MACKENZIE JAMIESON

'There is a third theory but it's so abysmal that I desperately try to forget it. It's the "Taylor Swift Just Sucks Now" theory.

The "Taylor Swift Just Sucks Now" theory:

She's a 27-year-old who can't seem to learn how to forgive and move on, despite her efforts to seem easy, breezy, beautiful covergirl in "Shake It Off." She's perfectly capable of writing an album that isn't simply one giant "heck off" to Kanye West and still being super successful and beloved, but she won't. Taylor Swift sucks now, but maybe she always has.'

'I don't like this new Taylor, I don't like this single and I definitely don't like that the album is set to drop on November 10th, the anniversary of Kanye West's mother's death. As anyone who's listened to *College Dropout* or *Graduation* knows, Donda West was the biggest influence on Kanye and his music. To drop a Kanye-diss album on the anniversary of the hardest day of his life is definitely too far by anyone's standards.'

'Taylor could claim ignorance before, but by now she's had to have heard this fact and if she doesn't move the album release date she's going to lose a lot of love from fans and defenders. Whether she does this and whether the rest of her album stands far above this garbage single is yet to be determined, but until then I think it's fair to say that Taylor is far, far from being out of the woods.'

In Kimye Vs. Taylor, No One Wins

'Swift's white victimhood complex and Kanye's gross misogyny are fueling this drama, and no one is a winner.'

'If Swift prefers the role of the innocent victim, West makes a perfect foil.'

'It's the 2009 VMA stage, redux: the innocent white woman being bothered by the black man who doesn't know his place.'

'If Swift had chosen to focus on West's misogynistic desire to control the images and bodies of women, she might have garnered more public sympathy. But that would have required her to care about all women—particularly women of color—and not just her own interests.'

'With just a few Snapchats, the cracks in Swift's white victimhood complex have become more visible.'

ELLE
ANGELICA JADE
BASTIÉN

Criticizing Taylor Swift Isn't About Negativity Towards Successful Women, It's About Vindication

'Kim Kardashian's big reveal doesn't "character assassinate" anyone; it liberates Kanye from the vilification that Taylor Swift has launched her career off.'

'Taylor was trapped in what seemed to be a complex and rotten lie.'

'Taylor was quick, almost too quick, to post a statement to her Instagram page'

'What we can unpack following Kim K's big reveal, is the way in which Taylor's team continually denied any claims that she had been approached for approval on "Famous" in any way.'

'The chronicle of Taylor, the innocent white girl, and Kanye, the bullying black demon.'

VICE
GRACE MEDFORD

'When it suited, Taylor was a victim of Kanye. When that no longer suited, she endeavored to ingratiate herself with him – she invited him to dinner, she publicly thanked him for a gift of a floral arrangement, she stood side by side with his wife as he performed at the BRIT Awards – and when he received a Vanguard at the same awards show that started the drama, it wasn't one of his many friends or peers that handed it to him, it was Taylor Swift. This shifting narrative is one that

Taylor has actively participated in, perpetuated and leveraged to her personal advantage. So that's perhaps why retconning herself as an unwilling passenger in light of the "Famous" lyrics doesn't wash in an Internet age of eternal memory'

'But the reductionist notion that this is all about Taylor being a woman – rather than about her being manipulative or caught in a lie – simply underpins the lazy and prejudice 'victim and aggressor' narrative that has always been the mainstream media's portrayal of the Kanye West and Taylor Swift story.'

'When the shoe went to the other foot, Kanye called Taylor as "a good person and a friend" to ask for her blessing regarding the lyrics on "Famous". Taylor appeared to give her approval, then turned her back on Kanye and her word, shifting the narrative back to her advantage. For seven years, she has relied on the fact that, historically, a white woman will always be taken at her word over a black man. You could say she was relying on it to ride her out on this "Famous" controversy, and, until Kim put the receipts on the table, it was working. Don't get me wrong, there is no glee derived from tearing down women, but there is vindication in seeing someone – who has been disingenuous and hypocritical at best, manipulative at worst – being played at their own game.'

VICE
RICHARD S. HE

Taylor Swift Isn't Like Other Celebrities, She's Worse: this title is not available on their page, however, I saved the article. You can find the original article.[155]

'But when Kanye says "Relationships are more important than punchlines", you can tell he means it.'

'Secondly, Taylor isn't feigning politeness. Her press statements painted a picture of disgust, but in the video, her initial response is anything but emotional. "I'm like, this close to overexposure", she says, a rational assessment of how the public will respond to the song. Everything else she says is positive, relaxed, spoken without hesitation. "Go with whatever line you think is better. It's obviously very tongue in cheek either way. And I really appreciate you telling me about it, that's really nice!" By the end of the video, Kanye and Taylor agree on the song's intent, and she implicitly agrees to support him. "It would be great for me to be like, 'Look, he called me and told me about the line before it came out.' Like, joke's on you guys, we're fine."'

'While the conversation's straightforward, Taylor's press statements since have been full of holes. What she objects to is, supposedly, being called "that bitch" in public. So was it "tongue in cheek" in their conversation, but misogynistic on the song itself? Memories distort, but the video's objective. Maybe her emotional response was authentic, maybe she manufactured it to claim a triumphant moment at the Grammys. But without acknowledging her and Kanye's

---

[155] Richard S. He, 'The Public Shaming of Taylor Swift (2016)', *Medium*, February 4, 2022, available at: https://medium.com/@kristenisshe/the-public-shaming-of-taylor-swift-2016-458c12c50fc0, last accessed: July 10, 2022.

conversation from day one, it's looked like she has something to hide. A truth told badly might as well be a lie.'

'Kanye's always practiced radical honesty, often to the detriment of his reputation: really? Why I can't trust you?'

'All Kim had to do was hang Taylor with her own rope, by releasing footage of her being really nice to Kanye. Is that so cruel?'

'She portrays herself as untouchable, above the bullshit of the tabloid media.'

'That's the beauty of being publicly shamed: it certainly can't get any worse.'

The Depressingly Predictable Downfall Of Taylor Swift

'It has been since last July, when Kim Kardashian West released videos of Swift approving the lyrics to Kanye West's "Famous," after Swift had sworn up and down she hated them, and claimed to have cautioned Kanye against the song's "misogynistic message" to boot.'

'I should lay my cards on the table here: I am, to put it mildly, not a Swift fan.'

'She elevates herself by portraying herself as a perfect patriarchal subject—white, polite, and virginal, or at least "romantic"—while bashing other women for their perceived impurity and carnality. Her racial politics are more than tone-deaf. She uses feminism to promote her work, but is not politically engaged when it doesn't benefit her financially.'

VICE
SADY DOYLE

'The backlash is arriving right on schedule, and at the same epic scale.'

'Make no mistake: There are serious and necessary critiques to be made of Taylor Swift. The lie she told about Kanye West was objectively wrong, and drew on a long history of white women perpetuating the idea that black men are predators.'

'Whether or not Swift was consciously aware of the structural racism she was playing into, people are right to be angry at her, and it's disturbing that she's never publicly apologized. It's also troubling that she made it through an entire two-year election cycle without warning her young fans away from Trump.'

'The Swift backlash may be happening in part because, in the age of Ivanka, we're all sick of rich white women who mean well but remain complicit to protect their own profits.'

'The only next step that leaves for her, in a culture that's profoundly threatened by female visibility and power, is to fail, fall apart, or die. Swift knows this. It's why her single — and probably her album cover — both reference the best-known example of the phenomenon, Britney Spears.'

When Did the Media Turn Against Taylor Swift?

VULTURE
NATE JONES

'In a concert review titled "Taylor Swift Is Not Your Friend," Evans wrote:

To think of [Swift] as womanhood incarnate is to trick oneself into forgetting about "Bad Blood" and "Better Than Revenge."
Swift isn't here to help women — she's here to make bank. Seeing her on stage cavorting with World Cup winners and supermodels was not a win for feminism, but a win for Taylor Swift. Her plan — to be as famous and as rich as she can possibly be — is working, and by using other women as tools of her self-promotion, she is distilling feminism for her own benefit.'

'Swift became an embodiment of "white feminism," a brand of progressivism that centers wealthy white women at the expense of everyone else. (Like a hipster or a neoliberal, no one identifies as a white feminist.) Critics soon fell over themselves pointing out that Swift's clique was really just an exclusive group of mostly white actresses and supermodels. As Mic now put it, Swift's #squadgoals were "totally disturbing."'

'instead of a vague sense of Swift controlling events to make herself the victim, there's actual video proof'

Now That Taylor Swift Is Definitely Less Innocent Than She Pretends to Be, What's Next?

THE CUT
FRANK GUAN

'The only point that matters is that Taylor Swift has been exposed as mendacious and disingenuous'

'The sales for her next album won't suffer — spurred by the anticipation of more drama, they'll rise to new heights.'

The War Over 'That Bitch'

THE ATLANTIC
SPENCER
KORNHABER

'Why did the plan fall through? Swift has said she didn't know the call was recorded, and so maybe she simply misremembered its details when her reps put out her initial anti-"Famous" statement. Or maybe she just decided the risks of spinning a story were outweighed by the benefits of objecting to the song.'

'For Swift to allow herself to be called that term in a rap song really would be a betrayal of her own brand.'

What Do Kim Kardashian's Snapchat "Receipts" Actually Prove About Taylor Swift and Kanye?

'Private Taylor is not really a person at all; there is only success robot Taylor.'

'Talking about how many likes an Instagram got is not cool—a cool person would pretend not to care about such things—but Taylor is numbers- and success-oriented. Later, when she cites the sales figures her album had before Kanye ever interrupted her ("It doesn't matter that I sold 7 million of that album before you did that, which is what happened," she says—you can imagine her turning to a camera and winking for that last part), that number, too, is one she has at the ready. It's a little passive-aggressive, a reminder to Kanye that she doesn't think she needs him.'

SLATE
HEATHER
SCHWEDEL

'That's our Taylor: always thinking strategically about her image, how this will affect the big picture of her brand.'

'There are parts of the video where Taylor sounds resigned. "You didn't know who I was before that, it's fine," she says, when that is clearly not fine. Even the effusive thank yous and vows of friendship Taylor offers can be seen in this light—she's used to laying it on thick, weaponizing her sweet personality as a way to further her business interests. When she says, "It's a really cool thing to do and a really good show of friendship," you can hear a hint of falseness in her voice, her willing herself to say what she knows she's supposed to say.'

'No one can pretend to understand her motivations for insisting that Kanye is in the wrong here—Who cares if he called you "that bitch"? Why make a big thing of it? Why continue to fight it?—but it seems like even after this umpteenth, mic drop of a chapter, there's probably still more to this story.'

How Keeping Up With the Kardashians Helps Kim Tell a Better Story Than Taylor

SLATE
KATHRYN
VANARENDONK

'Taylor is furious about something she apparently gave her full approval for. And maybe most importantly, Kim is merely trying to stand up for her husband, who is being publicly excoriated for something that's not his fault.'

'Plus, no matter how much you may wish to erase yourself from the narrative, posting a response to that effect sends a bit of a mixed message.'

Taylor Swift's Carefully Cultivated Image Is Starting To Crack

'Taylor Swift may have been a hard-working country star steadily making a name for herself in 2009, but prior to their now infamous MTV interaction, most of us hadn't a clue who she was. To the majority of the public, Taylor Swift came into being during that fateful moment where he stood on the stage beside her and claimed she was unworthy of the music award she'd worked so hard to win.'

FORBES
DANI DI PLACIDO

'In what must've been, initially, a humiliating experience for Swift, a valuable lesson was learned. Controversy is just another word for attention.'

'Swift doesn't appear to give permission to use the phrase "that bitch." Name calling aside, however, it's clear that Swift is giving her blessing to Kanye to make fun of her, and planning to allow the public to believe that she is offended, until she corrects the situation. Later, she appears to have decided that a full-blown artificial feud would be more lucrative. This time, playing the victim appears to have blown up in her face.'

'In her public appearances and music videos, Swift behaves like a blond bundle of positive energy, all sparkling smile, and ruby-red lips. Beneath the sugar-coating, however, is an incredibly shrewd and intelligent businesswoman with a ruthless streak.'

Taylor Swift is cold-blooded and calculating. That's what makes her a great pop star.

'Well, sure. We all knew she was fake. She's a celebrity. That's part of how being a celebrity works, yes?'

'But the video does seem to contradict much of Swift's original story, which is that West called to ask if he could release the song via her Twitter account, and that she not only declined but also cautioned him against "releasing a song with such a strong misogynistic message." It's within the realm of possibility that we didn't hear the whole phone call, and that West did indeed ask to release the song on Swift's Twitter and Swift told him not to be a misogynist, but there's no proof of that. And considering how chummy and ingratiating Swift sounds in the clips that Kardashian posted to Snapchat, it's difficult to imagine Swift saying something so confrontational within the span of the same conversation.'

VOX
CONSTANCE GRADY

'There's a lot to be said about Swift's reasons for (probably) lying in her initial statement, her history of presenting herself as the victim in every controversy involving her public life, and the racial and gendered nuances of her longstanding feud with West.'

"Hearing Taylor Swift think out loud about how to spin the story, to me, is more damaging than learning that Taylor Swift lied about Kanye West," Vox's Alex Abad-Santos writes. "Kim Kardashian's Snapchat video … confirms that underneath the thick coating of bubblegum pop known as Taylor Swift, there's a shrewd, savvy woman who puts a lot of effort into shaping and maintaining her public image."

'We have proof that Taylor Swift, one of the biggest celebrities in the world, thinks about the way the media perceives her. In the current state of news articles and the methods of interpretating evidence of the feud, it would be stupid not to think about how mass media perceives you.'

'Of course she curates the friends and boyfriends she's seen with in public; of course she thinks about how she'll spin this feud and that photo op into a good headline for the gossip mill. She does it because that's her job, and she's good at it.'

'But it's just as disingenuous for us, the audience, to pretend we're shocked to discover that Swift's persona is constructed — that when we look behind her mask, we're surprised to find she's put a lot of effort into cultivating her image. That's just us making the Taylor Swift Surprised Face at each other over and over again, into eternity.'

A unified theory of Taylor Swift's reputation

VOX
CONSTANCE GRADY

'And then Kim Kardashian West — Kanye West's wife and another celebrity who knows how to work a gossip cycle — released a series of videos that appeared to show Swift signing off on West's lyrics.'

'Swift tried to disavow the whole thing. "I would very much like to be excluded from this narrative, one that I have never asked to be a part of, since 2009," she wrote on Instagram in a now-deleted post. But the lie was too blatant to work. Because it was clear that Swift had asked to be a part of the narrative of her feud with Kanye West — had, if anything, amplified it by writing songs about it and talking about it in her Grammys speech — and that her public image had benefited as a result.'

'But at this point, Swift's ability to hold on to her appeal without uniting both halves of her persona is in serious doubt. The controlling and manipulative side of her persona has come into view to an extent that much of her audience is having trouble believing in the authenticity and intimacy of the other side. So even though Taylor Swift knows exactly what you think of her, for the first time in her career, she seems to be at a loss as to how to change your mind.'

Taylor Swift's internet rulebook

THE VERGE
KAITLYN TIFFANY

'she used the Grammys stage to call out men who wanted to take credit for her success. It was a cloying, cheap speech even before Kim Kardashian stepped up to say that West's phone call asking for permission for at least part of the lyric had been recorded, Swift's laughter and acquiescence included'

'And in the wake of the phone call's reveal on Snapchat, Swift's (since-deleted) tweeted screenshot from the Notes app — now a standard move for celebrities embroiled in controversy — only made things worse.'

The danger of Taylor Swift's privileged pop

'It's somewhat surprising to see the Kanye West vs. Taylor Swift saga reinvigorated by the pop star after West's wife — you may have heard of her, Kim (motherfucking) Kardashian — exposed Swift's conversation with West regarding "Famous" before its release, a conversation Swift conveniently forgot in her reaction to the lyric, "I feel like me and Taylor might still have sex / Why? I made that bitch famous."'

'But in practice, Swift's bid for feminism falls flat: leaving out women of color, women who aren't skinny, women who are poor, etc. etc.. She not only fails to acknowledge the possibility that her privilege as a skinny, attractive white woman has assisted in her rise to prominence, but basically refuses to acknowledge that the sociopolitical systems that benefit her make life and business more challenging for artists of color.'

MICHIGAN DAILY
CHRISTIAN
KENNEDY

'Additionally, when 1989 took Album of the Year over Kendrick Lamar's To Pimp A Butterfly'

'The privilege granted by their skin color that allows them to sacrifice the safety and peace of mind of Americans of color is the exact same privilege that allows Swift to "stay out of politics" and post a non-committal "make your voice heard" Instagram in one of the most critical elections in American history, guaranteeing that she is to lose no popularity or money due to the polarization of her audience.'

'While Beyoncé has the "choice" to stay mum on political topics, the reality is that she lives in a Black body, married to a Black man, raising Black children in 2017. In that reality, today's political climate (and all of American history) presents tangible ways in which her family and friends can be harmed, dehumanized and killed. Political apathy isn't always a "choice."'

'Swift's words and actions manipulate the truth and perpetuate the narrative of white-female victimhood at the hands of black, male villains at a time where it is especially dangerous. Whether she fails to see the sociopolitical tensions she is manipulating or she doesn't care, both of are equally unacceptable.'

FULCHER: Taylor Swift is creating trash, and we're letting it happen

'Between posting naked pictures of herself on Twitter (and embarrassing us all with her phenomenal hips) and defending racist makeup artists, there was only one time and one time alone Kim Kardashian did something that was actually important to me. Kim Kardashian ended Taylor Swift's "America's Sweetheart" phase."

'I have managed to be a Taylor Swift fan for more years than she deserved from me, but it looks that that may be coming to an end."

THE DAILY FREE PRESS
NASHID FULCHER

'After Kanye West's drunken mic-stealing of 2009, she drew the incident out for as many years as possible — writing a song about it, referencing it whenever she possibly could and playing the victim, as she does so well."

'Over the years, Taylor Swift has played her "fragile white feminist" card as often as possible."

'Fairly recently, Kanye West dropped "Famous," in which he claims his 2009 MTV Awards stunt was what made Taylor Swift famous. It didn't. It did help her career."

'Kanye West called to ask for permission and she said it was fine to put the line in the song and he did. Taylor Swift then said she wasn't aware of the line — that he never ran it past her. She accused him of trying to "take credit" for her success.'

'Kim Kardashian was not having that. Kim posted snapchats showing Taylor Swift's conversation with Kanye West, where she approved the lyric. Swift's credibility was shattered in that moment. I was utterly dismayed. I'd always trusted her to never get caught being a liar, so I could enjoy "We Are Never Ever Getting Back Together" and "Dear John" in peace, pretending they weren't about actual people whom she may have actually humiliated by writing a song about.'

'Either way, one thing is clear: accepting white mediocrity in the name of supporting women has been the very basis of her career and it's truly time for it to come to an end.'

Taylor Swift won't stop talking about Kanye West

CONSEQUENCE OF SOUND
ALEX YOUNG

'Taylor Swift's new album, Reputation, officially arrived today and one immediate takeaway is that the singer is still obsessed with Kanye West.'

'Upon the song's release in 2016, Swift claimed no prior knowledge of the lyrical content, but a phone call leaked by West's wife, Kim Kardashian, showed otherwise.'

Why is Taylor Swift still obsessed with Kanye West?

HIP HOP DX
KYLE EUSTICE

'Whatever her ongoing obsession is with West, it's been nearly nine years since West.'

'Not to mention, the Graduation mastermind endured a mental breakdown last year. It looks more like little "Tay Tay" is the bully in this case.'

'Word to the wise: just let it go.'

The business of Taylor Swift's 'Reputation'

THE STANDFORD DAILY
UGUR DURSUN

'As sincere as the letter might have been, there was a strategic reason behind the act. No, Taylor Swift did not care if Apple Music paid her for each of her listeners. She most likely did not care if they paid up-and-coming musicians, either, or any other ethical problem with streaming. Her earnings from the physical album and iTunes downloads, likely increased due to the album's inaccessibility on streaming platforms, did compensate for the lost streaming revenues and hence the lost streaming points on the multi-metric music charts like Billboard Hot 100 Singles Chart or Billboard 200 Albums Chart. "1989" ended up spending 11 weeks atop the albums chart and spawning five top-10 singles, three of which crowned the chart for a combined twelve weeks in 2014 and 2015; she calculated that she could survive without streaming and succeeded.'

Just Like Us: The Rise, Fall, and Future of Taylor Swift, America's Relatable Sweetheart

MEDIUM
DEVON MALONEY

'When Kanye West and Kim Kardashian dared challenge that image by claiming Swift had signed off on West's song "Famous" — "I feel like me and Taylor might still have sex/Why? I made that bitch famous"—and then lied about it to portray herself as West's victim again, it seemed like sour grapes of the highest order. Until it wasn't. And things began falling apart.'

There are also other unfair and hard critics about Taylor Swift, however, the journalist does not bother to criticise the actions of Kanye West and Kim Kardashian toward Taylor Swift.[156]

In the next two sections of this chapter, I used the official statements from Kanye West, Kim Kardashian, Taylor Swift (all available in the table with the timeline of the feud), the extracts of the articles found in the last section, other information available online such as albums released by the artists involved in the feud with the purpose to find strategies of communication and interpretation of the events from the *Famous* feud.

---

[156] Jennifer Gannon, *Taylor Swift: Why is it so difficult to support her?*, Irish Times, June 9, 2018, Available at: https://www.irishtimes.com/culture/music/taylor-swift-why-is-it-so-difficult-to-support-her-1.3520132, last accessed: January 15, 2022.

V.2 Kanye West, Kim Kardashian West and Western Mass-Media

Based on my research, I found similarities of strategies of communication and interpretation used by Kanye West, Kim Kardashian, Taylor Swift and the Western mass-media. As I wrote before, overall, Western mass-media was neutral in presenting the *Famous* feud. Not all the journalists from this report are part of the following strategies of communication and interpretation, even if you will find the word 'journalist', as it is an overall presentation of the strategies found.

1. *'Twist, Twist, Twist'* (Kanye West, Kim Kardashian and journalists):

Kanye West decided to release bits of information which included omitting parts of the conversation about the origins of the song which is valid at the time of publishing. Kanye West did not acknowledge publicly that he added a new line in the song and Taylor Swift was not aware of it. This strategy had a big impact and was used heavily by Taylor Swift's critics (negative) until the spring of 2020 when another video of the conversation between the two artists was leaked on Youtube and Twitter, and the truth came out: Taylor Swift did not know about the line 'I made that bitch famous.' This is a complicated strategy and Taylor Swift was trapped with little effort by Kanye West (the lead actor of this strategy); was used also by journalists.

DIAGRAM 1. *Twist, Twist, Twist*

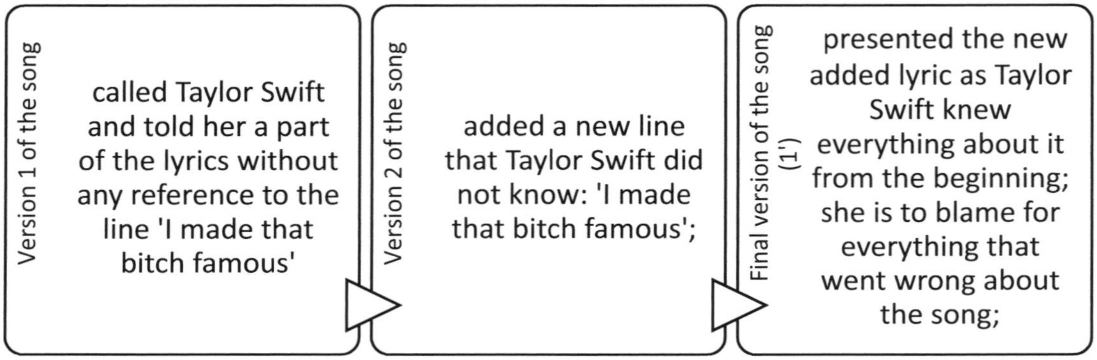

Version 1 of the song	Version 2 of the song	Final version of the song (1')
called Taylor Swift and told her a part of the lyrics without any reference to the line 'I made that bitch famous'	added a new line that Taylor Swift did not know: 'I made that bitch famous';	presented the new added lyric as Taylor Swift knew everything about it from the beginning; she is to blame for everything that went wrong about the song;

2. *'To Protect Kanye West from Taylor Swift'*: journalists and Kim Kardashian.

3. *'Passing the blame on Taylor Swift because she did not agree with Kanye and Kim's side of the story and journalist's expectations of statements regarding her involvement in the making of the song'*: Kanye West, Kim Kardashian and journalists.

4. *50/50*: more by journalists:

- shares Kanye West's mistake with Taylor Swift at the same level (a part of the journalists used in this report), however, for other journalists and bloggers Taylor Swift is to blame for the promotion and negative outcome of the *Famous* song.

DIAGRAM 2. *50/50*

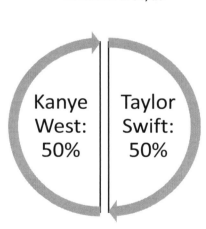

5. *'The Race Card: Black Man (Kanye West) Versus White Privileged Woman (Taylor Swift)'* (journalists):

- in a country presented as racist (USA) Kanye West has earned over a hundred million dollars, lives in multi million dollars house built according to his own vision; received lots of awards and one of the highest reviews in the music industry; the last concert, *Saint Pablo Tour* based on his album *The Life of Pablo*, had a box office of 52.8 millions of dollars[157];

- white woman (Taylor Swift) presented a bad image of a black man (Kanye West), and journalists need to speak the truth, even if Taylor Swift does not want the world to know, and Kanye West cannot do it because the general public does not believe a black man to tell his truth;
- in this feud the black man (Kanye West) is the victim of the white privileged woman (Taylor Swift);
- black man rejected by the society because of the persistent racism;
- black people are less appreciated than white people.

6. *'Stabbing in the Back While Shaking Her Hand'* (Kanye West, Kim Kardashian, journalists):

- was nice on the telephone with Taylor Swift but, after the telephone conversation, he added new lyrics and Taylor was not aware of them, yet Kanye presented the song as she agreed and knew everything about the song; during the telephone conversation Kanye asked Taylor to release his song on her Twitter account; also, Kanye said to Taylor: "Well, this is the thing where I'm calling you, because you're got an army. You own a country of mother—ing 2 billion people, basically, that if you felt that it's funny and cool and like hip-hop, and felt like just "The College Dropout" and the artist like Ye that you love, then I think that people would be like way into it. And that's why I think it's super-genius to have you be the one that says, "Oh, I like this song a lot. Like, yeah, whatever, this is cool, whatever";
- during *The Saint Pablo Tour* he presented his side of the story while people were chanting 'bitch' with reference to Taylor Swift;
- Kim Kardashian published a short video with her singing the lyrics of the *Famous* song: 'I made that bitch famous.'

7. *'Behind the Curtains'* (Kanye West and journalists):

---

[157] Pollstar, *Year End Top 100 Worldwide Tours, January 1, 2016 – December 31, 2016*, available at: https://www.pollstar.com/Chart/2017/01/2016YearEndTop100WorldwideTours_343.pdf, last accessed: October 24, 2020.

- doesn't include the fact that he added the line 'I made that bitch famous' without Taylor Swift's knowledge;
- the cover of his album is a picture with 'look like a white girl' (there are no proof to support that the model if definitely a white person) with a big bottom wearing a bath suit and a black family which depicts a matrimony, also it is written on the cover 'Which/One', the general meaning that readers might have is choosing between the white girl (which is lonely in the picture) or the black family: before the release of the album's cover, Kanye West launched the song with the infamous line ,I made that bitch famous' about Taylor Swift (she is white and according with her dress style in music videos and private life -where there are pictures published on different websites about her in private life- is in opposition with the picture from Kanye West's album cover, Taylor Swift never pictured herself in the way that the white girl (?) is pictured on Kanye West's album cover; maybe the 'look like a white girl' picture on the album cover is a metaphor and artistic representation of Taylor Swift; maybe it's an alternate reality that exists in Kanye West's mind, meaning, to him, that Taylor Swift is just a 'bitch'; maybe it's Kanye West's way of saying about Taylor Swift that in reality she is different from what she wants to promote and he managed to demonstrate her true personality;
- Kim Kardashian, in an interview with GQ magazine, talked about the existence of a telephone conversation between Kanye West and Taylor Swift and said: 'She totally approved that.' […] 'She totally knew that that was coming out. She wanted to all of a sudden act like she didn't': this interview (June 16, 2016) happened in the week that Kanye West started to sale tickets (June 14 for American Express cardholders, June 16 for Tidal members, June 18 for the general public) to his music tour named *Saint Pablo Tour*;
- Kim Kardashian presented a heavily edited video telephone conversation between Kanye West and Taylor Swift at a month after the start of Kanye West's sale of tickets for his music tour;
- a month before the start of Kanye West's *Saint Pablo Tour*, he and Kim Kardashian were on the cover of *Harper's Bazaar* September issue and when asked by editor Laura Brown about their favourite Taylor Swift song, Kanye West replied, 'For me? I don't have one.' Kim Kardashian replied: 'I was such a fan of hers';
- journalists through their negative articles about Taylor Swift.

8. *'The Narrative Line' (Kanye, Kim and journalists):*

- interfered in Taylor Swift's narrative line with negative views about her skills and character, ignoring Kanye's failure to keep his side: he did not send her the final version of the song and the lyrics;
- did not analyse Taylor's statements and her true involvement in the making of the song.

9. *'The Balance of Image and Fame' (Kim Kardashian, Kanye West and journalists):*

- Kanye West is the good black man while Taylor Swift is the bad white woman;

DIAGRAM 3. *The Balance of Image and Fame*

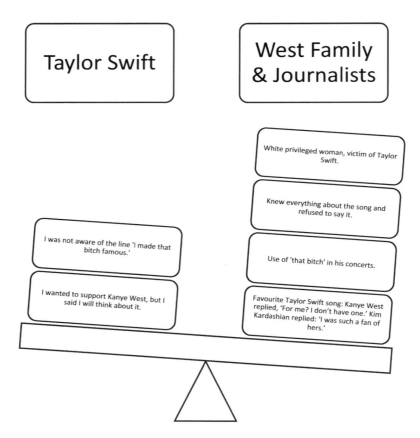

10. *"Til Her Sunshine Is Gone' (Kanye West, Kim Kardashian and journalists):*

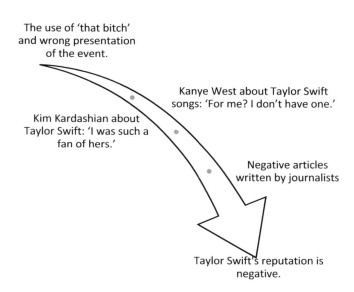

DIAGRAM 4. *Til Her Sunshine is Gone*

The use of 'that bitch' and wrong presentation of the event.

Kanye West about Taylor Swift songs: 'For me? I don't have one.'

Kim Kardashian about Taylor Swift: 'I was such a fan of hers.'

Negative articles written by journalists

Taylor Swift's reputation is negative.

11. *'I Want to be Famous!'* (Kanye West):

- this strategy of communication is based on Kanye's conversation with Taylor Swift encouraging her to accept his deal to promote his song; in other words, Kanye, the black man that made Taylor famous, is asking her to promote his song with the purpose to make people to like his song; if he is the God of rap/hip hop music, then why this act of humiliation in front of Taylor, a white woman? why does the white woman who should not get the award from MTV in 2009, should not win the *Album of the Year* in 2010 and 2016, have to promote and use her fame to persuade people to like the song of a God in rap and hip hop?

DIAGRAM 5. *I Want to be Famous!*

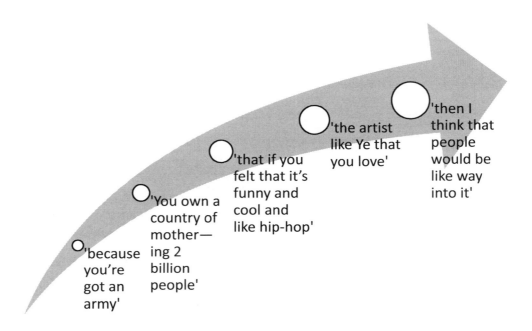

12. *'Controlling the Narrative Line'* (Kim and journalists):

- Taylor Swift is trying to control the narrative line through her music in her favour, and people should not believe her as she is not telling the truth: Kanye West is vindicated because Kim shared the edited conversation and it is the final truth.

13. *'Shine and Die'* (Kanye, Kim and journalists):

DIAGRAM 6. *Shine and Die*

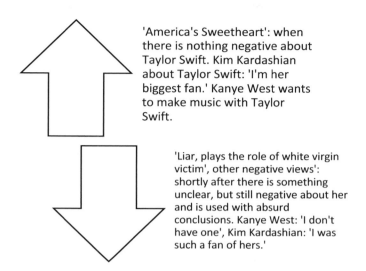

'America's Sweetheart': when there is nothing negative about Taylor Swift. Kim Kardashian about Taylor Swift: 'I'm her biggest fan.' Kanye West wants to make music with Taylor Swift.

'Liar, plays the role of white virgin victim', other negative views': shortly after there is something unclear, but still negative about her and is used with absurd conclusions. Kanye West: 'I don't have one', Kim Kardashian: 'I was such a fan of hers.'

14. *'Calculated'* (journalists):

- because Taylor Swift does not allow the false narrative about her to circulate free without her version of the truth; when Taylor Swift presented her version, journalists wrote in a way to not trust her version as she is *calculated* with the sole purpose to shift the narrative on her, the white victim, while ignoring the truth delivered by journalists and bloggers who were not there to see what happened, and the evidence available is not enough to draw final conclusion and pick the real perpetrator.

15. *'Impoverished people'* (Kanye West during the MTV VMA 2016 and journalists through negative articles):

- during the MTV VMA from 2016, Kanye West mentioned Taylor Swift: 'You know, like, people come up to me like, 'Yeah, that's right! Take Taylor!' But bro, like, I love all y'all. That's why I called her;' however, Kanye West failed to mention the full story behind the phone call and shared only bits of information that put him as the owner of the truth while Taylor is lying;

- Kanye West said: 'My friend Zekiah [sp?] told me there's three keys to keeping people impoverished: that's taking away their esteem, taking away their resources, and taking away their role models;'[158] at the end of his speech Kanye West released the song *Fade* which contains lyrics: 'Your love is fadin', Know it ain't no wrong, I feel it's fadin', I think I think too much, I feel it's fadin;'[159] at this time in 2016, Taylor Swift image is negative and Kanye West was the person behind it, digging her image with biased information about her true involvement in the *Famous* song;
- by presenting one biased side of the story, Kanye West matched at least one step of the strategy presented in his speech: he created a false narrative about Taylor Swift, which is a source of inspiration and model for millions of people; from the point of view of *only Taylor Swift*, through his negative actions, Kanye West maybe tried to take away her esteem.

DIAGRAM 7. *Impoverished people*

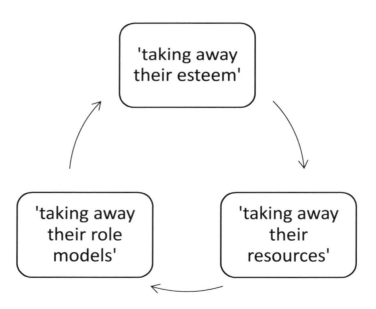

---

[158] For both quotes see: Patrick Hosken, 'Kanye West's 2016 VMA Speech – Here's the Full Transcript', *MTV*, September 28, 2016, available at: http://www.mtv.com/news/2925366/kanye-west-vmas-2016-full-speech-transcript/, last accessed: October 24, 2020.
[159] Kanye West, 'Fade', *Musicmatch*, available at: https://www.musixmatch.com/lyrics/Kanye-West/Fade, last accessed: October 24, 2020.

16. *The Spiral of Silence* (Kim Kardashian and journalists):

- it was used every time against Taylor Swift after she replied to people involved in the negative narrative either by comments or through lyrics of various songs to expose her part of the story;
- *The Spiral of Silence* is a deadly strategy because whatever the victim says is never good enough to prove innocence and the victim is for evermore the perpetrator; the roots of this strategy are found in the theory of Marxism and nowadays in the theory of Neo-Marxism.

DIAGRAM 8. *The Spiral of Silence*

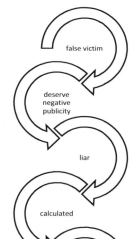

V.3 Taylor Swift

Based on my research, I found similarities of strategies of communication and interpretation used by Taylor Swift and Kanye West, Kim Kardashian and journalists. The difference between them and Taylor Swift is that Taylor's strategies contain a more truthful side of the story. As I wrote before, overall, the Western mass-media is neutral in presenting the

Famous feud. As in the first section of this chapter, with Kanye West, Kim Kardashian and journalists, here we have the same situation: not all the journalists from this report are part of the following strategies of communication and interpretation even if you will find the word 'journalist' as it is an overall presentation of the strategies found and the sources used in this report.

1. *'Long Story Short'*:

- posted short statements about her involvement in the *Famous* song which were not good enough for mass-media to use as evidence of her innocence;
- replied only when her name was mentioned;
- let the story to unfold as Kanye and Kim wanted;
- stopped using social media to talk about the *Famous* song;
- this strategy was used to prove her innocence, but in 2016 was not good enough for some journalists, and people who rejected her evidence and believed Kanye West and Kim Kardashian's side of the story.

DIAGRAM 9. *Long Story Short*

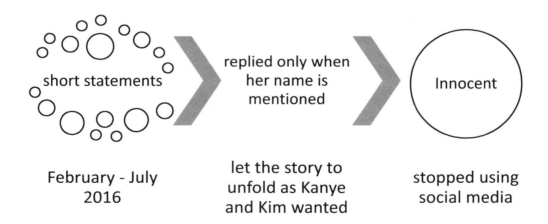

2. *'Meet Me Behind My Statements'*:

- Taylor Swift released various statements about her involvement in the creation of the *Famous* song, from February 2016 until 2020 and the leak of the video with the telephone conversation between her and Kanye West.

DIAGRAM 10. *Meet Me Behind My Statements*

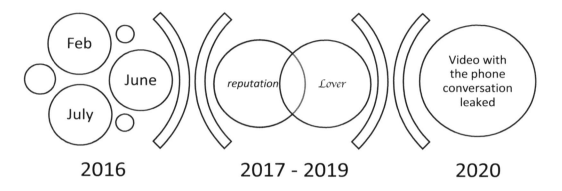

3. *'Teardrops On My Fame'*:

- Kanye West is the bad black man, Kim Kardashian is the bad white woman, while Taylor Swift is the good white woman.

DIAGRAM 11. *Teardrops On My Fame*

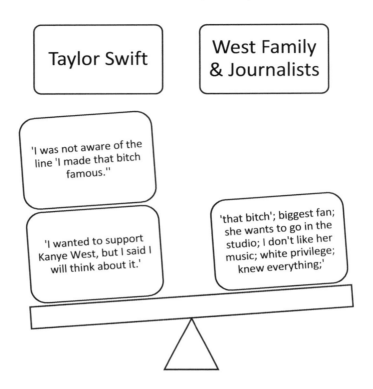

4. *'Speak Later'*:

- offered freedom of action to Kanye West and Kim Kardashian and responded only when her name was mentioned by a participant in the *Famous* feud; this strategy may have its roots in the short feud she was involved with Nicki Minaj in 2015 before the MTV VMA, when Taylor Swift wrote: 'I thought I was being called out. I missed the point, I misunderstood, then misspoke. I'm sorry, Nicki'[160];
- did not post anything on social media accounts for more than a year;
- to promote the *reputation* album from 2017, she created her own magazines which were available in two copies and only with the album at Target store;
- told her story through lyrics and videos more than a year after Kim Kardashian's post about the phone conversation between her and Kanye West;

---

[160] Jason Lipshutz, 'Taylor Swift & Nicki Minaj's Twitter Argument: A Full Timeline of the Disagreement', *Billboard*, July 23, 2015, available at: https://www.billboard.com/music/pop/taylor-swift-nicki-minaj-twitter-argument-timeline-6641794/, last accessed: January 22, 2022.

- in 2019 the album *Lover* is considered by critics and fans as a second answer for Kanye West and her involvement in the production of the *Famous* song;

DIAGRAM 12. *Speak Later*

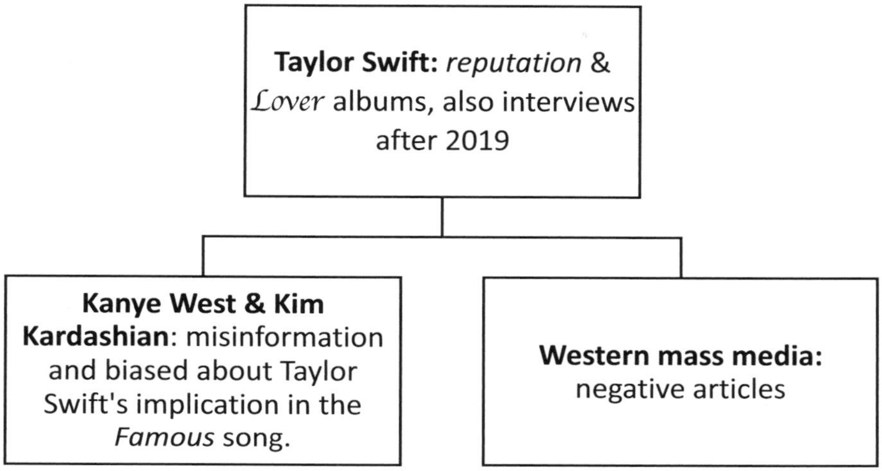

> **Taylor Swift:** *reputation* & *Lover* albums, also interviews after 2019

> **Kanye West & Kim Kardashian:** misinformation and biased about Taylor Swift's implication in the *Famous* song.

> **Western mass media:** negative articles

5. *'Out of the Woods'*:

- maybe the strategy of promoting her truth was made in two stages: the first stage through **reputation** and the darkest period of her musical life, and *Lover*: an album about her real personality;
- through *reputation* and *Lover* albums, Taylor Swift was caught in a journey from darkness (because Kanye West pushed and managed the feud in that direction) to the light (through her own thinking and the power of writing songs); she returned stronger and with the same well-being feeling and personality that she had before February 2016.

DIAGRAM 13. *Out of the Woods*

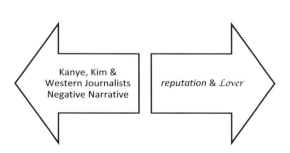

Kanye, Kim &
Western Journalists
Negative Narrative

reputation & *Lover*

6. *'Controlling the Narrative of Truth'*:

- this strategy is on long term and it started in January 2016 when the phone conversation between Taylor Swift and Kanye West took place and possible to exist as of today (it is impossible to determine whether the feud is over or not).

DIAGRAM 14. *Controlling the Narrative of Truth*

```
              ┌──────────────┐
              │    phone     │
              │ conversation │
              └──────────────┘
   ┌────────────┐         ┌────────────┐
   │ interviews │         │ statements │
   └────────────┘         └────────────┘
      ┌─────────┐       ┌────────────┐
      │  Lover  │       │ reputation │
      └─────────┘       └────────────┘
```

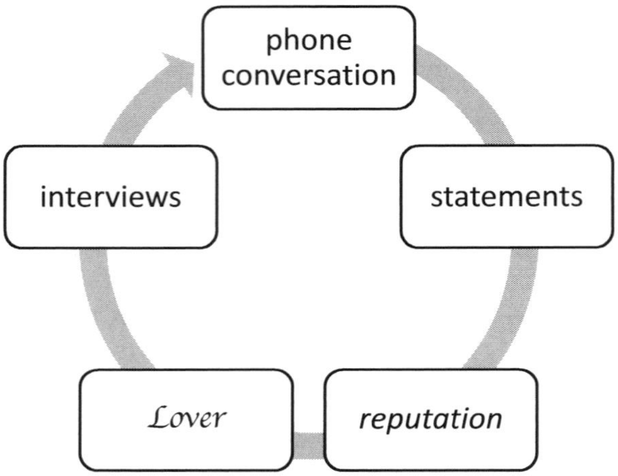

V.4 Kanye West, Beyoncé, Jay Z, Katy Perry and Taylor Swift: The Dynamic Reaction Strategy (DRS)

On August 21, 2017, more than a year after the post on Instagram about her participation in the song *Famous*, Taylor Swift returned to media attention by revealing a new song and a new music album named **reputation**, and on August 23, 2017 Taylor released the first song from the album, named *Look What You Made Me Do*; two years later, on August 23, 2019 Taylor Swift released the album, *Lover*. According to fans and journalists, these two albums are considered to be Taylor Swift's response to the negative effects of the *Famous* feud with Kanye West.

This strategy started in 2009 and may still exist as of today. *The Dynamic Reaction Strategy* is simple, but with serious consequences unleashed from the general public: each artist responded either by a statement on the official page, or through a song, video, album and interview.

In the next pages, I explored different patterns which show Taylor Swift in defence mode toward Kanye West, while Kanye West initiated offensive behaviour towards and in reference to Taylor Swift. In this subchapter, I used several examples to create a better understanding of Taylor Swift's behaviour toward Kanye West (I included Beyoncé, Jay Z and Katy Perry because they are players in the feud at some level).

DIAGRAM 15. *The Dynamic Reaction Strategy: Kanye West and Taylor Swift*

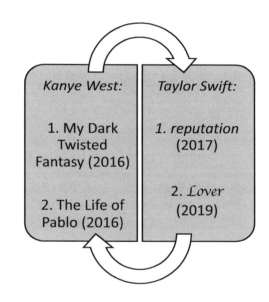

Examples to support the *Dynamic Reaction* Strategy (DRS) [161]:

---

[161] The examples of the *Dynamic Reaction* strategy were used/modified with new interpretation by the author of this report from the following sources: Christopher Rosa, '20 Taylor Swift 'Reputation' Fan Theories That Actually Make Sense', *Glamour*, September 8, 2017, available at: https://www.glamour.com/story/best-taylor-swift-reputation-fan-theories, last accessed: March 27, 2020; Rebecca Farley, 'Every Single Taylor Swift Clone That Appears In Reputation', *Refinery29*, November 10, 2017, available at: https://www.refinery29.com/en-gb/2017/11/180787/taylor-swift-reputation-taylors-theory, last accessed: March 27, 2020; Lauren Rearick, 'Taylor Swift's Reputation Sparks Multiple Fans Theories About Who She's Shading', *Teen Vogue*, November 10, 2017, available at: https://www.teenvogue.com/story/taylor-swifts-reputation-shade-fans-theories, last accessed: March 27, 2020; Dusty Baxter-Wright, '8 Fan Theories On What Taylor Swift's Reputation Lyrics Are About', *Cosmopolitan*, November 10, 2017, available at: https://www.cosmopolitan.com/uk/entertainment/a13514492/who-are-taylor-swift-reputation-lyrics-about/, last accessed: March 27, 2020; Nicole Pomarico, 'Fans Have Theories About Taylor Swift's "…Ready For It?' Video & It's Not Even Out Yet', *Bustle*, October 23, 2017, available at: https://www.bustle.com/p/theories-about-taylor-swifts-ready-for-it-video-from-kanye-references-to-reputation-connections-2971233, last accessed: March 27, 2020; Cady Lang, 'The 10 Most Convincing Theories About Taylor Swift's Album Reputation', *Time*, September 29, 2017, https://time.com/4944028/taylor-swift-reputation-album-theories/, last accessed:

There are many examples that can support the *Dynamic Reaction Strategy*, but I used enough examples to understand how it works. Unfortunately, despite the use of examples, this report cannot offer a clear causal link and the final evidence that this strategy was created with the sole purpose to answer to the allegations hold and promoted by all the parties involved in the feud, but have been illustrated by various fans on social media, articles published by Western mass-media, and my own interpretation based on lyrics, music videos and song titles.

1. References in the song/album/video:

- Taylor Swift wrote lyrics in which she described key situations that the audience knew and she confirmed them, refuted or added something unknown until the release of the song/album, for example:

Look What You Made Me Do[162]:

- Taylor Swift remade the scene with the phone call with Kanye West and added the lyrics: 'Taylor Swift can't come to the phone right now? Why? Oh, because she is dead:' this is a reference to the trend from July 2016, named *#TaylorSwiftOverParty*, and thousands of users who tweeted that Taylor Swift is dead because the truth is out and she is guilty: a mural was created in Australia and her birth and dead years were written on the left side: 1989 – 2016;

Endgame[163]:

- *'I'm one call away, whenever you need me'*: the phone call with Kanye West;

- *'Knew her when I was young'*: Kanye West met her at the age of 19 at the MTV VMA 2009;

March 27, 2020; Alyssa Bailey, 'All The Hidden Messages Taylor Swift Wants You To Notice In Her "End Game" Music Video', *Elle*, January 12, 2018, available at: https://www.elle.com/culture/music/a15069497/taylor-swift-end-game-hidden-messages-easter-eggs/, last accessed: March 27, 2020; Ashley Hoffman, 'The Internet Is Freaking Out About These Details in Taylor Swift's 'End Game' Video', *Time*, January 12, 2018, https://time.com/5100657/taylor-swift-end-game-video-theories/, last accessed: March 27, 2020; Jill Gutowitz, 'What Is Every Song on Taylor Swift's Lover Actually About?', *Vulture*, August 23, 2019, last accessed: March 27, 2020; Emily Yahr, 'Taylor Swift's 'Lover': A Track-By-Track Breakdown, From Coded Lyrics to Leonardo DiCaprio and Drake References', *The Washington Post*, August 23, 2019, available at: https://www.washingtonpost.com/arts-entertainment/2019/08/23/taylor-swifts-lover-track-by-track-breakdown-coded-lyrics-leonardo-dicaprio-drake-references/, last accessed: March 27, 2020.
[162] Taylor Swift, 'Look What You Made Me Do Lyrics', *Genius*, available at: https://genius.com/Taylor-swift-look-what-you-made-me-do-lyrics, last accessed: March 20, 2020.
[163] Taylor Swift, 'Endgame Lyrics', *Genius*, available at: https://genius.com/Taylor-swift-end-game-lyrics, last accessed: March 20, 2020.

- *'Reconnected when we were little bit older'*: in 2015 Kanye West called Taylor Swift and asked her to present the *MTV Michael Jackson Video Vanguard Award* and Taylor accepted his request; during this event, Taylor Swift stayed next to his wife, Kim Kardashian; after the ceremony Kanye West sent flowers to Taylor Swift;

- *'And I can't let you go, your hand print's on my soul'*: Kanye West used the private conversation to blame Taylor for not accepting the final version of the song, which included the lyrics 'that bitch'; Kim Kardashian released edited parts of the private conversation on Snapchat; Kanye West used a wax clone of Taylor Swift in the music video of the song *Famous* without her permission; during *Saint Pablo Tour* in various places in the USA, Kanye West encouraged people to shout 'bitch' in reference to Taylor Swift; in the end, Kanye West, in his speech to MTV in 2016, presented his position as the man who is telling the truth while Taylor Swift is a liar: 'That's why I called her';

Gorgeous[164]:

- same title as Kanye West's song 'Gorgeous' from the album *My Beautiful Dark Twisted Fantasy* (2010)[165];

Getaway Car[166]:

'We were jet-set, Bonnie and Clyde[167] *(oh, oh)'*: possible reference to Beyoncé and Jay Z; ''03 Bonnie & Clide' is a song performed by Jay Z, also connection with the concert *On the Run* and the Tidal platform; let's see the possible connections with the lyrics and the title of the songs[168]:

- Kanye West released the song *Famous* (*The Life of Pablo*) where Taylor Swift is called 'that bitch';
- Kanye promised that his album, *The Life of Pablo*, will be available exclusively on the *Tidal* platform (the platform owned also by Jay Z which is Beyoncé's

[164] Taylor Swift, 'Gorgeous Lyrics', *Genius*, available at: https://genius.com/Taylor-swift-gorgeous-lyrics, last accessed: March 27, 2020.

[165] Kanye West, 'Gorgeous Lyrics', *Genius*, available at: https://genius.com/Kanye-west-gorgeous-lyrics, last accessed: March 27, 2020.

[166] Taylor Swift, 'Getaway Car Lyrics', *Genius*, available at: https://genius.com/Taylor-swift-getaway-car-lyrics, last accessed: March 27, 2020.

[167] Bonnie Elizabeth Parker (October 1, 1910 – May 23, 1934) and Clyde Champion Barrow[1][2] (March 24, 1909 – May 23, 1934) were an American criminal couple who traveled the Central United States with their gang during the Great Depression, known for their bank robberies, although they preferred to rob small stores or rural gas stations.

[168] The following connections are from *Black and White Music*, pp: 185-191;

husband); however, on April 1, 2016, his album was made available on *Apple Music*, which led to the accusation that he cheated the audience, according to an article in Variety: „By the time Mr. West changed course and broadly released 'The Life of Pablo,' the deceptive marketing ploy had served its purpose: Tidal's subscriber numbers had tripled, streaming numbers were through the roof, and Tidal had collected the personal information, credit card numbers, and social media information of millions of deceived consumers […] Instead, they just wanted to boost Tidal's subscriber numbers – which indeed did get a big bump from the release. Tidal may have signed up as many as two million new subscribers thanks to the album, claims the lawsuit, arguing that this could have added as much as $84 million to Tidal's valuation;"[169]

- Beyoncé released the surprise album *Lemonade* on April 23, 2016; Taylor Swift is caught up in the negative narrative created and promoted by Kanye; *Lemonade* enjoyed success from critics being considered the best album released by Beyoncé, but also on Tidal: *Lemonade* was streamed 115 million times, setting a record for the most-streamed album in a single week by a female artist; what if Kanye West, through the exclusivity strategy for his album, plus the use of Taylor Swift (huge influence and at least a million fans) in his song, spread the narrative that in his album there could be something more about Taylor, which led to the growth of curious users (maybe most of them fans of Taylor Swift) and, in the end, some users decided to stay on the platform? At the same time, maybe the new number of users were used to justify the record number of streaming of his album, *The Life of Pablo*, and Beyoncé's *Lemonade*?

- in 2018 Tidal was accused of intentionally falsifying the streaming number of *The Life of Pablo* and *Lemonade*, according to Variety: "Tidal, which has rarely shared its data publicly, had a streaming exclusive on West's album for its first six weeks of release and continues to be the exclusive streamer for Beyoncé's album. It claimed that West's album had been streamed 250 million times in its first 10 days of release in February of 2016, while claiming it had just 3 million subscribers – a claim that would have meant every subscriber played the album an average of eight times per day; and that Beyonce's album was streamed 306 million times in its first 15 days of release in April of 2016." […] "Today's report, according to MBW's translation, says that "Beyoncé's and Kanye West's listener numbers on Tidal have been manipulated to the tune of several hundred million false plays… which has generated massive royalty payouts at the expense of

[169] Janko Roettgers, 'Kanye West Tricked Fans Into Subscribing to Tidal, Lawsuit Claims', *Variety*, April 18, 2016, available at: https://variety.com/2016/digital/news/kanye-west-tricked-fans-into-subscribing-to-tidal-lawsuit-claims-1201755580/, last accessed: February 25, 2021.

other artists;[170]" What if Kanye West and Jay Z's strategy to use Taylor Swift was also to increase the number of users? What if Kanye West and Jay Z used the new subscribers to falsify the number of streamings to make more money? Let's not forget that in the conversation with Taylor Kanye admitted that he has big debts (millions of dollars); what if the fake number of streaming was done in order to increase Beyoncé's profile and the records obtained? What if the false plays were made this route as on the other streaming platforms (Apple and Spotify) Beyoncé would not make the numbers to have new records to celebrate and maintain relevance in the music industry as Taylor Swift does? What if the fake number of streaming and the exclusive availability of her album, *Lemonade*, on Tidal was made to show the world that she is so loved that her fans follow her on the new platform and set new records in the music industry? What if Tidal is being used to justify a false point of view that black artists are not safe on other platforms because they are ruled by white people? What if behind Tidal the black artists from this report, Kanye, Jay Z and Beyoncé, used it to their own benefit, therefore, cheating the music industry and their fans?

- Kanye West interfered in the narrative of Taylor Swift with a negative story about her character, while Beyoncé has a positive image about her skills and character; Kanye West is behind the negative stories about Taylor Swift's character and skills in 2009 and in 2016; Kanye West in 2016 interfered in Taylor Swift's narrative line with a negative story while Beyoncé's narrative line is involved in releasing a new album; Kanye West negative behaviour toward Taylor Swift is after Beyoncé released an album (*I am … Sasha Fierce*, 2008) and before (*Lemonade*, 2016) she is out with a new album;

Dress[171]:

- contains one word from the song 'Devil in a New Dress'[172] by Kanye West from the album *My Beautiful Dark Twisted Fantasy* (2010).

---

[170] Jem Aswad, 'Tidal Accused of Falsifying Beyoncé and Kanye West Streaming Numbers', *Variety*, May 9, 2018, available at: https://variety.com/2018/biz/news/jay-z-tidal-accused-of-falsifying-beyonce-and-kanye-west-streaming-numbers-1202804222/, last accessed: February 25, 2021; Andy Cush, 'Tidal Accused of Generating 300 Million Fake Streams for Kanye and Beyoncé', *Spin*, May 9, 2018, available at: https://www.spin.com/2018/05/tidal-fake-streams-kanye-beyonce-investigation-300-million/, last accessed: February 25, 2021; Tim Ingham, 'Tidal 'Fake Streams': Criminal Investigation Underway Over Potential Data Fraud In Norway;, *Music Business Worldwide*, January 14, 2019, available at: https://www.musicbusinessworldwide.com/tidal-fake-streams-criminal-investigation-underway-over-potential-data-fraud-in-norway/, last accessed: February 25, 2021; Dagens Næringsliv's investigation can be found here: https://www.musicbusinessworldwide.com/files/2018/05/NTNU_DigitalForensicsReport_DN_Final_Version.pdf, last accessed: February 25, 2021.

[171] Taylor Swift, 'Dress Lyrics', *Genius*, November 10, 2017, available at: https://genius.com/Taylor-swift-dress-lyrics, last accessed: February 25, 2021.

[172] Kanye West, 'Devil in New Dress Lyrics', *Genius*, November 22, 2010, available at: https://genius.com/Kanye-west-devil-in-a-new-dress-lyrics, last accessed: February 25, 2021.

This is Why We Can't Have Nice Things[173]:

'This is why we can't have nice things, darling
Because you break them, I had to take them away
Did you think I wouldn't hear all the things you said about me?
It was so nice being friends again
There I was giving you a second chance
But you stabbed me in the back while shaking my hand
And therein lies the issue, friends don't try to trick you
Get you on the phone and mind-twist you.'

- Kanye West misinformed the public about the whole phone call and Taylor Swift cannot offer anymore her friendship and support;
- Kim Kardashian posted a video on her Snapchat while signing the part from the *Famous* song which Taylor Swift did not approve: 'I made that bitch famous'; during Saint Pablo Tour in various places in the USA, Kanye West encouraged people to shout 'bitch' in reference to Taylor Swift; during an interview for Harper Bazaar, Kanye West said he does not like Taylor's music and Kim Kardashian said that she is no fan of Taylor;
- in 2015 Kanye West called Taylor Swift and asked her to present the MTV Michael Jackson Video Vanguard Award and Taylor accepted his request; during this event, Taylor Swift stayed next to his wife, Kim Kardashian; after the ceremony Kanye West sent flowers to Taylor Swift;
- identic narrative of the song 'Runaway' by Kanye West (from the album *My Beautiful Dark Twisted Fantasy*, 2010) and *This is Why We Can't Have Nice Things* by Taylor Swift (reputation album, 2017): in both songs there is a party;

Runaway *(2010)*: it is a party with a ballerina (Taylor Swift played this role in 'Shake It Off' song, from her blockbuster album, *1989*, released in October 2014):

'Let's have a toast for the douchebags
Let's have a toast for the assholes
Let's have a toast for the scumbags
Every one of them that I know
Let's have a toast for the jerk-offs
That'll never take work off

---

[173] Taylor Swift, 'This Is Why We Can't Have Nice Things Lyrics', *Genius*, available at: https://genius.com/Taylor-swift-this-is-why-we-cant-have-nice-things-lyrics, last accessed: March 27, 2020.

Baby, I got a plan
Run away fast as you can'[174]

This is Why We Can't Have Nice Things: it is a party that in the end is ruined, but Taylor Swift offered her forgiveness and concluded the party with a toast:

'Here's a toast to my real friends
They don't care about the he-said, she-said
And here's to my baby
He ain't reading what they call me lately
And here's to my mama
Had to listen to all this drama
And here's to you
'Cause forgiveness is a nice thing to do
Haha, I can't even say it with a straight face'[175]

I Forgot That You Existed[176]:

'How many days did I spend
Thinkin' 'bout how you did me wrong, wrong, wrong?
Lived in the shade you were throwin'
'Til all of my sunshine was gone, gone, gone
And I couldn't get away from ya
In my feelings more than Drake, so yeah:
I forgot that you
Got out some popcorn
As soon as my rep starting going down, down, down
Laughed on the schoolyard
As soon as I tripped up and hit the ground, ground, ground
And I would've stuck around for ya
Would've fought the whole town, so yeah
Would've been right there, front row
Even if nobody came to your show'

---

[174] Kanye West, 'Runaway Lyrics', *Genius*, October 4, 2010, available at: https://genius.com/Kanye-west-runaway-lyrics, last accessed: March 27, 2020.
[175] Taylor Swift, 'This Is Why We Can't Have Nice Things Lyrics'.
[176] Taylor Swift, 'I Forgot That You Existed Lyrics', *Genius*, available at: https://genius.com/Taylor-swift-i-forgot-that-you-existed-lyrics, last accessed: March 27, 2020.

- during the phone conversation Taylor agreed to support Kanye West and waited for him to send her the song which never happened;
- during an interview for Harper Bazaar, Kanye West said he does not like Taylor's music and Kim Kardashian said that she is not anymore a fan of Taylor Swift;
- during Saint Pablo Tour in various places around USA, Kanye West encouraged people to shout 'bitch' in reference to Taylor Swift;
- Kanye West made a guest appearance at Drake's concert in Chicago, and spoke out about Taylor Swift; Kanye West told his fans, "All I gotta say is, I am so glad my wife has Snapchat!", "Now y'all can know the truth and can't nobody talk s–t about 'Ye no more." After his words, he performed the *Famous* song and people chanted 'bitch' in reference to Taylor Swift.[177]

Cruel Summer[178]: Kanye West has a compilation album with the same name released on September 14, 2012[179];

Lyrics:

'Shiny toy with a price, You know that I bought it': Kanye West wanted Taylor Swift's support by promoting his song on her Twitter account which she declined, however, she wanted to hear the full song and then to decide the next step; also, Kanye West told Taylor Swift that if she says the song is good and she likes it, the people will be into his song; Taylor Swift said to Kanye West that she will think about it and was positive about his song.

Lover[180]:

- in 2015 Kanye West called Taylor Swift and asked her to present the *MTV Michael Jackson Video Vanguard Award* and Taylor accepted his request; during this event, Taylor Swift stayed next to his wife, Kim Kardashian; after the ceremony Kanye West sent flowers to Taylor Swift;
- in 2016, at the MTV VMA, Kanye West was allowed to have a speech in which she mentioned the *Famous* song feud, by saying 'But bro, like, I love all y'all. That's why I called her', however, at the same time Kanye lied the people who love by saying only parts that are in his benefit, not the whole and true story of the phone conversation and what Taylor Swift really knew; during his entrance on the stage, the *Famous*

[177] Elias Leight, idem.
[178] Taylor Swift, 'Cruel Summer Lyrics', *Genius*, available at: https://genius.com/Taylor-swift-cruel-summer-lyrics, last accessed: March 27, 2020.
[179] Kanye West, 'Cruel Summer (GOOD Music Album)', *Wikipedia*, available at: https://en.wikipedia.org/wiki/Cruel_Summer_(GOOD_Music_album), last accessed: March 27, 2020.
[180] Taylor Swift, 'Lover Lyrics', *Genius*, available at: https://genius.com/Taylor-swift-lover-lyrics, last accessed: March 27, 2020.

song is being played and it contains the part where Kanye sings: 'I made that bitch famous', twice; at the end of his speech Kanye released the music video for *Fade*, a song from the album *The Life of Pablo*; *Fade* has the following lyrics: 'Your love is fadin', Know it ain't no wrong, I feel it's fadin', I think I think too much, I feel it's fadin', Ain't nobody watchin'[181]; in the video Teyana Taylor (born on December 10, 1990, one year and 3 days after Taylor Swift) is the main dancer;

- in the song *Swish, Swish* (Katy Perry reply song to Taylor Swift's *Bad Blood* song), Nicki Minaj sings the lyrics 'Don't be tryna double back, I already despise you, All that fake love you showin', Couldn't even disguise you, Ran? When? Nicki getting' tan, Mirror mirror who's the fairest bitch in all the land, Damn, man, this bitch is a Stan, Muah, muah, the generous queen will kiss a fan, Ass goodbye, I'ma be riding by, I'ma tell my n- Biggz, yeah that's tha guy, A star's a star, da ha da ha, They never thought the swish god would take it this far, Get my pimp cup, this is pimp shit, baby, I only rock with Queens, so I'm makin' hits with Katy[182]'; in 2015 Nicki Minaj was in a short feud with Taylor Swift, but Taylor apologised and Nicki accepted the apology and they both sang during MTV VMA in 2015, however, in 2017 Nicki featured in Katy Perry song; Nicki Minaj failed to achieve number 1 on Billboard with her album *Queen* released on August 10, 2018 and Taylor Swift music outperformed Nicki Minaj and Katy Perry's music on streaming platforms and sales;
- in 2019 Taylor Swift released the song *Lover* (also the name of the album) written by herself;
- in 2019 at the MTV VMA, Taylor Swift performed *Lover* and won (voted by fans) *Video of the Year Award* for *You Need to Calm Down* music video, which is 10 years from the first *Famous* feud event.

Miss Americana & The Heartbreak Prince[183]:

- *80s & Heartbreak* is the name of Kanye West album released on November 24, 2008.
- "I just wanted you to know": (Kanye West, 'Famous', *The Life of Pablo*, 2016)[184];
- "[…] Just thought you should know" (Taylor Swift, 'Miss Americana & The Heartbreak Prince', *Lover*, 2019).

False God[185]:

---

[181] Kanye West, 'Fade Lyrics', *Genius*, available at: https://genius.com/Kanye-west-fade-lyrics, last accessed: March 27, 2020.

[182] Katy Perry, 'Swish, Swish Lyrics', *Genius*, available at: https://genius.com/Katy-perry-swish-swish-lyrics, last accessed: March 27, 2020.

[183] Taylor Swift, 'Miss Americana & The Heartbreak Prince Lyrics', *Genius*, available at: https://genius.com/Taylor-swift-miss-americana-and-the-heartbreak-prince-lyrics, last accessed: March 27, 2020.

[184] Kanye West, 'Famous Lyrics', *Genius*, available at: https://genius.com/Kanye-west-famous-lyrics, last accessed: March 27, 2020.

[185] Taylor Swift, 'False God Lyrics', *Genius*, available at: https://genius.com/Taylor-swift-false-god-lyrics, last accessed: March 27, 2020.

- Kanye West presented himself many times as God of rap music and released one album *Yeezus* (close reference with Jesus); Kanye West released various gospel songs before 2019, however, Taylor Swift used the following lyrics:

'Religion's in your lips
Even if it's a false god
We'd still worship
You're the West Village
You still do it for me, babe'

the lyrics might be a reference to the following idea: despite Kanye lying the general public about her real implication in the *Famous* song and chanting 'bitch' in his concerts, there are still people who believe and bow their heads at Kanye's altar.

2. Songs/Album/Video music creation:

- she followed Kanye West steps to create the *Famous song*: phone call, samples, used the artwork created by other people.

Look What You Made Me Do:

- she called the artists of the song that she sampled just as Kanye West called her; however, the difference is that she recognized the real artists and the conversation between them was peaceful and true[186];
- eye for an eye/the other side of the coin: Kanye West used a sample from the song *Mi Sono Svegliato E...Ho Chiuso Gli Occhi*, by Il Rovescio Della Medaglia[187];
- Taylor Swift is afraid of being recorded, however, Kanye West did it and Kim Kardashian released to the general public edited parts of their conversation; in the music video Taylor used the scene of Kim's robbery from Paris in 2016, which is the worst event from Kim's life[188].

---

[186] Kory Grow, 'Right Said Fred on Taylor Swift's 'Cynical' 'Look What You Made Me Do'', *Rolling Stone*, August 23, 2017, available at: https://www.rollingstone.com/music/music-features/right-said-fred-on-taylor-swifts-cynical-look-what-you-made-me-do-205808/, last accessed: March 27, 2020.

[187] Il Rovescio Della Medaglia, 'Mi Sono Svegliato E...Ho Chiuso Gli Occhi', *Genius*, available at: https://genius.com/Il-rovescio-della-medaglia-mi-sono-svegliato-e-ho-chiuso-gli-occhi-lyrics, last accessed: March 27, 2020.

[188] Aurelie Corinthios, Julia Emmanuele, Lanford Beard, 'Everything We Know About Kim Kardashian West's Paris Heist', *People*, December 2, 2020, available at: https://people.com/tv/kim-kardashian-robbery-questions-answered/, last accessed: December 5, 2020.

Endgame music video[189]:

In the *Famous* song Kanye West used a sample from the song *Rock the Boat* by Aaliyah[190] which is dancing on the boat with other girls; in the music video of *Endgame*, Taylor is dancing on a yacht with other girls[191].

Delicate:

Kanye West used samples and ideas from other artists[192], then promoted himself as somehow the owner of those ideas and was accused of copying other artists without their permission; Taylor Swift maybe used the same strategy for *Delicate* music video: she was accused of copying and ripping off a Kenzo advert.[193]

However, maybe Taylor Swift did it before *Delicate* music video with *Shake It Off* music video in 2014: there is a similarity between her music video and Kanye West's music video *Runaway*: Taylor is dressed as a ballerina and she is dancing; in Kanye West's song ballerinas are also playing, while Kanye is using the piano. Also, the videos *Bad Blood* by Taylor Swift and *Stronger* by Kanye West have one similarity: in the beginning of the video, both artists are using technology to repair their bodies and to become stronger (it is like *Bad Blood* from 2014 is one video with two blows: Kanye West and Katy Perry, exactly like *Look What You Made Me Do* from 2017: references to Katy Perry and Kanye West, but also other people).

---

[189] Taylor Swift, 'Engame', *Youtube*, January 12, 2018, available at: https://www.youtube.com/watch?v=dfnCAmr569k, last accessed: March 27, 2020.

[190] Aliyah, 'Rock the Boat', *Youtube*, September 10, 2021, available at: https://www.youtube.com/watch?v=3HSJU5fDg0A, last accessed: September 14, 2021.

[191] Taylor Swift, 'Endgame', *Youtube*.

[192] Some accusation: Wenn, 'West Accused Of Copying French Film In New Video', *Contact Music*, February 22, 2011, available at: https://www.contactmusic.com/kanye-west/news/west-accused-of-copying-french-film-in-new-video_1203310, last accessed: March 27, 2020; BBC, *Kanye West accused of copyright theft by Hungarian rock singer*, May 24, 2016, available at: https://www.bbc.co.uk/news/entertainment-arts-36367591, last accessed: March 27, 2020; Cassidy Mantor, 'Kanye West's Yeezy sued for copying camo print', *Fashion Network*, March 19, 2018, available at: https://ww.fashionnetwork.com/news/kanye-west-s-yeezy-sued-for-copying-camo-print,959797.html, last accessed: March 27, 2020; Susanna Heller, 'Kim Kardashian and Kanye West are being accused of copying famous designers with their new kids' clothing line'', *Insider*, December 6, 2017, available at: https://www.insider.com/kim-kardashian-kanye-west-accused-of-copying-famous-designers-2017-12, last accessed: March 27, 2020; Clemence Michallon, 'Seeing double? Kanye West's fashion label Yeezy is SUED over accusations that it 'ripped off' another brand's camo designs', *The Daily Mail*, March 16, 2018, available at: https://www.dailymail.co.uk/femail/article-5506945/Kanye-Wests-Yeezy-accused-ripping-designs.html, last accessed: March 27, 2020; Samantha Ibrahim, 'Kanye West accused of stealing 'Donda' logo from black-owned company', *New York Post*, August 31, 2021, available at: https://nypost.com/2021/08/31/kanye-west-accused-of-allegedly-stealing-donda-album-logo-design/, last accessed: September 12, 2021.

[193] BBC, *Taylor Swift: Delicate Video Accused of Copying Kenzo Advert*, March 13, 2018, available at: https://www.bbc.co.uk/news/newsbeat-43382742, last accessed: March 27, 2020; Diana Samson, 'Is Taylor Swift's 'Delicate' Music Video A Rip Off Of A Perfume Ad?', *Music Times*, March 13, 2018, available at: https://www.musictimes.com/articles/78315/20180313/is-taylor-swift-s-delicate-music-video-a-rip-off-of-a-perfume-ad.htm, last accessed: March 27, 2020.

Use of sample from same category of music:

- Taylor Swift used samples from 'Humpty Dumpty' which is a character in an English nursery rhyme and one of the best known in the English-speaking world;
- Kanye West used sample in the song 'Bad News' (from the album *808s & Heartbreak*, 2008) from 'Sea Lion Woman' which is a traditional African American folk song originally used as a children's playground song.[194]

3. Album theme: dark and light; Taylor Swift followed the path of two albums released by Kanye West and in which she was one of the characters who inspired songs from the album:

- *Kanye West*:

  My Beautiful Dark Twisted Fantasy (2010): an album that tries to erase the mistakes of the past and an apology to Taylor Swift (I tried to find a specific, clear lyrics and song dedicated to Taylor Swift as apology, however, I did not find anything to support his statement'; from Taylor Swift there is a specific, clear lyrics and song dedicated to Kanye West about the incident and her forgiveness: 'Innocent' on *Speak Now* album); it is the album of a man with a negative reputation obtained after interrupting Taylor Swift's speech at the MTV VMA Awards in 2009; the album was created during self-imposed exile;

  The Life of Pablo (2016): an album describing the overall life (family, love, faith, importance) of a man named Pablo (possible Kanye West);

- *Taylor Swift*:

  reputation (2017): an album with a dark theme and design that describes the life of a person with a negative reputation based on gossips and lies and the search for love in a dark period of her life; the album was created during self-imposed exile due to negative media articles about her involvement in the song *Famous,* and the failure to respond according to the expectations of Kanye, Kim and some Western journalists who unjustly sanctioned her;

---

[194] Sea Lion Woman, *Wikipedia*, available at: https://en.wikipedia.org/wiki/Sea_Lion_Woman, last accessed: February 25, 2020. This paragraph was first use in Casian Anton, *Black and White Music.*

Lover (2019): covers all facets of love and represents a character who loves life and comes to conclusions that help her to overcome the state of negativity and realises that 'it is morning' and 'love is golden'.

Through two albums, *reputation* and *Lover*, maybe Taylor Swift is closing the circle started by Kanye West in 2009 and 2016.

4. Marketing:

- first, Kanye West used Taylor Swift in the *Famous* song, interviews and the musical tour, *Saint Pablo Tour* 2016; second, Taylor Swift used references in her songs, music videos and the musical tour, *Taylor Swift's Stadium Reputation Tour*, 2018;
- in 2018, Kanye West released his eight album, *ye* which is stylized with lower letters as Taylor Swift's *reputation*; in 2020, on October 27 (same release date as Taylor Swift with *Speak Now* album in 2010) released the album *Jesus is King*, which has 27:04 minutes[195], which (based on how Taylor Swift includes easter eggs in her statements, lyrics and music video) calculated as individual numbers we have the following maths calculation: 2+7+4=13 (the birth date of Taylor Swift and her lucky number).

Katy Perry, *Witness* album in 2017[196]:

Weeks before the release of the album, Katy Perry confessed that she wrote a song about Taylor Swift, named *Swish, Swish* as a reply to Taylor Swift's song *Bad Blood* with the following lyrics:

'You're calculated
I got your number
'Cause you're a joker
And I'm a courtside killer queen
And you will kiss the ring
You best believe
Your game is tired
You should retire

---

[195] Kanye West, 'Jesus is King', *Wikipedia,* available at: https://en.wikipedia.org/wiki/Jesus_Is_King, last accessed: October 30, 2020.
[196] The Late Show with James Corden, 'Katy Perry Carpool Karaoke', *Youtube*, May 23, 2017, available at: https://www.youtube.com/watch?v=5tvxzLK3rFs, last accessed: October 30, 2020.

You're 'bout cute as
An old coupon expired
And karma's not a liar
She keeps receipts.[197']

On the day of her album release, the world witnessed Taylor Swift's decision to release her entire music catalogue on streaming services for the first time: 'In celebration of 1989 selling over 10 million albums worldwide and the RIAA's 100 million song certification announcement, Taylor wants to thank her fans by making her entire catalogue available to all streaming services tonight at midnight;' furthermore, in August 2017, Taylor Swift released the first single, *Look What You Made Me Do*, from the new album, *reputation*, which fans and mass-media think it is also a reply through music to Katy Perry.

---

[197] Katy Perry, idem.

VI. **FAMOUS** REASONS FOR A **FAMOUS** FEUD[198]

In this chapter I wrote various reasons why the *Famous* feud was created and supported for more than 10 years. The reasons are based on the data used in this report. All the reasons are speculative and some negative, maybe there is a possibility that these speculative reasons have some truth and could help in making a better understanding of the events between Kanye West and Taylor Swift.

There are more negative reasons for Kanye West because he started the feud and Taylor Swift is in defence mode.

***Kanye West*:**

- wanted to have enough publicity to get customers for his album: Kanye West lost half of his popularity in the USA first week pure sales in 1 year (from 2007 to 2008, and after three successful albums and high increase) and remained low (in comparison with the first three albums); also, in September 2009 (the start of the feud) Taylor Swift was on the natural path of increasing as global pop artist, while Kanye West was decreasing as global rap artist;
- does not make enough money from music (used many samples from many artists and has to share the money, which means much less money for him and he is need of financial resources) to live up to the level he aspires to and, if music doesn't help him, he resorts to other methods including the shoes business with Adidas, plus the deliberate and aggressive intervention in Taylor Swift's narrative line;
- to maintain his presence (even negative) on the music market and business with clothes;
- played the victim's card to sell clothes, shoes and music to make money to pay his debts and to become a free person;

---

[198] Parts of this chapter were used also in Casian Anton, *Black and White Music*.

- distracted the negative attention from him to Taylor Swift to fulfil his dreams, while Taylor Swift had to fight the lies he told and credited/promoted by mass-media (only based on the negative articles used in this report);
- what if the 'bitch' idea came up during the telephone conversation based on Taylor Swift's word: 'That stupid, dumb bitch'? did he change his mind because Taylor Swift refused him (until she thinks about the song), and his plan would have been ruined because he wanted the song to be released before the Grammy Awards, and everyone to know that she approved the song, so he can make profit, because Taylor Swift's fans will buy the song?
- what if Kanye West interfered in Taylor Swift's album release pattern a year earlier (2007), and then justified the release of the next album (2008) in the same timeframe as Taylor Swift in order to create a racial comparison: Kanye West (black man) received better reviews than Taylor Swift (white woman), and that Taylor Swift success is because she is white, not because she has better music than him? yet, Taylor Swift came with her lyrics, and Kanye West came with samples from other artists;
- what if Kanye West accused Taylor Swift of doing what he did in order to cover his track and other artists that he is supporting by creating a negative view about her? the end of this strategy is to create a negative wave about Taylor Swift, hoping that her fans will get sick of her negative stories that she is involved too often, and switch to his favourite artists, such as Beyoncé, because there are no negative stories about her?
- MTV VMA 2015: what if Kanye West tried to humiliate Taylor Swift by asking her (the girl who should not get the award, despite being voted by fans) to give him the award, even though he was the one who didn't give her the courtesy to end the speech of thanks to her fans?
- if *My Beautiful Dark Twisted Fantasy* was the apology album offered to Taylor Swift, then what are the specific lyrics with the necessary apologies dedicated to Taylor Swift? according to my research, Kanye West does not provide specific details of his apology that is easy to observe and understand by fans and the general public; on the contrary, Taylor Swift wrote the song 'Innocent' and her fans know (and maybe to a larger extend by the general public) that this song is addressed to Kanye West as a sign of forgiveness;
- what if Kanye West found out that Taylor Swift would release the *folklore* album and came sooner with the announcement that on July 24th, 2020 he would release the album *Donda* (in her mother's memory) in order to create a negative narrative in Taylor Swift's line? the negative narrative is as follows: the purpose for which Taylor Swift intervenes in his narrative is to show disrespect and lack of manners to the memory of his mother, *Donda*, as it happened on November 10, 2017? (this is the

day of Kanye West's mother's death; also, this is the day of the release of her album *reputation*: some Kanye West's fans accused Taylor Swift, and the release of the album on the day of Donda's death, as being disrespectful and an insensitive method of attack on Kanye West; Big Machine's (former Taylor Swift's label at that time) response was: 'It is standard practice that releases come out on Fridays and we locked in this release date based on other Universal Music Group releases' […] There is no correlation.' [199]); Kanye West did not finally release the album in July 2020, but on August 29, 2021: what if the name *Donda* came to his mind after learning that Taylor Swift would be releasing a new music album, that she is involved in a new musical genre for her, and he decided to intervene, so that people would hate her and give up listening to her music? well, if that was the plan, it didn't work: in the end, the *folklore* album was a resounding worldwide success and won the *Album of the Year* at the Grammy Awards in 2021 (for Taylor Swift this is her third win, the only female in the music history to achieve this record); what if in July 2020, Kanye West had only the title of the album and no songs written and no samples available to use, and that's why he released the album a year later in 2021? from July 2020 until August 28, 2021 Kanye West had enough time to create music and plans to justify the existence of the album and not be considered a persistent liar (because he does not release the albums on the promised day);

- what if Kanye West refused to publicly say that Taylor Swift has the right to publicly challenge the new line he added and without informing Taylor Swift, 'I made that bitch famous', with the purpose of using the video recording to influence people to buy his concert tickets being a black man who tells the truth and deserves to play concerts in the USA? Kim Kardashian spoke about the video evidence the week his concert tickets went on sale;
- what if Kanye West refused to publicly say that Taylor Swift has the right to publicly challenge the new line he added without informing Taylor Swift, 'I made that bitch famous', because otherwise he wouldn't have had a great source of publicity (Taylor Swift, America's Sweetheart) for at least 6 months before his *Saint Pablo Tour* started? Kanye West's public acknowledgment, of the topics during his conversation with Taylor Swift, immediately after the release of the song *Famous* in February 2016, would have been a per se erasure of any negative feeling towards Taylor Swift from the general public, a self-incrimination of the decision to record the telephone conversation and using it against Taylor Swift; finally that he wrote a new line that Taylor didn't know; in the long run, Kanye West's self-admission of the actual phone conversation with Taylor Swift would not have helped him to create a high interest of

---

[199] Roisin O'Conner, 'Taylor Swift: Reputation release date coinciding with anniversary of Donda West death is a 'coincidence'', *The Independent*, August 26, 2017, available at: https://www.independent.co.uk/arts-entertainment/music/news/taylor-swift-donda-west-reputation-release-date-kanye-kim-kardashian-album-tour-dates-a7914191.html, last accessed: March 27, 2020.

the general public and the Western mass-media in his music and tour: from February (the release of the song *Famous*) – to November 2016 (the last month of the musical tour);

- what if Kanye West has no mental health problems, but it is a long-term scam? the strategies used towards Taylor Swift and in his private life, published by various news agencies, show the ability to successfully follow the flow of logic and has too well thought out movements for a person facing mental problems;
- what if his mental health problems is the ultimate strategy to cover up and justify the dirty tricks used on Taylor Swift, on the general public to forgive him for what he did/does to Taylor Swift and Kim Kardashian (maybe he forced her to publish the edited videos to hurt an innocent woman which contradicts the pro-women ideas promoted by Kim Kardashian, and has a negative impact on her mental health and her public image) to be able to sell albums and clothes, to hide behind the release of albums with poor quality, because his talent expired and used all the samples that could have brought him more financial and critical success than before, and now he has nothing valuable and real worthy of attention?
- what if his divorce from Kim Kardashian's is the second ultimate marketing strategy for both? both maintain their popularity and visibility in the Western mass-media, the world loves a scandal between rich people; what if in the end, both will end up together, a sort of family reunion due to Kanye West's mental problems: but now that is in the past, Kanye West is cured, Kim Kardashian is more mature than before, the money and public attention are in their lockers, and have a new story to present, new clothes, new music and new purchases by fans, and a higher bank account?
- what if he abuses fans through Stem Player: the base of the stem player it is not his invention, but he continues the old and traditional strategy of success: attach himself to other ideas and present them as his; makes money not music; takes advantage of people who want to believe in him and, in return, he rewards them with low quality music; what if he does it because he knows people are paying attention to his behaviour and, in return, he gets their money?

Kanye West, Beyoncé and Jay Z:

- what if Beyoncé and Jay Z were part of the plan in 2009 for the MTV Awards?
- what if Kanye West and Jay Z developed the plan for MTV Awards in 2009 without Beyoncé's knowledge?
- what if Kanye West played The Bad Man (interrupted the speech) and Beyoncé the Good Woman (offered the chance to Taylor Swift to thank the fans for the award) at

the MTV Awards? And if that was the plan, let's see how it could have been done in practice:

- ○ *Step 1*. Kanye West (black man) entered the stage and interrupted Taylor Swift's speech (white woman) on the grounds that she does not deserve the award, even if it was voted by the public, and that Beyoncé deserved the award;
- ○ *Step 2*. Taylor Swift does not end the speech to thank her fans;
- ○ *Step 3*. Beyoncé (black woman) fixed the narrative and gave Taylor Swift (white woman) her time to finish her speech (time that she received because she won *Video of the Year*), but first she mentioned her success: "I remember being 17 years old, up for my first MTV Award with Destiny's Child, and it was one of the most exciting moments in my life, so, I'd like for Taylor to come out and have her moment "; this is a situation where the black artist, with the award of the year, offered the opportunity to the white artist (with the negative image that she doesn't deserve the award) to finish her speech; what if the staff behind the curtain knew that Beyoncé will get the award and the plan was set up before the award ceremony?

- what if Taylor Swift's career and progress was closely watched by Kanye West and Jay Z (probably with other people in their circle) and came to the idea that she would be the next famous pop artist in the USA and in the world (because she has the power to write her songs), and interfered in her narrative to destroy it or to insert in the audience's memory that Taylor Swift could not have been a successful artist without a black artist (through Kanye West)?
- what if the release of Beyoncé 's album on November 12 was her idea, but also Jay Z and Kanye West were involved in making this decision (the day after the release of Taylor Swift's album, *Fearless*) and then November 18 (in the USA)?
- what if Beyoncé's album release pattern (November 18, 2008) and Kanye West's album release pattern (November 24, 2008) were made in order to block Taylor Swift (November 11, 2008) to reach number 1 for several weeks in the USA, to reduce the popularity she enjoyed and grew every year since her debut in 2006?
- what if Beyoncé (maybe got an idea from her husband Jay Z) changed her album name and included the word *Fierce*, which has a similar meaning to *Fearless*, and entered into direct and planned competition with Taylor Swift? in 2008 both artists used the same theme: fear, and in 2009 both artists competed for an award at the MTV VMA;
- what if the release with different dates of the album *I am… Sasha Fierce* was made in order to gain ground and influence in front of Taylor Swift? what if the album release took place the day after Taylor Swift in order to insert the idea: first comes Taylor

Swift with *Fearless*, but Beyoncé will come with *Fierce* and will be better than Taylor Swift, then later Kanye West will release his album in the third week, and the world will forget about Taylor Swift?

- what if Beyoncé released the surprise album, *Beyoncé*, intentionally on Taylor Swift's birthday (December 13, 2013) as a sublime message: look who Beyoncé is and I'm coming after you (she didn't win the Grammy Awards for the *Album of the Year*);

- what if Kanye West and Jay Z knew Taylor Swift would receive the *Best Female Video Award* before the ceremony and Kanye West decided to bring a bottle of alcohol with him to cover his plan? just as he probably knew Taylor Swift wrote a song for him and said that he also wrote a song for her (I did not find information that he really wrote a song for Taylor Swift (maybe he said it as a marketing strategy, to not to be lower than Taylor Swift in the eyes of the general public)), and may have known some of the lyrics: CBS[200] wrote an article with content from Kanye West published on his Twitter account: "When I woke up from the crazy nightmare I looked in the mirror and said GROW UP KANYE… ", after a few days Taylor Swift sang the lyrics of the song *Innocent* written for Kanye West at the MTV Awards: "32 and still growin'up now"; what are the chances for Kanye West to use words so close to Taylor Swift's lyrics? if there was a leak about the lyrics written by Taylor Swift for Kanye West, who provided the information?

- what if the release of the album by Kanye West and Beyoncé in 2008, then the disagreement with the MTV award in 2009, and finally the release of the album in 2010 (for Kanye West), respectively in 2011 (for Beyoncé), was actually a long-term plan in order to present themselves as better than the white artist Taylor Swift, to diminish her popularity and creativity in the music industry?

- what if Jay Z and Kanye West are actually fighting Taylor Swift's influence over people and the music industry in which they do not accept her records and do whatever it takes to keep Beyoncé on top?

- what if Kanye West, Jay Z and Beyoncé are too desperate to win the awards and be recognized more than they are in reality? what if they create all sorts of plans that in the end do not work, create more damage for themselves and blame other people?

- in 2017 the relationship between Kanye West and Jay Z was not so good, however, in 2019 it was reported that they are again on good terms; what if this tension between them is false and was created as a solution to change the focus on a different topic considering *Tidal* was the platform where Kanye exclusively released his song with lyrics that put him and Taylor Swift in difficulty, also about the *Tidal* false plays? more, what if the new better terms of the relationship between Kanye and Jay Z (from December 2019) happened as a sublime and reply message to

---

[200] Devon Thomas, 'Kanye West Writes Song in Honor of Taylor Swift', *CBS*, September 7, 2010, available at: https: // www. cbsnews.com/news/kanye-west-writes-song-in-honor-of-taylor-swift/, last accessed: February 25, 2021.

Taylor Swift which she could have a line about their bad relationship in one of her songs from *reputation*, 'This Is Why We Can't Have Nice Things': "but I'm not the only friend you've lost lately/if only you weren't so shady"?

- what if Kanye and Jay Z are behind the feud and everything that the album patterns show in this report? what if Beyoncé has no idea about the tricks behind the curtains, even if it benefits her by having a positive image because of Kanye and Jay Z's intentional involvement?

- what if Beyoncé 's *Lemonade* album (including Jay Z) were part of Kanye West's strategy against Taylor Swift in 2016? and if this was the plan, let's see how it could have been carried out in practice:

    Step 1:

    - Kanye West released the song *Famous* (The Life of Pablo) where Taylor Swift is called 'that bitch'; Taylor entered the narrative created and promoted by Kanye by writing the truth: she did not know the lyrics in which she is called 'that bitch';

    Step 2:

    - Taylor was assailed by negative comments on social media, and the preferred term to address her is 'bitch';

    Step 3:

    - Kanye promised that his album, *The Life of Pablo*, will be available exclusively on the *Tidal* platform (the platform owned also by Jay Z); however, on April 1, 2016, his album was made available on *Apple Music*, which led to the accusation that he cheated the audience, according to an article in Variety: „By the time Mr. West changed course and broadly released 'The Life of Pablo,' the deceptive marketing ploy had served its purpose: Tidal's subscriber numbers had tripled, streaming numbers were through the roof, and Tidal had collected the personal information, credit card numbers, and social media information of millions of deceived consumers […] Instead, they just wanted to boost Tidal's subscriber numbers – which indeed did get a big bump from the release. Tidal may have signed up as many as two million new subscribers thanks to the album, claims the lawsuit, arguing that this could have added as much as $84 million to Tidal's valuation;"[201]

Step 4:

- Beyoncé released the surprise album *Lemonade* on April 23, 2016; Taylor Swift was caught in the negative narrative created and promoted by Kanye West; the album enjoyed success from critics being considered the best album released by Beyoncé; on Tidal, *Lemonade* was streamed 115 million times, setting a record for the most-streamed album in a single week by a female artist; what if Kanye West, through the exclusivity strategy of his album, plus the use of Taylor in his song, spread the narrative that in his album there could be something more about Taylor, which led to the growth of curious users and, in the end, some users decided to stay on the platform? at the same time, maybe the new number of users were used to justify the record number of streaming of his album, *The Life of Pablo*, and Beyoncé's *Lemonade*?

Step 5:

- in July 2016, the positive popular opinion is on Kanye's side, especially after Kim Kardashian (Kanye's wife at the time of the event) published edited parts of the phone conversation between Kanye and Taylor, here the conclusion of the published videos is that Taylor knew about everything (only in March 2020 an extended of the video was released and the whole planet found out that Taylor told the truth since February 2016); Taylor's image worldwide is negative;

Step 6:

- based on her previous pattern release, Taylor releases the first song in August or September, but the *Famous* feud and the negative image obtained as a result of Kanye's song, her strategy and public image do not allow her to release a new song every two years (the last album released was in the fall of 2014, so the next album should have been in the fall of 2016), and therefore Beyoncé has no competition, and has a

---

[201] Janko Roettgers, 'Kanye West Tricked Fans Into Subscribing to Tidal, Lawsuit Claims', *Variety*, April 18, 2016, available at: https://variety.com/2016/digital/news/kanye-west-tricked-fans-into-subscribing-to-tidal-lawsuit-claims-1201755580/, last accessed: February 25, 2021.

positive image while Taylor does not release a new album and has a negative image;

Step 7 (unexpected shift of the plan and not possible to change the course of their plan):

- although *Lemonade* received the most positive reviews in her career, Beyonce does not win the *Album of the Year* (although she has 12 songs on the album, this number was not lucky) and lost in favour of the white artist, Adele;

Step 8 (unexpected shift of the plan and not possible to change the course of their plan):

- in 2018 Tidal is accused of intentionally falsifying the streaming number of *The Life of Pablo* and *Lemonade*, according to Variety: "Tidal, which has rarely shared its data publicly, had a streaming exclusive on West's album for its first six weeks of release and continues to be the exclusive streamer for Beyoncé's album. It claimed that West's album had been streamed 250 million times in its first 10 days of release in February of 2016, while claiming it had just 3 million subscribers – a claim that would have meant every subscriber played the album an average of eight times per day; and that Beyonce's album was streamed 306 million times in its first 15 days of release in April of 2016." […] "Today's report, according to MBW's translation, says that "Beyoncé's and Kanye West's listener numbers on Tidal have been manipulated to the tune of several hundred million false plays… which has generated massive royalty payouts at the expense of other artists;[202]" what if Kanye West and Jay Z's strategy to use Taylor Swift was also to increase the number of users? what if Kanye West and Jay Z used the new subscribers to falsify the numbers of streaming to make more money? let's not forget that in the conversation with Taylor Kanye admitted having big debts (millions of dollars); what if the fake number of

---

[202] Jem Aswad, 'Tidal Accused of Falsifying Beyoncé and Kanye West Streaming Numbers', *Variety*, May 9, 2018, available at: https://variety.com/2018/biz/news/jay-z-tidal-accused-of-falsifying-beyonce-and-kanye-west-streaming-numbers-1202804222/, last accessed: February 25, 2021; Andy Cush, 'Tidal Accused of Generating 300 Million Fake Streams for Kanye and Beyoncé', *Spin*, May 9, 2018, available at: https://www.spin.com/2018/05/tidal-fake-streams-kanye-beyonce-investigation-300-million/, last accessed: February 25, 2021; Tim Ingham, 'Tidal 'Fake Streams': Criminal Investigation Underway Over Potential Data Fraud In Norway; *Music Business Worldwide*, January 14, 2019, available at: https://www.musicbusinessworldwide.com/tidal-fake-streams-criminal-investigation-underway-over-potential-data-fraud-in-norway/, last accessed: February 25, 2021; Dagens Næringsliv's investigation can be found here: https://www.musicbusinessworldwide.com/files/2018/05/NTNU_DigitalForensicsReport_DN_Final_Version.pdf, last accessed: February 25, 2021.

streaming was done in order to increase Beyoncé's profile and the records obtained? what if the false plays were made this route as on the other streaming platforms (Apple and Spotify) Beyoncé would not make the numbers to have new records to celebrate and maintain relevance in the music industry as Taylor Swift does? what if the fake number of streaming and the exclusive availability of her album, *Lemonade*, on Tidal was made to show the world that she is so loved that her fans follow her on the new platform and set new records in the music industry? what if Tidal is being used to justify a false point of view that black artists are not safe on other platforms because they are ruled by white people? what if behind Tidal the black artists from this report, Kanye, Jay Z and Beyoncé, used it to their own benefit, therefore, cheating the music industry and their fans?

Taylor Swift:

- what if the telephone interview with Ryan Seacrest about Taylor Swift where Kanye West said: 'She wants to get in the studio and we're definitely going to go in', […] 'I don't have an elitism about music, I don't discriminate' is a lie and Taylor Swift was not aware of it? in an interview with Entertainment Tonight, Cameron Mathison asked Taylor Swift about the rumoured collaboration between her and Kanye West. Taylor Swift answered: 'He has said that… *(was not so sure about it: author interpretation)*' and then she was nice about Kanye West? Taylor Swift: 'We're never been in the studio together, but he's got a lot of amazing ideas, he's one of those people who's just like idea, idea, idea, like what you think of this, what you think of that, he's very creative and like I've think *(not so sure, author interpretation)* we've talked about it but we've also about so many other things, I think I completely respect his vision as a producer, so that's all I know now, I have no idea how the next album is gonna be though;'
- what if Taylor Swift came up with the *1989* album (the year of her birth) to complete Beyoncé 's cycle, to reply and show who she is: an original lyricist and her first pure pop album that will eventually win the *Album of the Year* at the Grammy Awards?
- what if Taylor Swift is using samples in her songs to prove to Kanye West that she can do it too, it is not something hard, and she does it better and has a higher popularity than him?
- what if the mole inside Taylor Swift's team leaked the lyrics of the song *Dear John* (dark twisted games) to Kanye West and he decided to use them to name his album

My Beautiful Dark Twisted Fantasy? Kanye West has a long list of songs based on other's artists ideas;

- what if Taylor Swift found out the name of Kanye West's album and she decided to use it slightly differently in her song *Dear John* in order to remind people of the person who ruined her moment, therefore, positioning herself as a long-term white victim of a black man?

- Taylor Swift mentioned that she wanted to use existing musical methods in the 80's for her own music: is it possible to say this as a subtle hit to Kanye West? Kanye West said that he is inspired by the music of those years ('70, '80, '90, '00), but he used instruments that did not exist at that time and Taylor Swift came to show him how the music should sound like in those years? Kanye West presented himself as a genius in music, but he wrongly combined the instruments for the years from which he is inspired? and Taylor Swift came and gave him a subtle lesson of the correct use of musical instruments specific to the period from which he is inspired?

Kanye West, Taylor Swift, Beyoncé and Western mass-media:

- what if the prediction of the album sales for Kanye West in 2013, Yeezus, of 500,000 copies sold in the first week was made with the purpose to encourage people to buy it as it will be popular anyway? what if the prediction of the album sales for Taylor Swift in 2014 (album *1989*), of 600,000 to 750,000 copies sold in the first week was made with the purpose to discourage people to buy it as it is a lower number than the last album, and as subtle message that she lost her fans and popularity, so there is no need to bother with her album? If we look at the number of sales in the first week of each artist before 2013 and 2014, Kanye West has a lower number of albums sales in 2010, 2011 and 2012 with below 500,000 copies in the first week, and yet in 2013 the prediction increased to half a million copies sold first week; for Taylor Swift is the opposite: in 2010 and 2012 the number of album sales is over one million, and yet in 2014 the prediction decreased to half of the last number of albums from 2012, 600,000 to 750,000. The common point of the two predictions is both were not true: in 2013 Kanye West's final album sales was below the prediction, while in 2014 Taylor's final albums sales was higher than the prediction (double to be precise). The failed prediction for the first week sales happened first with Kanye West in 2005 when his album, *Late Registration*, was predicted to sale over 1.6 million copies in the first week, however, it sold over half of the prediction, 860,000 copies; this model of prediction was used with Taylor Swift too in 2014, but with the opposite expectation; what if there are people who intentionally play with the prediction (maybe a person of interest (maybe from Kanye's team or Taylor's team;

or unrelated to them), but could profit somehow from the outcome) to modify fans' intentions and get lower and higher album sales?

- what if the *Famous* event from February 2016 offered the opportunity for envious journalists and bloggers to take revenge on Taylor Swift for the success they do not have? what if there are journalists and bloggers who are being paid for negative articles, they do not have a permanent job, and this scandal gave them the chance to use their negative imagination, which is based on their own frustrations and dissatisfaction, to project it onto a woman who did not do anything wrong to them, nor to the general public to justify the high interest in the case?
- what if an unknown number of songs and maybe even the name of the albums released by Kanye West, Beyoncé and Taylor Swift is a subtle/behind the curtain message to each other and the information we already know about the pattern of album release and the interference in Taylor Swift's pattern is the real evidence available to see it?

In the following table I found a pattern that is happening in 2008 and 2016 and involves Taylor Swift, Kanye West and Beyoncé. The pattern is exposed in Figure 27.

TABLE 47. A FAMOUS ATTACK ON TAYLOR SWIFT?

EVENT/ NAME OF THE ARTIST:	TAYLOR SWIFT	BEYONCÉ	KANYE WEST
RELEASE PATTERN	Fixed pattern	Fixed pattern Changing pattern Surprise pattern	Fixed pattern Changing pattern
ALBUM RELEASE NARRATIVE LINE	2008: She followed her fixed pattern and released her album in November 2008. 2016: Taylor releases the first song in August or September, but the *Famous* feud did not allow her to release a new song every two years (the last album released was in the fall of 2014, so the next album should have been in	2008: She released the album in the same month as Taylor Swift, the second day and a week after Taylor Swift; she followed this release one time. 2016: Surprise album like in 2013 (December 13, Taylor Swift birthday). Released exclusively on Tidal; Kanye's album was	2008: A year before (2007), he changed his pattern and released the album in the same month as Taylor Swift; in 2008 he followed the new pattern for the last time. 2016: Released the album a couple of days before the Grammy Awards ceremony where Taylor Swift will win the Album

	the fall of 2016). The *Famous* feud ruined Taylor's album release pattern.	also exclusive on this platform.	of the Year for her album *1989.*
THE PUBLIC IMAGE NARRATIVE LINE	**2008 - 2009:** Positive before the MTV award ceremony from 2009; a little bit negative after the ceremony from 2009: Kanye told the whole world that she does not deserve the award, Beyoncé is better. **2016:** Positive before the *Famous* song was released; she walked to Grammy Awards while being called in Kanye's song 'that bitch'; Negative at high level after the release by his wife, Kim, of edited parts of the telephone conversation between Taylor and Kanye.	**2008 - 2009:** Positive, and also seen (through free promotion by Kanye West) as an artist that deserved the award won by Taylor Swift, the MTV ceremony was unfair with her talent and creativity. **2016:** Positive at high levels, she received the highest reviews in life for her album *Lemonade*.	**2008 - 2009:** Positive image before the MTV award ceremony from 2009; Negative image after MTV award ceremony from 2009 because of his view about the 'true' winner of the MTV award. **2016:** Little negative image, and more negative after the release of the song *Famous*, but with positive changes after the release by Kim Kardashian, of edited parts of the telephone conversation between him and Taylor.
AWARDS LINE	Taylor's music was nominated for MTV in 2009, in 2010 she won the Grammy Award for the Album of the Year for *Fearless,* in 2016 she won the Grammy Award for Album of the Year for *1989*. During and after these events, Kanye West interfered in Taylor Swift's narrative with a negative view about her music and character.		

Discussion about another pattern personal: meaning of the album

In 2013 Beyoncé and Kanye West released their albums which has full name (*Beyoncé* album by Beyoncé), and combination of his last two letters 'Ye' with 'Jesus' (*Yeezus* from Kanye: himself, people in his circle and fans around the world called him 'Ye') to promote himself as 'Ye' (Kanye) the Jesus (God) = Yeezus as God of rap music, which in reality he is a one of the gods in music: he is one of the few people in the USA to be awarded over twenty Grammy Awards. In 2014 Taylor Swift released her album *1989* which is the year of her birthday. What if these albums are actually connected: Beyoncé and Kanye West through their albums took a shot at Taylor Swift, while Taylor Swift, with her the year of birth, replied to Beyoncé and Kanye West? Beyoncé took the shot by releasing her surprise album on Taylor Swift's birthday (December 13, 2013), while Kanye West said, few days before the release of his album *Yeezus,* in June 2013, in a *New York Times* interview about Taylor Swift VMA's moment the following: he doesn't have any regret about his interruption and that it was a situation where he gave into peer pressure to apologise; when asked if he'd take back the original action or the apology, if given the choice, he answered, „You know what? I can answer that, but I'm – I'm just -- not afraid, but I know that would be such a distraction. It's such a strong thing, and people have such a strong feeling about it. *My Beautiful Dark Twisted Fantasy* was my long, backhanded apology. You know how people give a backhanded compliment? It was a backhanded apology. It was like, all these raps, all these sonic acrobatics. I was like: 'Let me show you guys what I can do, and please accept me back. You want to have me on your shelves.'[203]

CONCLUSIONS:

Kanye West interfered in the narrative of Taylor Swift with a negative story about her skills and character, while Beyoncé had a positive image about her skills and character; Kanye West is behind the negative stories about Taylor Swift's character and skills in 2009 and in 2016; Kanye West in 2016 interfered in Taylor Swift's narrative line with a negative story while Beyoncé's narrative line is involved in releasing a new album; Kanye West negative behaviour toward Taylor Swift is after Beyoncé released an album (*I am … Sasha Fierce,* 2008) and before (*Lemonade,* 2016) she is out with a new album.

[203] Jon Caramanica, 'Behind Kanye's Mask', *New York Times*, June 11, 2013, https://www.nytimes.com/2013/06/16/arts/music/kanye-west-talks-about-his-career-and-album-yeezus.html?_r=0, last accessed: May 28, 2018.

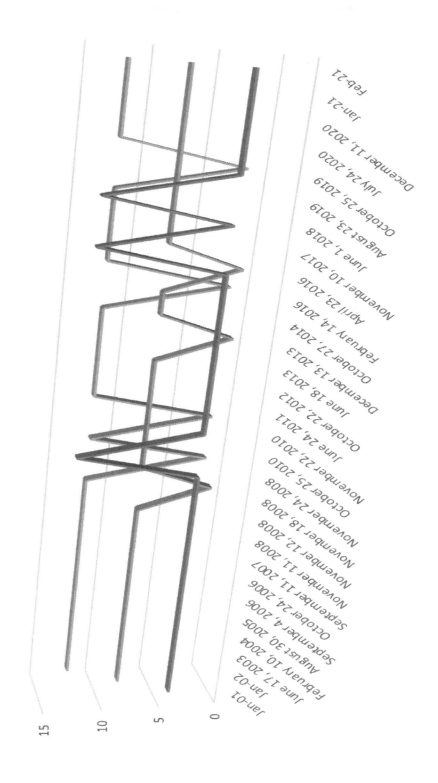

FIGURE 27. THE NARRATIVE LINE OF THE ALBUMS RELEASED

■ TAYLOR SWIFT'S NARRATIVE LINE   ■ BEYONCÉ'S NARRATIVE LINE   ■ KANYE WEST'S NARRATIVE LINE

VII. Conclusion: Who is the **FAMOUS** victim and who is the **FAMOUS** perpetrator?

In this report I investigated the *Famous* feud between Kim Kardashian, Kanye West and Taylor Swift from the perspective of ten items of research. Below you will find the conclusions I reached for each item of research.

1. ***To expose, to extract, to understand the role of the Western mass-media about: a. the key moments of the Famous feud; b. detailed and specific information about the Famous feud; c. to find what is missing from the Famous timeline:***

   a) ***key moments of the Famous feud:*** the Western mass-media, overall, was neutral and focused on the important elements and dates such as accusation, response to the accusation and proof; fortunately, there are few news agencies who delivered a more advanced view of the narrative line of the feud; at the same time, the Western mass-media does not have any obligation toward the players of the feud, in the sense of creating a profound analysis of the events and the narrative line of their feud with the sole purpose to satisfy pretentious readers or anyone else interested in the feud, because most of the events were available online on Twitter and Instagram, ready to be consumed; also, some journalists and bloggers asked and encouraged the readers to make their own judgement about the feud;

   b) ***detailed and specific information about the Famous feud***: as with the narrative line, the Western mass-media was overall neutral, however, there are negative articles with focus *only* on Taylor Swift while *ignoring* the acts of Kanye West and Kim Kardashian which was the first and second to mislead the general public about Taylor Swift's intervention and the type, length, conditions and support for a song she never heard, but promised by Kanye West to send it to her after the telephone conversation; this report show a small, but visible number of journalists and bloggers who spectacularly failed to show who is the real perpetrator and the real victim of the feud and exaggerated with absurd interpretations that portrayed the participants of the feud in the wrong role; few journalists ignored the neutrality role and sided with the perpetrators, presented final conclusions while the feud was in motion and with big gaps in the narrative, failed to hold Kanye West and Kim Kardashian accountable rightly at the same level they did wrongly with Taylor Swift; in March 2020, 25 minutes of the telephone conversation with Taylor Swift and Kanye West was leaked on Twitter and Youtube, and yet there are no negative articles about Kanye West with similar or identic language design and structure as it was used with Taylor Swift in July 2016 and onwards; why the Western mass-media failed to analyse Kanye West's behaviour toward and in reference to Taylor Swift for what he did in reality: he misled the general public with a negative view about Taylor Swift's character? from this point of view, I can suggest that Kanye West enjoyed of a 'black privilege' by not being sanctioned by the Western mass-media at the same level they did with Taylor Swift; what if there is a 'black privilege' offered, supported and promoted by the Western mass-media against the white people from the music industry?

c) **what is missing from the Famous feud**: the lack of Taylor Swift's view expressed during the interview in April 2016: it is important in the timeline of the feud because it shows a character that does not want to be part of the events put in motion by Kanye West, which is in strong relation with her expression on the telephone conversation with Kanye West about the song 'I will think about it'; the Western mass-media should update the articles with the timeline of the feud and add the missing interview from April 2016, because it can help the readers to understand the point of view of Taylor Swift toward and in reference to Kanye West; also, Western mass-media should update the timeline and add the telephone conversation (25 minutes from Youtube) from March 2020 to January 2016 while keeping the short version of the telephone conversation published by Kim Kardashian on her Snapchat account to its original date, July 2016: doing this move, the readers can reach a better understanding of the strategies of communication and interpretation of each player, who is the real perpetrator and who is the real victim and if Taylor Swift deserved the negative treatment from Kim and Kanye's fans, ordinary people, journalists and bloggers.

2. **To analyse the narrative line of the feud in order to identify patterns of behaviour: Kanye West's behaviour toward Taylor Swift, and Taylor Swift's behaviour toward Kanye West:**

- o **for Kanye West**: I observed 10 patterns of an *overall negative behaviour* created, maintained and promoted worldwide toward and in reference to Taylor Swift since 2009 until today; maybe he attempted to destroy a younger woman (character and skills, he was 32 years old when he actioned verbally against Taylor Swift, 19 years old) that did nothing wrong against him before the start of the feud in 2009 and after 2009 to justify his actions;
- o **for Taylor Swift**: I observed 8 patterns of an *overall defence mode behaviour* created, maintained and promoted worldwide toward and in reference to Kanye West's negative behaviour about her character and skills since 2009 until today; she attempted to show that she is not guilty and does not deserve the negative behaviour of Kanye West, because she was famous before he met her and earned the awards because of the vote from her fans for the music she wrote and composed.

3. **To assess and evaluate three points of view of Kanye West, Kim Kardashian and Taylor Swift:**

   a. **Kanye West wrote on Twitter: '3rd thing I called Taylor and had a hour long convo with her about the line and she thought it was funny and gave her blessings'**; the information shared with the general public was partially true, biased, misleading and failed to mention the real discussion about the line that Taylor Swift disagreed with: 'I made that bitch famous'; the reason of this omission is because Taylor Swift was not aware of it; Kanye West used her verbal agreement for the two lyric lines: the one lyric line she heard over the phone and was good with it, and the second line 'I made that bitch famous' that she was not aware of; Kanye West failed to send her the full song and instead he published the song online, and she heard the new lyrics at the same time with the general public;

   b. **Kim Kardashian in the interview with GQ magazine** from 16 June 2016 and during her show *Keeping Up with The Kardashians* (season 12, episode 11): **'She totally approved that. [...]** **'She totally knew that that was coming out;'** the information shared with the general public was partially true, biased, misleading and failed to mention that Taylor Swift was not aware of the full song and lyrics as she claimed in the interview; also, Taylor Swift said she will think about it and Kanye West failed to keep his side of the bargain by sending her the full song as he said during the telephone conversation;

   c. **the affirmation made by Taylor Swift in July 2016**: **'Being falsely painted as a liar when I was never given the full story *or played any part of the song* (underline by author) is character assassination'**; this information is mostly true as Kanye West did not share with her the whole story, failed to keep his side of the bargain and blamed her for his actions; however, the part ***'played any part of the song':*** she knew some lyrics and suggested a change of the lyrics; however, this support for the lyrics does not offer a clear causal link that she played a part because she *really* wanted or because she tried to be *nice* and *supportive* with Kanye West; she was unaware of Kanye West's intention to record the telephone conversation and keeping it as evidence of her involvement, ready to be shared with the general public on his terms, without any information given to her; eventually, Taylor Swift found out at the same time as the general public that Kanye West had indeed recorded their telephone conversation, edited it and released it to show only the parts that benefited Kanye West and Kim Kardashian.

4. ***To analyse the Famous song to see how much Taylor Swift knew about the song before its release:***

   o by using various mathematical formulas (subtraction, percentage conversion, average method) Taylor Swift knew between 8% to 8.27% about the *Famous* song; this level of knowledge about the song does not offer a clear causal link that she played a part because she *really* wanted or because *she tried to be nice* and *supportive* with Kanye West.

5. ***To analyse the impact of the Famous feud on the albums sales and songs for Kanye West, Taylor Swift and Katy Perry:***

   o on long term, despite all the negative behaviour and attitude of Kanye West, then later Katy Perry, toward and in reference to Taylor Swift, there is a higher negative impact of the albums and songs sales for Kanye and Katy Perry than for Taylor Swift.

6. ***To discover mechanisms and strategies of interpretations and communications used by Kim Kardashian, Kanye West, Taylor Swift and Western mass-media:***

   o ***for Kanye West, Kim Kardashian, journalists and bloggers***: I found 16 strategies of communication and interpretation of the *Famous* feud, and all of them are against Taylor Swift's version of the story; each player used either their own strategy that was not used by other player, for example we have *The Race Card: Black Man versus White Privileged Woman* strategy used visible only by journalists, or all three players of the feud used the same strategy: *Stabbing in the Back While Shaking Her Hand* and *The Balance of Image and Fame*;

- o **for Taylor Swift**: I found 6 strategies of communication and interpretation of the *Famous* feud, and all of them are in defence mode toward and in reference to Kanye West, Kim Kardashian and journalists with the purpose to share her side of the story which is mostly true (less true for the 'played any part of the song');

- o **for all the player of the Famous feud**: there are similar strategies of communication and interpretation of the events, however, each part is presenting their own view; overall, Taylor Swift's strategies are mostly true in comparison with the strategies of the other players of the feud;

- o **the most used strategy of communication and interpretation** *was The Dynamic Reaction Strategy*: each player of the feud responded by a statement on the official page, or through a song, video, music album or interview;

- o **intelligence of the strategy**: all players have shown intelligence and creativity in their strategies of communication and interpretation of the feud;

- o **side effects**: on long term, Taylor Swift's strategies of communication and interpretation of the feud are more powerful than Kanye West's strategies (because he started the feud) and the general public sided with her side of the story: we know this due to high number of sales of her songs, albums and concert tickets in comparison with Kanye West since 2009 until today.

7. *To explore possible reasons for creating, supporting and promoting the Famous feud by Kim Kardashian, Kanye West, Taylor Swift and Western mass-media:*

- o **for Kanye West**: for publicity, to maintain his presence in the music industry and online, to distract the negative attention from him to Taylor Swift; to create headlines written and published by the Western mass-media; to generate income from publicity and own businesses (music, clothes, shoes) even if it is done through negative publicity because, in the end, the only person that can sue him is Taylor Swift, the general public can only judge his actions and make a choice: on his side or Taylor Swift's side;

- o **for Kim Kardashian West**: for publicity, to maintain her presence online and in the mind of the general public which creates headlines written and published by the Western mass-media; to generate income from publicity and own businesses even if it is done through negative publicity because, in the end, the only person that can sue her is Taylor Swift, the general public can only judge her actions and make a choice: on her side or Taylor Swift's side;

- o **for Western mass-media**: for income through incendiary and clickbait articles: being on the side of the perpetrators, Kanye West and Kim Kardashian, the reaction of Taylor Swift's fans was negative, with lots of them being angry and upset about the conclusions of the journalists, and engaged a massively in the comment section of the articles, which, in return, generated views, increased the economic profile of the news agencies, and increased the profit from the taxes to run ads on their own websites; to spread their own agenda: the comparison between two races, white and black (which generate a lot of interest through online debates (comments) and views of the articles; to attract users to consume their services (online and print); to keep the number of users and their subscription because there is content to read, so there is a reason to keep the subscription; to show interest in various topics and create a profile of a diverse news agency capable of accommodating users with different interests;
- o **for Taylor Swift**: to present her side of the story; because she is the victim of the *Famous* feud and her actions are in defence mode toward and in reference to Kanye West, Kim Kardashian and Western mass-media, it is hard to suggest that Taylor Swift is trying to capitalise on this feud for the sole purpose to earn more money from fans and maintain a vivid presence online.

8. *To confront and challenge the core argument of the false white victimhood attributed to Taylor Swift:*

- o this core argument was widely spread by the Western mass-media; indeed, the feud started because of Kanye West, however, there is no mention in his responses that the reason why he put in motion 'look like planned negative behaviour' toward and in reference to Taylor Swift is because Taylor Swift is white and she is to blame for the poor choices of Kanye West, nor that his life suffered at the hand of Taylor Swift's actions (a white woman) before he interrupted her speech at the MTV Music Video Awards in 2009 and he wanted to get a sort of well-deserved justice;
- o the white victimhood attributed to Taylor Swift is *solely* made by the Western mass-media due to their biased, misleading and sleazy interpretations of the events of the *Famous* feud despite not having clear causal links and enough evidence to *at least suggest* that Taylor Swift might have played the race card to advance her side of the story and career;

- o the core argument of the white victimhood attributed to Taylor Swift is a false creation of the Western mass-media and the authors own a full frontpage apology to Taylor Swift;

- o based on Taylor Swift statements, music (all albums) and strategies of communication and interpretation, there is no clear causal link and evidence that she intentionally presented herself as a *white victim* of a *bad black man* for the specific reason to create a racial comparison, and that she is a white victim of the black man, Kanye West, because she planned this strategy before she met Kanye West in September 2009 and after, with the sole purpose to advance her career;

- o the narrative line of Taylor Swift is the most advanced evidence to support the conclusions above: she interfered in Kanye West's narrative line only *after* his actions and with the purpose to *defend herself* from his negative accusations and opinions about her character and skills;

- o the Western mass-media (based on the negative articles used in this report) interfered in Taylor Swift's narrative line with a false argument to advance their *own* worldview about Taylor Swift's strategies of communication and interpretation *while totally ignoring* the reason of her responses: because of Kanye West.

9. ***To confront and challenge the core argument of Ellie Woodward about the existence of a false worldview attributed to Kanye West which is that of a: 'black man terrorising the "innocent" white woman' because of Taylor Swift:***

- ***i.*** there are rich reasons and comments provided by Kanye West to create at least a good suggestion that he is the bad/evil black man (The Narrative Line, the patterns of negative behaviour, the strategies of communication and interpretation);

- ***ii.*** based on Kanye West's patterns of negative behaviour in reference to Taylor Swift, I found Ellie Woodward statement false and lacks of substantial evidences to support it; in contrast, Kanye West's patterns of negative behaviour in reference to Taylor Swift are a rich resource of creating at least a satisfactory suggestion that there could be a picture of a 'black man terrorising the innocent white woman': he started the feud, he continued the feud, he controlled the feud, while Taylor Swift's pattern of behaviour was to defend herself from his negative views about her character and skills; he called her 'bitch' in front of the entire world while falsely claiming that Taylor Swift approved it; he called her 'bitch', presented her as a 'bitch' in every concert from Saint Pablo Tour and spread the negative presentation toward and in reference to her character through various statements during his concerts and interview;

iii. **'black man terrorising'**: this part of the statement, however, cannot be taken in the entirety written by Ellie Woodward, due to the issue regarding the acceptance from experts about the clear existence of a universal concept of 'terror', 'terrorism' and 'terrorising'[204]: a part of the definition is in the eye of the beholder; for Ellie Woodward, despite the existence of a rich evidence of persistent patterns of negative behaviour, Kanye does not terrorise Taylor Swift, it's the other way around and we should not believe Taylor Swift; however, from the point of view of Taylor Swift and Kanye West's patterns of negative behaviour toward and in reference to her character and skills, (although she presented all the time a positive image about him and tried her best to support him), she might have a different view about him, it might be the view of a 'black man terrorising her' despite trying to help him out; he betrayed his word and misled the general public about her true implications in the creation of the *Famous* song;

iv. **'black man terrorising'**: this statement is exaggerated by Ellie Woodward in relation with Kanye West's worldview and added an unnecessary evil/bad view for him as his fans (on both camps) and the general public are capable of seeing and understanding the events of the feud and can be influenced to reach conclusions, surprisingly, against Kanye West, because he started the feud against Taylor Swift which was in defence mode in relation to his patterns of negative behaviour; maybe through Ellie Woodward's opinion and her lack of following the logical flow of Taylor Swift's statements about her involvement, Kanye West's negative public image grew more than the effort and reaction of the general public;

v. it is possible that Kanye West's worldview of a **'black man terrorising the "innocent" white woman'** to exist more after Ellie Woodward's article than only by his actions as the general public might attribute simple words to describe Kanye West's negative behaviour such as

---

[204] Andrew Heywood, *Global Politics*, Palgrave Macmillan, New York, 2011, p. 282; David Brown, 'Terrorism', In Trevor C. Salmon, Mark F. Imber (eds), *Issue in International Relations*, Second Edition. New York, Routledge, 2008, pp. 107-120; Colin Wight, 'Theorising Terrorism: The State, Structure, and History', *International Relations*, 23:1 (2009), p. 99; Thomas J. Badey, 'Defining international terrorism: A pragmatic approach', *Terrorism and Political Violence*, 10:1, 1998, p. 90; Ben Saul, 'Attempts to Define 'Terrorism' in International Law', *Netherlands International Law Review*, Vol. 52, No. 1, 2005, pp. 58-59; Myra Williamson, *Terrorism, War and International Law the Legality of the Use of Force Against Afghanistan in 2001*, The Ashgate International Law Series, Asgate, England, 2009, p. 49; Joshua Woods, 'What We Talk About When We Talk About Terrorism: Elite Press Coverage of Terrorism Risk from 1997 to 2005', *The Harvard International Journal of Press/Politics*, 12: 3, 2007, p.3.

'bad/evil man' or 'perpetrator', but, with Ellie Woodward's rich imagination, his worldview might have changed in the eyes of the beholder;

vi. **Ellie Woodward statement: 'The dominant reaction, however, was a reflection of what the world has been conditioned to see: the "threat" of an "angry" black man terrorising the "innocent" white woman. Even their clothes reflected the racially fuelled victim/villain framework that would define the incident: The image of West, wearing dark shades and an entirely black outfit, accosting sweet Swift in her white and silver party dress, remains an iconic one':** I found it to be biased and misleading toward and in reference to Taylor Swift 'false white woman victimhood'; Kanye West initiated the events of the *Famous* feud (evidence: the patterns of behaviour and the strategies of communications and interpretations) for which Taylor Swift is not guilty; Taylor Swift interfered in the narrative line of Kanye West *only after he initiated* and *perpetuated* the events, she interfered to protect herself from his malicious, biased and misleading information spread to the general public in his own terms; there is nothing wrong for a white woman to reply to a black man who she did not nothing wrong to him to justify his malicious actions from 2009 until and after 2016;

vii. **'black man terrorising the "innocent" white woman':** if this perception exist in the mind of the general public about Kanye West, then Ellie Woodward should provide more explanations about the reasons and evidence behind her statement and the connection that she tried to create in reference to Taylor Swift 'white victimhood' and the 'black man terrorising';

viii. **'black man terrorising the "innocent" white woman':** if this perception exist in the mind of the general public about Kanye West, then Kanye West is to blame because he initiated the events of the *Famous* feud in his own terms.

10. To find out who is the Famous victim and who is the Famous perpetrator of the Famous feud:

o   to find out the answer to this item of research, I used the strategy presented below:

▪   *perpetrator points*:

- ***13 September 2009***: Kanye West: 1 point; Taylor Swift: 0 points;
- ***11 February 2016***: Kanye West: 1 point; Kim Kardashian West: 1 point; Taylor Swift: no points (because Kanye West initiated the new event of the feud);

- ***final perpetrator points***:

  - *Kanye West*: 2 points;
  - *Kim Kardashian West*: 1 point;
  - *Taylor Swift*: 0 points.

- ***conclusions***:

  - Kanye West was the first to misled the general public about Taylor Swift's involvement in the creation of the *Famous* song, then Kim Kardashian and Taylor Swift (for 'played any part of the song');
  - for Kanye West the advices and suggestions received by Taylor Swift (she sold millions of albums before he met him; she will think about the song) via the telephone conversation did not matter: he decided to record the telephone conversation and to continue with his plan; he allowed Kim Kardashian to edit the telephone conversation and to publish it online according with their needs;
  - Taylor Swift is the *Famous victim* of the *Famous perpetrators*: Kanye West and Kim Kardashian (due to their intentional interference in her narrative line with a negative view about her skills and character in front of the entire world);
  - *Kanye West is the big perpetrator in the **Famous** feud* because he had the power and the evidence to respond to Taylor Swift's publicly disputed lyric line and he never did it; had plenty of chances to publicly acknowledge Taylor Swift's right to publicly challenge the song's final lyrics: they spoke on the phone about the song, but not the new line 'I made that bitch famous' and he decided to add it; he did not send Taylor Swift the final version of the song; he is the author of the song and, therefore, it is his duty to say exactly what happened;

- Kanye West, Kim Kardashian and some Western journalist and bloggers own a deep, genuine and classic apology to Taylor Swift for publishing and spreading biased and misleading information about her character.

Other conclusions & discussions:

- **The cause of Kanye West's negative view about his personality**: based on the figure *The Narrative Line of the Famous Feud*, I found that **lack of manners** is to blame for everything bad that came for Kanye West from the general public since September 2009 until today and forevermore; by walking on the stage and interrupting the speech of Taylor Swift, Kanye West showed **lack of manners** toward a person who did not do anything wrong to him and this might be the real reason of Kanye West's fall in the eyes of the general public;
- in the first event of the *Famous* feud, in September 2009, many artists expressed their personal opinion towards all participants, for example Pink and 50 Cents expressed a negative opinion about Kanye West's interruption of Taylor Swift's speech; in 2016, Kanye West initiated a second major event, the *Famous* song, and in 2019 Wendy Williams (black woman; before 2008 she worked as radio DJ; since 2008 she has her own show, *The Wendy Williams Show*) had an interesting opinion about Kanye West and Taylor Swift: 'I didn't really know her until Kanye West brought her on stage all those years ago'[205]; Wendy Williams worked as a radio DJ while Taylor Swift started her musical career and her albums (*Taylor Swift* and *Fearless*) were included for many weeks in the music charts like those published by Billboard and Nielson; it is possible that a former radio DJ, then later her own public show with guests from almost every industry category, including music, to miss all the news about the success of Taylor Swift, a new artist in the music industry who managed to sell more albums than other artists considered better than her? she did not read the Billboard charts, and if she did, how did she skip the name Taylor Swift? can you be a radio DJ without reading news about new artists who influenced millions of people? what if Wendy Williams sided with Kanye West because it was the right moment for her to pour out all her internal dissatisfaction accumulated over the years toward a person who did nothing wrong to her? what if Wendy Williams took advantage of the *Famous* feud to project her discriminatory attitude toward a white artist, towards a white woman with greater success than hers and Kanye West? what we know for sure is that Wendy Williams decided to draw final conclusions

[205] Celebs Today, 'Wendy Williams says it's 'unbelievable' Taylor Swift is named AMAs Artist of the Decade', *Youtube*, November 26, 2019, available at: https://www.youtube.com/watch?v=YUJbMnZ_qbU, last accessed: November 27, 2019.

while the event was in motion and without having the whole story, which suggests a lot about her state of mind (reasoning) and character; Wendy Williams said that Kanye West brought Taylor on the stage, but Taylor was already on the stage when Kanye interfered in her speech, also the award was earned because of the vote of her fans, which indicate that she was known by people before the events, and her music was appreciated and available to the general public; Wendy Williams might have sided with the perpetrators, Kanye West and Kim Kardashian; this is interesting side of view because her show is presented as a source of credibility for events with a high interest for the general public;

- surprisingly, the negative articles written about Taylor Swift did not have a negative effect on long term; in 2021 Taylor Swift won for the third time the *Album of the Year* with an album that she owns, *folklore*; the number of pure albums sales decreased in the last 14 years, however, she is still in top of various charts and world records;
- Taylor Swift (the victim) was criticised head to toe while Kanye West (the perpetrator) got away with it; imagine the reaction of the Western mass media and Black Lives Matter if Taylor Swift was indeed the perpetrator and Kanye West the victim;
- Taylor Swift is being accused that she is following 'only the money', yet, in this report, I showed and described the opposite picture: Kanye West, Jay Z and Beyoncé are involved in various strategies (such as Tidal false plays) where 'money' are involved in their narrative and the end of their narrative;
- Kanye West interfered in Taylor Swift's increasing and positive narrative line, after and while his narrative line of success was decreasing;
- in this report I discovered that Fake News is real and it's happening inside the most prestigious news agencies of the Western world and involves a white woman which contradicts the argument of the Black Lives Matter that 'white people have a higher privilege than black people'; from the point of view of the *Famous* feud and the sources used in this report, there is not enough evidence to create at least a satisfactory argument that Taylor Swift is the privileged white woman and Kanye West is the exiled black man who does not deserve to be treated negatively by the Western mass-media: for example, although the leak of the conversation between Kanye West and Taylor Swift supported her side of the story more than Kanye's story, The Wall Street Journal decided to keep Kanye West on the main cover[206];
- there are people involved in criminal organisations and activities and do not get the same malicious treatment as the one offered for free to Taylor Swift by the Western mass-media;
- Kanye West called Taylor Swift 'I made that bitch famous', yet he was not cancelled, but he got support from American Express and Tidal with exclusive tickets for

---

[206] 'The Creation and the Myth of Kanye West', *The Wall Street Journal*, March 25, 2020, available at: https://www.wsj.com/articles/the-creation-and-the-myth-of-kanye-west-11585138241, last accessed: March 26, 2020.

customers and other venue places; Adidas continues to support Kanye West; this a good reason to suggest that Kanye West does not experience discrimination in the USA from companies; the higher number of tickets sold for his *Saint Pablo Tour* is another good evidence to suggest that people does not discriminate Kanye West because he is black; his public behaviour toward and in reference to Taylor Swift might weight more for people in making the decision to support or not his music and concerts;

- the 25-minute telephone conversation available on Youtube does not change the conclusion of the first version of this report from 2017, but confirms them: the evidence available is good to create at least a satisfactory argument that Kanye West and Kim Kardashian are the perpetrators and Taylor Swift is the victim of the *Famous* feud;

- in this report there is evidence to create a good suggestion regarding the following statement: Kanye West is not the famous black artist who is fighting to calm the race problem in the USA and build a peaceful world, but he interfered brutally and negatively in the narrative line of a famous white artist and refused to accept the negative consequences towards other people due to his behaviour, which extends and continues the negative narrative line of the race problem in the USA; people who want a better world must look for another source of inspiration; Kanye West failed to build a better world in the USA for black and white people; on long term, can Taylor Swift, through her music, influence black and white people to leave the past behind and to embrace a common and a brighter future forevermore?

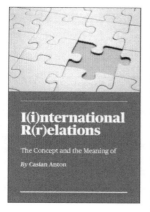

The Concept and the Meaning og I(i)nternational R(r)elations (2022): In this paper I explored the concept of 'I(i)nternational R(r)elations', with the aim (i) to show the two techniques of writing and their representation, (ii) the meaning that is attached to each technique; (iii) the process of creation of a concept based on two terms. Through this paper: (i) I return to theorizing the concept of 'I(i)nternational R(r)elations' but from its etymological bases; (ii) the terms 'relation' and 'international' is based on a wide range of concepts that help its formation, and I want to *show this formation*; (iii) I contribute to the existing literature that discusses the concept; (iv) I contribute to the historical development of the interdiscipline and (v) I respond to the crisis of ideas that haunts science. If you started reading this paper it means that it is time to look with greater clarity and objectivity to all the elements and the process of creating a concept. To *see* the concept of 'I(i)nternational R(r)elations' *as it is.*

Black and White Music: A Journey Behind the Musical Notes (2022): In this report I explored a very small part of the music industry from the USA, more precisely, I investigated the contribution, greater or lesser, of black and white artists in the production and writing of their albums. The artists investigated in this report are Taylor Swift, Kanye West, Beyoncé, Kendrick Lamar, Macklemore & Ryan, Adele and Beck. I selected these artists because the music produced and released by them were used by various artists and journalists as examples of racial discrimination that takes place in the music industry. For example, Kendrick Lamar (black man) was promoted by western journalists the winner of the Best Rap Album days before the 2014 ceremony, but was defeated by Macklemore & Ryan (white artists) and in 2016 by Taylor Swift (white artist); Beyoncé (black artist) lost in 2015 to Beck (white artist) and in 2017 she lost to Adele (white artist). In other words, today's music industry is caught in a difficult situation that is severely undermining The Recording Academy's credibility and the Grammy Awards.

The full experience of ***Revi Project 88*** is available online:

Printed in Poland
by Amazon Fulfillment
Poland Sp. z o.o., Wrocław

17168188R00132